This ·is the fourth volume to appear in a new series of plays edited with the same critical standards and the same physical presentation as the Arden Shakespeare.

Ben Jonson's great comedy *Bartholomew Fair*, which, after holding the stage for over a century, is now less well known than it deserves to be, is here offered in an edition, based on the text of the first edition, which affords every help to the modern producer and reader.

The editor is Professor of English in the University of Otago.

THE REVELS PLAYS

General Editor: Clifford Leech

BARTHOLOMEW FAIR

Bartholomew Fair

BEN JONSON

EDITED BY

E. A. HORSMAN

THE REVELS PLAYS

METHUEN & CO LTD
LONDON

This edition first published 1960

Introduction, Apparatus Criticus, etc.
© 1960 E. A. Horsman
Printed in Great Britain by
The Broadwater Press Ltd, Welwyn Garden City, Herts
Methuen Catalogue No. 6128/U

General Editor's Preface

The aim of this series is to apply to plays by Shakespeare's predecessors, contemporaries, and successors the methods that are now used in Shakespeare editing. It is indeed out of the success of the New Arden Shakespeare that the idea of the present series has emerged, and Professor Una Ellis-Fermor and Dr Harold F. Brooks have most generously given advice on its planning.

There is neither the hope nor the intention of making each volume in the series conform in every particular to one pattern. Each author, each individual play, is likely to present special problems—of text, of density of collation and commentary, of critical and historical judgment. Moreover, any scholar engaged in the task of editing a sixteenth- or seventeenth-century play will recognize that wholly acceptable editorial principles are only gradually becoming plain. There will, therefore, be no hesitation in modifying the practice of this series, either in the light of the peculiarities of any one play or in the light of growing editorial experience. Nevertheless, in certain basic matters the plan of the series is likely to remain constant.

The introductions will include discussions of the provenance of the text, the play's stage-history and reputation, its significance as a contribution to dramatic literature, and its place within the work of its author. The text will be based on a fresh examination of the early editions. Modern spelling will be used, and the original punctuation will be modified where it is likely to cause obscurity; editorial stage-directions will be enclosed in square brackets. The collation will aim at making clear the grounds for an editor's choice in every instance where the original or a frequently accepted modern reading has been departed from. The annotations will attempt to explain difficult passages and to provide such comments and illustrations of usage as the editor considers desirable. Each volume will include either a glossary or an index to annotations: it is the hope of the editors that in this way the series will ultimately provide some assistance to lexicographers of sixteenth- and seventeenth-century English.

But the series will be inadequately performing its task if it proves acceptable only to readers. The special needs of actors and producers will be borne in mind, particularly in the comments on staging and stage-history. Moreover, in one matter a rigorous uniformity may be expected: no editorial indications of locality will be introduced into the scene-headings. This should emphasize the kind of staging for which the plays were originally intended, and may perhaps suggest the advantage of achieving in a modern theatre some approach to the fluidity of scene and the neutrality of acting-space that Shakespeare's fellows knew. In this connection, it will be observed that the indications of act- and scene-division, except where they derive from the copy-text, are given unobtrusively in square brackets.

A small innovation in line-numbering is being introduced. Stage-directions which occur on separate lines from the text are given the number of the immediately preceding line followed by a decimal point and 1, 2, 3, etc. Thus the line 163.5 indicates the fifth line of a stage-direction following line 163 of the scene. At the beginning of a scene the lines of a stage-direction are numbered 0.1, 0.2, etc.

'The Revels' was a general name for entertainments at court in the late sixteenth and seventeenth centuries, and it was from the Master of the Revels that a licence had to be obtained before any play could be performed in London. The plays to be included in this series therefore found their way to the Revels Office. For a body of dramatic literature that reached its fullest growth in the field of tragedy, the term 'Revels' may appear strange. But perhaps the actor at least will judge it fitting.

CLIFFORD LEECH

Durham, 1958

Contents

Preface

No editor of *Bartholomew Fair* can fail to be in debt to the editors of the Oxford Jonson, C. H. Herford, and Percy and Evelyn Simpson. My acknowledgement of this is plain in commentary and apparatus (even though at every turn I have gone back to the original materials, sometimes to produce a different result from theirs). I am also indebted to their predecessors, particularly to Gifford, and to Cunningham who went over Gifford's work in 1871 and added some notes in 1875. In preparing the commentary, where brevity was essential, I have been much helped by being able to give references to the *Oxford English Dictionary*, to the Oxford Shakespeare (ed. W. J. Craig, 1913), and to volumes I and II of Fredson Bowers's edition of *The Dramatic Works of Thomas Dekker* (Cambridge, 1953–5). (The two latter have been used for quotations from these authors.)

I would like to thank the Librarians and their assistants of the Bodleian, the British Museum, and Trinity College, Cambridge, of the Alexander Turnbull Library, Wellington, the Public Library, Auckland, and the Otago University Library. The Librarians of Oriel and All Souls Colleges, Oxford, and Trinity College, Dublin, have given ready answers to small textual inquiries. The General Editor has throughout been the genial embodiment of Horace's advice—*cum tabulis animum censoris sumet honesti.*

E. A. HORSMAN

University of Otago, 1959

Abbreviations

C.S.A.	*Bartholomew Fayre*, ed. C. S. Alden, *Yale Studies in English*, xxv, 1904.
Chambers	Sir Edmund Chambers, *The Elizabethan Stage*, Oxford, 1923.
Cotgrave	*A Dictionarie of the French and English Tongues*, London, 1611.
F	*The Workes of Benjamin Jonson. The Second Volume*, London, 1640.
F3	*The Works of Ben Jonson*, London, 1692.
G.	*The Works of Ben Jonson*, ed. William Gifford, 9 vols., London, 1816.
Grose	Francis Grose, *A Classical Dictionary of the Vulgar Tongue*, London, 1785.
H. & S., H.S.	*Ben Jonson*, ed. C. H. Herford, Percy and Evelyn Simpson, 11 vols., Oxford, 1925–52.
J.	Ben Jonson:

	A.	*The Alchemist*, 1610.
	C.	*Catiline*, 1611.
	C.R.	*Cynthias Reuells*, 1600.
	D.A.	*The Diuell is an Asse*, 1616.
	E.H.	*Eastward Hoe*, 1605.
	E.M.I.	*Every Man in his Humour*, 1598.
	E.M.O.	*Every Man out of his Humour*, 1599.
	Ep.	*Epigrammes*.
	M.L.	*The Magnetick Lady*, 1632.
	N.I.	*The New Inne*, 1629.
	Poet.	*Poetaster*, 1601.
	S.	*Sejanus*, 1603.

J.   Ben Jonson (*cont.*):
                     S.N.   The Staple of Newes, 1626.
                     S.W.   The Silent Woman, 1609.
                     V.   Volpone, 1605.

Johnson   Samuel Johnson, *A Dictionary of the English Lan-
                    guage,* London, 1755.

Markham   Gervase Markham, *Markhams Maister-peece* ...
                    *Containing all Knowledge belonging to a Smith,
                    Farrier, or Horseleach,* 1610.

McKerrow   *The Works of Thomas Nashe,* ed. R. B. McKerrow,
                    1904–10.

Morley   Henry Morley, *Memoirs of Bartholomew Fair,*
                    London, 1859.

O.E.D.   *Oxford English Dictionary.*

S.R., Arber   *A Transcript of the Registers of the Company of
                    Stationers of London,* ed. Edward Arber, 5 vols.,
                    London and Birmingham, 1875–94.

Stow   John Stow, *A Survey of London,* 1598, 1603; ed.
                    C. L. Kingsford, Oxford, 1908.

Stubbes   *The Anatomie of Abuses,* 1583, ed. Furnivall (New
                    Shakspere Soc., Series VI, Nos. 4, 6, 12), 1877–82.

W.   *The Workes of Ben Jonson,* ed. Peter Whalley,
                    7 vols., London, 1756.

1716   *The Workes of Ben Jonson,* 6 vols., London, 1716.

Introduction

I. BEN JONSON AND 'BARTHOLOMEW FAIR'

In *Bartholomew Fair*, written and acted in 1614, Jonson produced
his first comedy since *The Alchemist* in 1610. Both that play and
Volpone (1605) had presented an extraordinary variety of corrupt
energies controlled within an intricate moral and aesthetic structure. To some critics the looser construction and the less trenchant
satire of *Bartholomew Fair* have seemed to show Jonson returning
'towards the loose multiplicity of *Every Man out of his Humour* or
Cynthia's Revels.'[1] But these earlier plays (of 1599 and 1600) were
'comical satires' depending as much upon characters described and
morals pointed as upon stage presentation. The action in them (particularly in the second) involved an ingenious starting of hares, as if
to justify the use of stage and actors at all; it had hardly shaped their
varied material into a unified comment. In *Bartholomew Fair*, on
the other hand, the action does just this. Centring upon the Fair, it
enables Jonson to group his personages into those to whom Smithfield is their native element and those who come to it from outside,
and to group these latter according to their diverse reasons for coming. The result is a play full of varied 'humours' which preserve the
appearance of freedom without getting out of hand. Moreover, the
sense and structure of the play arise from their interaction, not from
any comments of the playwright himself.

Compared with the moral issues in *Volpone* or *The Alchemist*, of
course, those in *Bartholomew Fair* may appear slight—the mere
follies of a fair instead of the absurd and terrible permutations of
greed and lust. The outcome of the play in good-natured disillusion-
ment and reconciliation may seem beneath the Jonson who could so
uncompromisingly dismiss his earlier villains. But this play depends less upon the exploration or indictment of vice itself than

[1] H. & S. i. 70.

upon the discovery of certain relations between would-be moralists and those people or habits they attack. In particular, moral indictment is shown to be misguided when those who indict lack the understanding of unregenerate flesh and blood which those they attack already have. These would-be moralists fail because of their imperfect knowledge of the old Adam not only in those they attack but also in themselves. The Fair embodies in lively action and vigorous language this old Adam, these nefarious energies which the outsiders encounter to their pain and profit.

Such a subject, which allows for both satire of and sympathy with unregenerate humanity, gives Jonson the opportunity to evoke in his audience, according to their capabilities, a simple amusement or a more intellectual delight. It may even have been this which recommended the subject to him. For there is some evidence in the play (see p. xxvii below) that he remembered the failure, three years before, of the tragedy, *Catiline*, of which he himself had thought so well. This had been his last public play before *Bartholomew Fair* and, if he now needed to work for popular success, the problem would be to do so without losing face with the more discerning part of his audience, without compromising his moral or literary standards. His subject, as we shall see, safeguards the former; the latter he preserves by persistently satirizing the taste he is forced to serve. With these considerations in mind, we may look more closely at the whole work.

From the very beginning of the Induction, ironical play is made with the grounds of judgement in the theatre of 1614, in lively patter to deceive the unsuspecting. Jonson has been doing this kind of thing, of course, since at least *The Case is Altered* (see II. vii. 68–71) in the 1590's, but in much more simple and scornful terms. Here he is trying to placate as well as to indict the popular taste. The first speaker is picked out as a representative of the theatre itself. Although only a stage-keeper—a cleaner, we would call him—he offers to show the 'fashion' in 'stage-practice', to save from his 'absurd courses' one of 'these master-poets' who 'will be inform'd of nothing' (ll. 26–7). He recommends either a simple realism which will bring on stage well-known 'Bartholomew-birds' like little Davy, the bully, or Kindheart, the tooth drawer, or an obscene pan-

tomime staged with the help of 'my witty young masters o' the Inns
o' Court' (ll. 34–5 and n.)—whom we might rather expect to form
the more judicious part of the audience. The stage-keeper's judgement depends upon his recollections of 'Master Tarlton's time',
back in the 1580's (ll. 36–7 and n.) and upon his appreciation of the
stock figures who hold the stage at the moment (ll. 42–5). It seems
reasonable to him that his judgement should have been asked by the
'understanding gentlemen o' the ground here'. These are, on the
one hand, the standers under, or below, the stage, in the pit, and,
on the other, those who understand the play, the second sense recalling the form sometimes used in printed books—as in Dekker's
A Strange Horse-Race (1613), offered 'Not to the Readers . . . but to
the Understanders'. Jonson ingeniously telescopes in one word the
two parts of the public which he had addressed separately in the
quarto of *Catiline* as 'the Reader in Ordinarie' and 'the Reader extraordinary'. But there he had perforce to oppose judgement, 'the
trying faculty', to 'commendation'. Here he is attempting, with
ironical good humour, to unite them. He brings on the prompter to
question the judgement of a mere stage-keeper—'Your judgement,
rascal ? For what ? Sweeping the stage ?'—and yet to turn round and
remember that it is to this man's 'meridian', the full stretch of *his*
drudging faculties, and 'the scale of the grounded judgements here,
his play-fellows in wit' that the author has written. This contrasts
with the serious use of *meridian* in the court Prologue to *The Staple
of News*, 'A worke . . . writ to the *Meridian* of your *Court*', and with
the straightforward justification of the audience's viewpoint in the
Prologue to *The Silent Woman*—

> Our wishes, like to those make publique feasts,
> Are not to please the cookes tastes, but the guests (ll. 8–9).

Equally it contrasts with the straightforward depreciation in *The
Case is Altered, loc. cit.*, of

> the rude barbarous crue, a people that have no braines, and yet
> grounded judgements, these will hisse any thing that mounts
> aboue their grounded capacities.

Nevertheless, Herford and Simpson take altogether too simple a
view in claiming that the *Bartholomew Fair* Induction shows

> the most masterful of playwrights . . . disposed to meet his unruly

audience more than half-way; to give them as much as he in conscience could of what they wanted; instead of as much as they
would stomach of what they ought to want; and above all, to
resent no man's disapproval. . . The . . . censor has stripped off the
robes of his authority and of his chartered scorn; he mingles
with . . . the mob of 'ordinary readers' (ii. 132–3).

Rather has Jonson managed adroitly to placate the less discriminat-
ing part of his audience while having his say at their expense, and in
terms which the 'understanders' proper will appreciate.

It is the same with the so-called 'genial compact' which is made
with the audience. It is comical in its parade of legal longwinded-
ness, leading up only to the undertaking that they shall remain 'in
the places their money or friends have put them in'. But it is depreciatory too, for Jonson has in mind the disturbances created by
those who do not like a play, and possibly the rowdy behaviour of
spectators at the bear-baiting for which this very stage at the Hope
Theatre could be removed: at any rate, the recommendation of the
play to come, 'as full of noise as sport', catches up the earlier reference to the 'bears within' which had called in question the stage-
keeper's judgement. In this context, too, the disclaimer that it is
'made to delight all, and to offend none; provided they have either
the wit or the honesty to think well of themselves' (ll. 83–5) can be
read as haughtily patronizing at the expense of both their wit and
their honesty. Certainly, whatever their honesty, their wit is depreciated by being not valued but priced—it should not 'get above'
the place each has paid for.

The agreement that each member of the audience 'exercise his
own judgement, and not censure by contagion' is depreciatory because to Jonson this is an impossibility, at least on the view presented in the address 'to the Reader in Ordinarie' in the quarto of
Catiline:

The commendation of good things may fall within a many, their
approbation but in a few; for the most commend out of affection,
selfe tickling, an easinesse or imitation: but men judge only out of
knowledge.

His intention is made plain when he switches in a satirical direction
the item which is linked with it—'that he be fix'd and settled in his

censure'—to the ridicule, this time, of those whose judgement has stood still since the early days of *Titus Andronicus* and *The Spanish Tragedy*. Those who want the latest fashions '[*Winter's*] *Tales, Tempests*', 'to make Nature afraid', are equally condemned: to please them the author would have to forgo his own judgement and 'mix his head with other men's heels'. The charges glance backward, of course, to the homely comedy of Tarlton's times which the stage-keeper had recalled and to the obscene pantomime which he had recommended. And instead of the unheightened realism he had wanted, and the topicality of known names, Jonson presents the types—drunkards, roarers, cutpurses, hypocrites—which will provide caps to fit those who cannot think well of themselves. At the same time, he warns against attempts to search out any particular cap as made for any particular wearer. On a suspicion of this kind (in his part of *Eastward Ho*) Jonson had nine years before gone to prison.

Perhaps it should be said that comment on the play from Selden's time to the present has made the disclaimer appear necessary, from the very number of such fitting caps Jonson was thought to be offering. For instance, a connection between Lantern Leatherhead and Inigo Jones has commonly been made since the remark of Selden's reported in *Table Talk* (1689), sig. F4 verso, that

> Ben Jonson satyrically express'd the vain Disputes of Divines by *Inigo Lanthorne* disputing with his puppet in a *Bartholomew Fair*.

But this hardly shows the personal satire to be more than incidental. There seems to be no evidence, so early as 1614, of strained relations between Jonson and the designer of the scenery for his masques, though two epigrams printed in the 1616 Folio (cxv, cxxix) may be aimed at Jones (who is not named) and Jonson in *An Expostulation with Inigo Jones* of 1631 (H. & S. viii. 402 ff.) goes to *Bartholomew Fair* for ammunition (I normalize his spelling):

> I am too fat t'envy him. He too lean
> To be worth envy. Henceforth I do mean
> To pity him, as smiling at his feat
> Of Lanterne-lerry: with fuliginous heat
> Whirling his whimsies, by a subtlety
> Suck'd from the veins of shop-philosophy.

B

> What could he do now, giving his mind that way
> In presentation of some puppet play!   (ll. 69-76)

But that this connection of Jones with Leatherhead was made after rather than before the play seems indicated by the further *ad hoc* comparison with Justice Overdo—

> Should but the king his Justice-hood employ
> In setting forth of such a solemn toy!
> How would he firk? like Adam Overdo
> Up and about? Dive into cellars too
> Disguis'd? and thence drag forth Enormity?
> Discover Vice? Commit Absurdity?
> Under the Moral?   (ll. 77-83)

Again, Fleay confidently identified Littlewit with Daniel, and even Herford and Simpson allow some connection (ii. 147-8) on the slender ground that Jonson uses the phrase 'little or . . . noe braine at all' in the introduction prefixed in 1606 to the quarto of his masque *Hymenaei*, probably in reply to Daniel's Preface to his *Vision of the Twelve Goddesses* (1604). In Wasp and Cokes, Herford and Simpson (ii. 142) see Jonson himself and his pupil (the son of Sir Walter Raleigh) with whom he had gone abroad a year before. Fortunately the part of these personages in the structure of the play is not limited by the ways in which they may perhaps recall contemporaries.

To return to the Induction, Jonson makes a final hit at an oversimple realism in the ironical claim to have 'observ'd a special decorum' in staging a play about the Fair in a (bear-baiting) theatre 'as dirty as Smithfield and as stinking every whit'. In thus taking up one by one the despised stage-keeper's points, Jonson has indicated plainly what the popular demands are and yet in such a way as to keep the populace on his side.

The element of continuity between the Induction and the play is visible when Jonson introduces a lawyer (no doubt from the Inns of Court depreciated in the Induction) who claims to be a rival of 'your Three Cranes, Mitre and Mermaid men', on the strength of friendship with the actors. Not even Mr I. A. Shapiro seeks to deny[1] that these were haunts of Jonson's, and it is no surprise to

---

[1] In his articles on the 'Mermaid Club', *Modern Language Review* XLV (1950), pp. 6-17, XLVI (1951), pp. 59-63.

learn before the first act is out that Littlewit himself has written a
'popular' play—for the puppets at the Fair. It is this which brings
to the Fair Littlewit's wife and, for dependent reasons, her mother
and her mother's suitor Zeal-of-the-Land Busy. Although, after
this, Littlewit's play falls out of sight until Act V, some of the hits
at Leatherhead, 'parcel-poet, and an inginer' (II. ii. 16), and the
ridiculous game of vapours, with its travesty of dramatic repartee,
in IV. iv, keep in view the inadequacies of the popular stage of which
Jonson is to make final mockery in the puppet play. It serves, too,
in Act I, to prompt in the audience two of those views of the Fair
out of which Jonson constructs his own play—the Fair as the proper
field for the talents of a popular playwright (with wit enough to
entertain it though not to understand it) and the Fair as attracting
those who, like Busy, claim to repudiate it on principle. Throughout, Jonson plays upon *our* judgement of the Fair, while grouping
and defining his main personages according to *theirs*; and the crude
vitality of the Fair, in turn, challenges the moral views which urge
repudiation or restraint. Thus, as has been suggested, the Fair not
only makes dramatic the disabusement of each of the main characters in turn, but directs it to the reinforcing of a single comment.
In Act I, then, along with Busy and Littlewit, Jonson 'places' in relation to the Fair the bird-witted Cokes, agape for pleasant variety,[1]
and his fussy 'governor', Wasp, who thinks that the Fair is to be re-
sisted by mere railing and good advice. Quarlous is neither attracted
nor repelled; his long attack on widow-hunting (I. iii. 62 ff.), translated from Jonson's favourite satirists, stamps him as representative of the reasonable man; yet he is to gain more from the Fair than
anyone except Winwife—by marrying the richest of its detractors,
and a widow.

Act II widens the gap between the extremes of the play by pre-
senting, on the one hand, the Fair itself and, on the other, Justice
Overdo. It is significant of Jonson's intention that Overdo should
appear first, for the contrast is not between Busy's denunciation of

---

[1] Cf. '*Expectation* of the *Vulgar* is more drawne, and held with new-
nesse, then goodnesse; . . . so it be new, though never so naught, and de-
praved, they run to it, and are taken' (*Discoveries*, ll. 405–9, H. & S.
viii. 576).

idolatry, and the trivial get-pennies of Smithfield, but between the attitudes of the two moralists. On the face of it, the similarities are perhaps more striking than the differences: both use, for instance, an extravagantly rhetorical language which is meant to put the audience on its guard against accepting what they say at its face value; both, that is, break 'decorum'. But they do this in rather different ways; Busy attacks the trivialities of the Fair in Old Testament terms ('. . . you make the Fair no better than one of the high places. . .' I. vi. 55) which only accentuate the travesty of argument by which he veers round to justification. For he changes his mind with a mere metaphor—'it . . . hath a face of offence . . . but that face may have a veil put over it. . .' (ll. 66–9)—of no more force than Littlewit's attempt at a pun—'. . . place should give place' (l. 57).

The subject of Overdo's opening soliloquy, on the other hand, is, within its limits, important—the doing of justice. But, like Littlewit with his 'ambitious wit', the justice grows 'insolent with it, and overdoing' (I. v. 71). Overdo is after all only a Justice of the Peace, an inferior magistrate, presiding over the lowest, if the most expeditious, court in the kingdom, the Pie-powders (II. ii. 22 n.) and even there only as representative of the Lord of the Fair. Yet he sees himself as hidden in a cloud, like a god, and acting 'in the King's name, and for the Commonwealth'. For his disguise, he invokes the example of 'a worthy worshipful man, sometime a capital member of this city'. This may be, as C. S. Alden thought, a reference to Sir Thomas Hayes, Lord Mayor of London in 1614. A letter of his, dated 8 July that year, to the Lord Chamberlain is summarized in the *Analytical Index to the Series of Records known as the Remembrancia preserved among the Archives of the City of London* (London, 1878, pp. 358–9):

> He had informed himself by means of spies, of many lewd houses, and had gone himself disguised to divers of them, and, finding these nurseries of villainy, had punished them according to their deserts, some by carting and whipping, and many by banishment.
>   . . . Finding the gaol pestered with prisoners, and their bane to take root and beginning at ale-houses, and much mischief to be there plotted, with great waste of corn in brewing heady and strong beer, 'many consuming all their time and means sucking

that sweet poison', he had taken an exact survey of all victualling
houses and ale-houses which were above a thousand, and above
300 barrels of beer in some houses, the whole quantity of beer in
victualling houses amounting to above 40,000 barrels, he had
thought it high time to abridge their number . . . whereby the price
of corn and malt had greatly fallen.

. . . The Bakers and Brewers had been drawn within bounds, so
that, if the case continued, men might have what they paid for, viz.
weight and measure. . .

Hayes went in disguise only for the first purpose quoted, not the
others, but this may nevertheless be the source of a story that he
had gone to work in the same way against victualling abuses. A
letter of 15 October 1614 (*Remembrancia*, pp. 543–4) requires

every Alderman in his Ward to call before him the innholders,
victuallers, ale-house-keepers, cooks and all those who brewed
and sold again in bye-places, and to examine the quantity and
prices of such ale and beer as they had received into their houses
and cellars since Christmas, 1613. . .

so that the issue was still alive in the month of the play. Of course, it
is not quite the same issue as that in Overdo's speech. He trivializes
the whole matter into measuring puddings, cans and custards 'with
a stick; and their circumference, with a thread' (ll. 21–2): this concern for triviality is to be his constant fault. That Jonson has in
mind the parallel with, and the difference from, Busy's tirade in i.
vi seems clear from the appearance in each of the same key phrase,
'high place'. Meaning a place of idolatry, it is Busy's ridiculous
phrase (l. 56) for a pig-booth; meaning a high station in society, it is
Overdo's equally incongruous description of his status and importance in his own eyes (l. 37). There is careful parallelism too in
the central paradoxes which each uses to justify his decision: in
Busy's case, 'we may be religious in midst of the profane' (ll. 71–2),
in Overdo's, 'There is a doing of right out of wrong' (ll. 11–12). The
different terms of debate in each case are thus sharply underlined at
the same time as their similarities are suggested. It is to be the business of the play to show that neither of them really understands the
terms he uses.

Despite his attempt, in disguise, to see the Fair from the inside,
Overdo is hopelessly isolated from it, as Jonson makes plain by

having him deliver his first soliloquy alone (except for the eaves-dropping Mooncalf who may put his head through the curtains of the inner stage). When the Fair breaks in upon him in II. ii his behaviour answers our expectations. He portentously discovers 'enormity' in the 'stale bread, rotten eggs, musty ginger, and dead honey' which are mentioned only in a slanging match between two hucksters. From the same slanging match he is, equally foolishly, glad to draw evidence that 'my name is their terror yet'. These things, and his Ciceronian reprobation of Ursula's overcharging ('O tempora, o mores!') carry on the incongruous excesses of his soliloquy. In trying to address the inhabitants of the Fair (ll. 118–24), he is just as rhetorical, though in a rather different style. The ridiculous classical references are dropped, but the circumlocutions become more fatuously rotund, the similitudes are drawn self-consciously from common life, as if this were the way to come to terms with it—'oily as the King's constable's lamp, and shining as his shoeing-horn'; isocolon and alliteration contrast equally ludi-crously with the humble subject-matter—'Hath thy ale virtue, or thy beer strength ? that the tongue of man may be tickled ? and his palate pleas'd in the morning ?' The bombast carries its own criti-cism, in contrast with the language 'such as men do use' all round it; and, even before he is taken for a fool, the Justice is picked out as a 'roarer', which means a blusterer or 'big talker', as well as a rois-terer. Mooncalf, who has overheard him in II. i, recognizes him at once, ' 'Tis mad Arthur of Bradley, that makes the orations.' How much Mooncalf has heard and understood we are not told, but, when a mere tapster pricks these pretensions to astuteness in a 'high' cause, we are reminded of an aphorism from the *Discoveries* which serves as an apt comment on the situation:

> *Imposture* is a specious thing; yet never worse, then when it faines to be best, and to none discover'd sooner, then the simplest (ll. 236–8, H. & S. viii. 570).

The Fair soon overwhelms the Justice, the very language taking us into a realm of animal energies and appetites which he is power-less to 'correct' or even correctly to observe—the vigorous horsey lingo of Knockem, the likening of Ursula to a whale or Mooncalf to a polecat, the linking of punk and pig (both hot), and the lusty invective of the pig-woman-bawd herself. In this 'debauch'd company', all the Justice can single out for assistance is 'a civil young man' who is in fact a cutpurse. The climax (II. vi) comes in a harangue about bottle ale and tobacco, which is wholly in keeping with Overdo's obstinate concern for trivialities, while the fool applauds and the 'civil young man' picks his purse. It is tempting to suspect that the attack on tobacco was added to please James I, whose views were known, at the court performance; but this seems ruled out by the uncomplimentary resemblance between James and the Justice which would then lie open to 'any politic pick-lock of the scene'.

Act III adds to the satire upon the doing of justice in the Fair by bringing in the watch and their paid informer Whit, who, once they have gone out, reverts to his proper trade of pimp. Then the Puritan visitors redirect our attention to the hypocritical attempt to enter the Fair without contamination. The movement of spurious logic, aided by 'the famelic sense, which is the smell', between Busy's first words in Scene ii and his last, dramatizes an aim and an outlook which we now see to be neatly opposite to Overdo's: the latter's rhetoric is directed towards convincing himself that he will learn about the Fair by becoming involved in it, Busy's towards convincing other people that he remains ignorant about the Fair in his religious repudiation of it; but it is Overdo who remains hopelessly separated from the Fair by his own bombastic stupidity while Busy and his crew become increasingly involved in it. In III. ii Busy's rhetoric, in its exaggerated use of the figures which A. H. Sackton[1] has pointed out—epizeuxis ('it were a sin of obstinacy, great obstinacy, high and horrible obstinacy, to decline, or resist . . .', ll. 80–1), isocolon ('let not your eyes be drawn aside with vanity, nor your ears with noises', ll. 29–30), and paraphrasis ('satisfy your wife's frailty. Let your frail wife be satisfied', ll. 84–5)— gives us the very feel of hypocritical corruption. For 'wheresoever manners . . . are corrupted, Language is.'[2] In making us directly aware of the contrast between appearance and reality by his use of the verbal medium itself as well as of carefully chosen sensory refer-

---

[1] Alexander H. Sackton, *Rhetoric as a dramatic Language in Ben Jonson* (New York, 1948), p. 156.

[2] *Discoveries*, ll. 954–5, H. & S. viii. 593.

ence, Jonson has much in common with Dickens here. We think of the charm of 'a sweet delicate booth with boughs', or the steam of pig after which '*Busy scents like a hound*'. But the greater clarity of focus in Jonson is plain in the very brevity of the scene, as also in the comparison which he makes between Busy's reaction to the Fair and that of Quarlous, or of the Justice. Quarlous, in his plain reasonableness, has been something of a point of stability in the play, yet even he is made aware of the lascivious promptings of the Fair. He goes clean against his earlier advice and urges Winwife 'to lay aboard' his widow, for, in the Fair, modesty is 'disease . . . , not judgement' (ll. 142–3). Overdo on the other hand appears, in Scene iii, incongruously chastened. But, as with Emma after the ignominious failure of her plans for Harriet and Mr Elton (just half way through the work, as here), the partial nature of Overdo's reformation only underlines its ineffectiveness. Again a chain of spurious logic dramatizes his attitude. At the beginning, with 'I will make no more orations', his repetition of Mooncalf's phrase in II. i seems to imply acceptance of the Fair's judgement, but by the end of the scene he is making orations again: 'as I said ever, in Justice' name, and the King's, and for the Commonwealth'. The transition is made by self-satisfied and garrulous contemplation of the figure he will cut when all is known (ll. 6–13) and thence by his customary inflation of his own moral importance, blown up this time by no fewer than six metaphors on end (ll. 26 ff.), to vainglorious welcome of 'beating, . . . imprisonment, . . . infamy, . . . nay, . . . the rack, . . . the hurdle'.

The rest of the Act takes us into the underworld of the jest-books and coney-catching pamphlets. Parallels with the play of *Sir Thomas More*[1] and with the inset play in Act V of Middleton's *The Mayor of Queenborough* show that Jonson is drawing on traditional material, and Edgworth's boast that he will steal from Wasp either the box or the licence from it is in direct line of descent from the 'master thief' tales of the jest-books (e.g. *The Merie Tales of Skelton*, 1567, xiii). But though this simple concentration on the humours of the underworld is diverting enough, it goes on rather

---

[1] Pointed out by C. R. Baskervill in *Modern Philology*, July 1908, and discussed in H. & S. x. 167 ff.

longer than its importance in the play demands. Structurally, it is there to provoke Wasp's jeers when Cokes loses his purse—as if to defeat the sharpers of the Fair were merely a matter of the commonplace watchfulness they make it their business to circumvent—with the result that Wasp takes charge of the licence and meets his own reversal when Edgworth gets it from him. For showing up Wasp's schoolmasterly short-sightedness, his over-emphasis on commonplace precept, one picking of his master's purse would be enough. The repetitiveness is underlined by, for instance, the quite unchanged context in which the Justice again finds Edgworth, his 'proper', his 'civil' young man, in 'debauch'd company', though there is one delightful moment of contrast when Edgworth himself picks up Overdo's phrase and uses it in self-justification: 'Good gentlemen, do not undo me; I am a civil young man, and but a beginner, indeed' (III. v. 244–5). As before, too, the Justice gets the blame.

Act IV brings near to the full circle each of those wheels of ignorance and self-deception out of which the play is made. '*I know* of no disease of the *Soule*', writes Jonson in the *Discoveries* (ll. 801 ff., H. & S. viii. 588), 'but *Ignorance*; not of the Arts, and Sciences, but of it selfe', and he is interested in the Fair as a place where unquestioned appetites and impudent vitality may bring this kind of ignorance to light. The proper inhabitants of the Fair are untouched by it. They know themselves and the world to which they belong, and Jonson does not repudiate them, however he may mock. But, if it is their strength to know their world, they know nothing beyond it, 'no better ware than they have, nor better customers than come' (II. v. 15–16). They are not expected to make the adjustments to a more civilized order of life which are demanded of those who come from outside the Fair. Each of these is changed by what happens to him in it. In Act IV, the Justice is brought nearer to self-knowledge by finding that the only person who respects his petty jurisdiction is mad, though he does not yet see a connexion between this and his own high Stoicism, corrupted by the anticipation of public praise—'The world will have a pretty taste by this, how I can bear adversity. . .' (IV. i. 28–9).

The plot centring on Grace Wellborn, which brings Winwife and

Quarlous to their respective reversals, is too much subdued, for some tastes, to the Fair in which it works. From his own viewpoint, Quarlous recognizes this when he must keep company with the thief who has stolen Cokes's licence for him: 'Facinus quos inquinat, æquat' (IV. vi. 29 and n.); and other characters suffer a similar levelling with the evil that pollutes them. Grace Wellborn is a ward who has been bought by Overdo and is about to be sold to Cokes; her contribution to the play would be strengthened if Jonson could persuade us that it is the bargain and not merely the buyer that she resents. As it is, she is given modesty and honesty, but in a rather masculine sense of the words; and there is no hint of anything to make her admirable wish for 'a husband I must love' (IV. iii. 16) of emotional importance to us. So she escapes being the subject of a bargain only to become that of a lottery. Moreover, Winwife eventually gets her only because Quarlous, the other party to the gamble, sees better possibilities in a rich widow. As Herford and Simpson say (ii. 143), 'Bargaining and fraud make up all the circumstance of the story'. And it is all rather externally done, without our being made aware *through the language* of the kind of moral life involved. Jonson's habit of verbal repetition still works, but only on the periphery of this part of the action—when, for instance, at the end of v. ii, both Quarlous and the Justice (ll. 121, 126) use the word 'conscience', the first with the overtones of '(good) sense' which Shakespeare uses in *Timon*, II. ii. 185, the second with the common meaning of today, though ironically, for he has requited not the madman but Quarlous in disguise.

It is very different with the corrupting effect of the Fair on Mistress Littlewit and Mistress Overdo, who become 'mistresses o' the game'. Here the quality of the whole unsavoury transaction is fully realized. Knockem, for instance, itemizes (IV. v. 21–6) the 'points' of a woman as he would those of a horse, leaving the implication that a horse needs a rider (whether or not Jonson is echoing *Venus and Adonis*) to hang unspoken till the last words in the scene: 'Hide, and be hidden; ride, and be ridden, says the vapour of experience' (ll. 101–2). By that time, brisk discussion of assignations and the attacks of Alice (the professional, custom-shrunk) have given full meaning to the line. The verbal echoes which tie the episode into the rest of the play are fuller, too. Mistress Overdo imitates her husband in manner and speech when she thanks the watch for making their second mistake of the day (i.e. taking Wasp to join her husband in the stocks); and a little later, with Whit, she is 'distempered with these enormities' and goes on at once to 'entreat' from him the 'courtesy' from which stem the following double entendres, culminating in 'Master Overdo shall thank her!' (IV. iv. 184–221). Ursula in her turn catches up and makes punningly precise a phrase which has echoed through the play, 'We are undone for want of fowl ['plover or quail', i.e. prostitutes] i' the Fair' (IV. v. 14, cf. II. ii. 134, III. vi. 83). It is all done with an eye to the lively quality of the moment as well as to the piquant connexions with the rest of the play. At revivals after the Restoration these episodes in IV. v and V. iv must have seemed quite modern in tone. Even to us the spectacle of the simpleton inducted into the loose ways of the world—though of a lower world—recalls Prue or Mrs Pinchwife, despite the lack of the forthrightness of the one and the shrewdness of the other.

The puppetry which is central to the final act takes up again the first strand of the play. As Jonson put it in the *Discoveries*, 'A man cannot imagine that thing so foolish, or rude, but will find, and enjoy an Admirer; at least a Reader, or *Spectator*. The Puppets are seene now in despight of the Players' (ll. 608–11, H. & S. viii. 582). But Jonson does not simply take up, unchanged by the play between, his earlier scheme of satirizing the popular stage. Littlewit's piece, when it comes, has, for instance, a bawdiness which carries on one interest of Acts IV and V, but so feebly as to contrast well with their vigour and irony. At the same time, the comments of Leatherhead and his audience, particularly of Cokes, neatly recall the Induction and seem to have glancing reference to the learning for which *Catiline* had been damned: 'Your home-born projects prove ever the best, they are so easy, and familiar; they put too much learning i' their things now o' days' (v. i. 14–16). Even the puppet Dionysius takes up this charge in his disputation with Busy—'I have as little to do with learning as he; and do scorn her helps as much as he' (v. v. 104–5)—and Busy's capitulation is less a comment upon him than upon the popular stage which in Jonson's view makes the charge unanswerable. For Busy's conversion is less of an event than it would have been if Jonson had not expended all his art on the earlier capitulation to roast pig. The reasoning which leads from 'Down with Dagon' (v. v. 1) to 'I am changed, and will become a beholder with you', may be cleverer but is less amusing because less spurious; it is not activated with a sense of commonplace appetite corrupting even the shreds of logic. Busy has been all along a mere balloon, and his deflation is unexpected only in being sudden and under pressure of reasoning. We would prefer him, no doubt, to go out like Ananias in *The Alchemist*:

> may dogs defile thy walls,
> And waspes, and hornets breed beneath thy roofe,
> This seat of false-hood, and this caue of cos'nage (v. v. 113-15).

But that would be to ask for a stronger character in a different kind of play.

The Justice, on the other hand, however ridiculous his hyperboles, does serve a genuine ideal. He only mistakes its relevance and misreads the evidence before his eyes. For him to be disabused is an event of importance. Jonson gives him his moment of triumph in unmasking enormity (v. vi. 33-69), but only that he may, when in turn his own wife is unmasked, find how much he is 'the dupe of everyone else's disguise and the victim of his own'.[1] He capitulates not to the logic of a puppet but to the good sense of Quarlous:

> ... remember you are but Adam, flesh and blood! You have your frailty, forget your other name of Overdo... (ll. 99-101).

The invitation to supper is like the conventional dance to end a play. Jonson leaves us with the reflection that we are but Adam, flesh and blood—for the whole play backs up the phrase. We have entered, in the Fair, an underworld of amoral human energies, and brought back the sense that, in a strict count, none does offend, none, more than another, and that the recognition of that fact is a more secure basis for an un-self-righteous morality than those moral schemes which, working *a priori*, fail to come to terms with flesh and blood.

[1] H. & S. ii. 144.

II. THE TEXT

The only authoritative text for *Bartholomew Fair* is the folio printed in 1631 by John Beale for Robert Allot but not published[1] till its inclusion in the Second Folio of Jonson's *Works* in 1640. There the 1631 title page was retained (see facsimile) and another was printed on A1 recto[2] of the 1631 text:

The / Workes / of / Benjamin Jonson. / The second Volume. / Containing / These Playes, / *Viz.* / 1. Bartholomew Fayre. / 2. The Staple of Newes. / 3. The Divell is an Asse. / *London,* / Printed for Richard Meighen, / 1640.

The collation is A1 recto, (originally blank) Meighen's title page; A1 verso, blank; A2 recto, title page of *Bartholomew Fair*; A2 verso, blank; A3 recto, the Prologue; A3 verso, the Persons of the Play; A4 recto to A6 verso, the Induction; B to M in fours, paged 1 to 88 (with pp. 12, 13, 31 misnumbered as 6, 3, 13 respectively), the text of the play and the Epilogue.

For the present text, photostats have been used of the copy in the library of Trinity College, Cambridge (T), and of one with press mark Douce I. 303 in the Bodleian (D), collated with one copy in the Grey Collection, Public Library, Auckland (G), one in the Alexander Turnbull Library, Wellington (AT), three in the British Museum with press marks C 39.k.9 (BM1), 79.l.4 (BM2), and 642.l.29 (BM3), and one further copy in the Bodleian with press mark Don.d.66 (B). The librarians of Oriel and All Souls Colleges, Oxford, and of Trinity College, Dublin, have kindly answered letters on special points.

The play was very badly printed: misspelling is common, through letters being dropped (e.g. '*eners*', I4 verso, IV. v. 62.1) or added (e.g. 'trifle', E 1 recto, II. v. 60) or misplaced (e.g. 'Soueragine', A5 recto, Ind. 69); the punctuation (in which, as we know

---

[1] It was not entered in S.R., though it was transferred to John Legatt and Andrew Crooke, along with sixty other books, on 1 July 1637 (Arber, iv. 387). There is no record of the further transfer to Richard Meighen.

[2] The existence of a copy with this page blank (in the possession of Sir Walter Greg) shows this general title to have been added later. See *Proceedings of the Oxford Bibliographical Society*, i. 259.

from the MS. of the *Masque of Queens* and from more carefully printed plays, Jonson was scrupulous) is most casual, to the frequent detriment of the sense (e.g. II. ii. 16). Some of the worst errors occur only in some copies (D, G, AT, BM1, of those in question here) and show that the type for the forme containing L2 recto and L3 verso was accidentally disturbed and had to be reset. Only in this way can the oddities of spacing, changes of type, mispunctuation, and textual errors be explained (see app. crit. to v. iv. 96–110, though it has not seemed necessary to give a full account of these variants). Other differences amongst the copies collated reveal a few haphazard proof corrections, all of them in Act II and in the first two scenes of Act IV. The Act IV errors seem to have been picked up early in the printing, as they occur, to my knowledge, only in the Trinity Cambridge copy, where on sig. H2 'asweare' (IV. i. 63) appears for 'answere' and 'Tryumph' (l. 43) for 'Triumph'. Some of the Act II corrections may be Jonson's, like the attempts to mend the punctuation at ii. 46 and 59 ('Heere,' and 'morning,'[1] for 'Heere.' and 'morning.'[2]) and at iv. 38 and 61 (by inserting commas after 'sing' and 'here'[1]). These would hardly have troubled the printer, considering the things he was content to leave.[3]

In this edition, printer's errors of which one correction alone seems possible or overwhelmingly probable have been corrected silently. The Folio punctuation has been modernized, though sparingly[4]; it is given in the apparatus whenever alteration has made a difference to the sense. Spelling, including that of proper names, has been modernized, except for a few cases where the older form is a means of avoiding a misleading modern sense (e.g. 'inginer', 'cattel', II. ii. 16, 18).

All the stage directions given in the copy text have been kept; any addition to them has been enclosed in square brackets. The copy text masses at the head of each scene the names of all the char-

---

[1] In G, AT, BM2, BM3, B, T.   [2] In BM1, D.

[3] The presupposition is strengthened by errors which are corrected in all but one copy in the possession of Mr Percy Simpson (see H. & S. ix. 108): e.g. misspellings like 'Egdeworth' (D1 verso, II. ii. 56) which the printer would scarcely notice, and an omitted stage direction (II. iv. 39.1) which he would be unlikely to supply.

[4] It is often a guide to the pauses and pace of realistic dialogue.

acters participating in it, regardless of the times they enter. These have had to be distributed throughout the scene according to their entries (and/or exits). The apparatus notes the massed names, together with the occasionally added 'To him', 'To them', at the beginning of each scene, but makes no reference to their subsequent redistribution. Hence when a stage direction like that at 1. i. 18.1, '[Enter] to him WIN', is compared with apparatus to 1. i. 0.1, it can be seen that, with the exception of the bracketed word, the direction comes from the head of the scene, unlike the similar one at Ind. 45.1 which appears in the body of the scene in the original.

III. STAGE HISTORY

The history of *Bartholomew Fair* on the stage is a record of success until the second quarter of the eighteenth century and of relative neglect since then.

The day after the first performance at the Hope on 31 October 1614, *Bartholomew Fair* was acted at Court,[1] but there is no record of any other performance of the play during the reigns of James I or Charles I, and it was not until after its publication in the Folio of 1640–1 that it was used as the basis of a pamphlet account of the Fair (see Appendix I). But 'since the Restauration', wrote Langbaine,[2] 'this Play has frequently appear'd on the Stage . . . , with great applause'. In 1661 the King's players under Killigrew gave it in Gibbon's tennis court, Vere Street, on 8 and 27 June, on 7 September, 12 November, and 18 December[3]: Pepys, who saw all but the second and the last of these performances, admired the play, but not the puppets which were reintroduced on 7 September. A reference in the list of plays entitled 'Sir Edw. Browne's Memorandum Book, 1662'[4] in BM. MS. Sloane 1900 f.63v, shows it to have

[1] See Ind. 68, H. & S. ix. 245, Chambers, iv. 183. The players were the Lady Elizabeth's Servants, recently united with the Children of the Queen's Revels for whom, under their earlier title of the Children of the Chapel, Jonson had written *Cynthia's Revels* (1600), *Poetaster* (1601), and *Epicoene* (1609).

[2] *The English Dramatick Poets*, 1691, pp. 287–8; see too R. G. Noyes, *Ben Jonson on the English Stage 1660–1776*, Cambridge, Mass., 1935.

[3] J. Q. Adams, *The Dramatic Records of Sir Henry Herbert*, 1917, p. 117.

[4] See Sir Walter Greg, 'Theatrical Repertories of 1662', *Gentleman's Magazine* CCCI (1906), pp. 69–71.

been in performance in 1662 'At the New Theatre in Lincolnes Inne fields'. Pepys saw it again on 2 August 1664 and 4 September 1668. In between, a command performance on 27 April 1667 is recorded[1] in a warrant of 29 August 1668, for plays acted from 10 December 1666 to 31 July 1668 (L.C. 5/139, p. 129). Dryden's allusion in the same year in *Sir Martin Mar-All* (v. i: 'Now he is as earnest in the quarrel as Cokes among the puppets') shows that he expected the play to be well known, as other allusions show that it was: for instance *The English Rogue*, 1668 [by Francis Kirkman and Richard Head], pp. 228–9, where the old woman by whom Merton Latroon is taken up has her cheeks 'so bathed . . . with tears . . . that you would have sworn she was the representation of the Pig-woman in Ben's *Bartholomew-fair*'. In a list of the following year it is among the plays[2] 'now allowed of to His Maties Servants at ye New Theatre' (i.e. in Bridges Street, Covent Garden, whither they had moved from Vere Street on 7 May 1663), and a performance is recorded[3] at the Cockpit in Whitehall on 22 February—again attended by Pepys. After this, except for the command performance of 30 November 1674,[4] there is no exact record of performances during the remainder of the century. Downes tells us that the 'mixt Company', formed when the Patentees (Killigrew and Davenant) of each company united Patents in 1682, revived it among 'the several old & Modern Plays, that were the Property of Mr *Killigrew*.'[5]

Mention should perhaps be made of a farce based on the play. A letter[6] of 12 October 1661, from a certain Rev. William Hooke to a New England friend, describes a court performance of it. From the *Reliquiae Baxterianae*[7] of Richard Baxter (after whom one of the Puritans in it was said to be named), it seems that this was revived in Dublin nine years later.

[1] Allardyce Nicoll, *A History of English Drama*, Cambridge, 1952, i. 343.
[2] Allotted c. 12 January 1668/9 (L.C. 5/12, p. 212), *ibid.*, p. 353.
[3] *Ibid.*, p. 344.
[4] Warrant dated 27 January 1674/5, *ibid.*, p. 345, L.C. 5/141, p. 116.
[5] *Roscius Anglicanus*, 1708; ed. Summers, 1928, pp. 39–40.
[6] Mather Papers, 4th Series, viii. 177–8 (Massachusetts Historical Society).
[7] 1696, part III, p. 84.

In the eighteenth century[1] it was in continuous performance up to 1731. There were performances at Drury Lane on 18 August 1702, 25 March, 8 April, and 28 September 1704, and on 8 January 1705, and at the Haymarket on 12 and 14 August and 22 October 1707. Between 1708 and 1722 the play was given at Drury Lane every season except for 1714 and 1721. There was a performance at Court on 21 December 1722; for one at Drury Lane on 30 October 1731 the play was announced as 'not acted seven years'.

Except for an altered version of the play put on at Lincoln's Inn Fields on 25 August 1735, it then passed out of the repertoire until the revival by the Phoenix Society, under the direction of Montagu Summers, on 26 and 27 June 1921, at the New Oxford Theatre. Littlewit was played by Eric Cowley, Win by Angela Baddeley, Dame Purecraft by Margaret Yarde, Busy by Ben Field, Winwife by Tristan Rawson, Quarlous by Howard Rose, Cokes by Ernest Thesiger, Wasp by Stanley Lathbury, Overdo by Frank Cellier, Dame Overdo by Helena Millais, Grace Wellborn by Clare Harris, Leatherhead by H. K. Ayliff, Joan Trash by Elsie French, Edgworth by Edward Combermere, Nightingale by John Clifford, Ursula by Roy Byford, Mooncalf by Edwin Greenwood, Knockem by Eugene Leahy, Whit by Richard Grenville, Alice by Sylvia Young, Trouble-all by Edwin Greenwood, Stage-keeper by P. H. Vernon, Book-holder by F. Harker, and Scrivener by Allan Wade (the producer).

The play was performed by the Old Vic Company at the Edinburgh International Festival in 1950 (in the Assembly Hall) and from 18 December to 13 January following at the Old Vic Theatre, London. Littlewit was played by Anthony Van Bridge, Win by Dorothy Tutin, Dame Purecraft by Dorothy Green, Busy by Mark Dignam, Winwife by John Ebdon, Quarlous by Douglas Wilmer, Cokes by Robert Eddison, Wasp by Alec Clunes, Overdo by Roger Livesey, Dame Overdo by Ursula Jeans, Grace Wellborn by Heather Stannard, Leatherhead by George Speaight, Edgworth by Paul Hansard, Nightingale by Leo McKern, Ursula by Nuna Davey, Knockem by William Devlin.

[1] What follows is indebted to Noyes, *op. cit.*, and to Allardyce Nicoll, *op. cit.*, ii. 128–37.

C

There have too been a number of amateur performances: on 30 April 1940 at Bryn Mawr College, Pennsylvania, in March 1947 by the Marlowe Society at Cambridge, produced by Donald Beves, and on 26 and 27 September 1952 by the Dunedin Teachers' College in the Wallace Hall, Dunedin, produced by Jean Ballard.

BARTHOLMEW FAYRE:

A COMEDIE,

ACTED IN THE
YEARE, 1614.

By the Lady *ELIZABETHS*
SERVANTS.

And then dedicated to King IAMES, of
most *Blessed Memorie*;

By the Author, BENIAMIN IOHNSON.

Si foret in terris, rideret Democritus : *nam
Spectaret populum ludis attentiùs ipsis,
Vt sibi prabentem, mimo spectacula plura.
Scriptores autem narrare putaret asello
Fabellam surdo.* Hor. lib. 2. Epist. 1.

LONDON,
Printed by *I. B.* for ROBERT ALLOT, and are
to be sold at the signe of the *Beare*, in *Pauls*
Church-yard. 1631.

Title page of the play in the 1640 Folio

BARTHOLOMEW FAIR

THE
PROLOGUE
TO
THE KING'S
MAJESTY.

Your Majesty is welcome to a Fair;
Such place, such men, such language and such ware,
You must expect: with these, the zealous noise
Of your land's Faction, scandaliz'd at toys,
As babies, hobby-horses, puppet-plays,   5
And such like rage, whereof the petulant ways
Yourself have known, and have been vex'd with long.
These for your sport, without particular wrong
Or just complaint of any private man
(Who of himself or shall think well or can),   10
The Maker doth present: and hopes tonight
To give you for a fairing, true delight.

PROLOGUE] for the performance at court, 1 November 1614.
4. Faction] the Puritans.
toys] rubbish, trumpery.
5. babies] dolls.
12. fairing] a present at a fair.

THE PERSONS
OF THE PLAY.

JOHN LITTLEWIT.	*A Proctor.*	
SOLOMON.	*His man.*	
WIN LITTLEWIT.	*His wife.*	
DAME PURECRAFT.	*Her mother, and a widow.*	
ZEAL-OF-THE-LAND BUSY.	*Her suitor, a Banbury man.*	5
WINWIFE.	*His rival, a gentleman.*	
QUARLOUS.	*His companion, a gamester.*	
BARTHOLOMEW COKES.	*An Esquire of Harrow.*	
HUMPHREY WASP.	*His man.*	
ADAM OVERDO.	*A Justice of Peace.*	10
DAME OVERDO.	*His wife.*	
GRACE WELLBORN.	*His ward.*	
LANTERN LEATHERHEAD.	*A Hobby-horse-seller.*	
JOAN TRASH.	*A Ginger-bread-woman.*	
EZEKIEL EDGWORTH.	*A Cutpurse.*	15
NIGHTINGALE.	*A Ballad-singer.*	
URSULA.	*A Pig-woman.*	
MOONCALF.	*Her Tapster.*	
JORDAN KNOCKEM.	*A Horse-courser, and Ranger o'*	
	Turnbull.	20

Puritan

2. SOLOMON. *His man.*] *G; not in F.*

1. Proctor] an agent or attorney.

5. Banbury] noted for Puritans (cf. III. ii. 96); 'Banbury Zeal, Cheese and Cakes' was the proverb.

7. gamester] rake; cf. l. 23.

8. *COKES*] cf. I. v. 50; Ford, *The Lovers Melancholy*, IV. ii: 'A kind of Cokes, which is, as the learned term it, an Asse, a Puppy . . . a Dolt'.

18. *MOONCALF*] mis-shapen birth, monster.

19. Horse-courser] a 'scourser' of (cf. III. iv. 22) or dealer in ridden horses.

Ranger] (*a*) keeper of a park; (*b*) rake, cf. *O.E.D.*, s.v.[1], 1599: 'Accusing his father . . . for an whore-master and . . . a raunger'.

20. Turnbull] a street in Clerkenwell noted for brothels: cf. Falstaff on Shallow who 'hath done nothing but prate to me of the wildness of his youth, and the feats he hath done about Turnbull Street' (*2 Henry IV*, III. ii. 330).

VAL. CUTTING.	*A Roarer.*	
CAPTAIN WHIT.	*A Bawd.*	
PUNK ALICE.	*Mistress o' the game.* ~~Prostitution~~	
TROUBLE-ALL.	*A madman.*	
HAGGIS. } BRISTLE. }	*Watchmen.*	25
POCHER.	*A Beadle.*	
FILCHER. } SHARKWELL. }	*Doorkeepers.*	
PUPPY.	*A Wrestler.*	30
NORDERN.	*A Clothier.*	
	Costermonger.	
	Tinderbox-man.	
	Corncutter.	
	Passengers.	35
	Puppets.	

25-7. HAGGIS . . . *Beadle.*] *G;* WHTCHMEN, three. *F.*   28-9. FILCHER . . . *Doorkeepers.*] *G;* DOORE-KEEPERS. *F.*   30. PUPPY. *A Wrestler.*] *G;* WRESTLER. *F.*   31. NORDERN. *A Clothier.*] *G;* CLOTHIER. *F.*   33. *Tinderbox-man.*] *This ed.;* MOVSETRAP-man. *F.*   34. *Corncutter*] *G; not in F.* 35. *Passengers.*] *G;* PORTERS. *F.*

---

21. Roarer] bully, roisterer.
23. the game] prostitution.
32. Costermonger] seller of costards, i.e. apples.

Bartholomew Fair

THE INDUCTION
ON THE STAGE

[*Enter*] STAGE-KEEPER.

[*Stage.*] Gentlemen, have a little patience, they are e'en upon
coming, instantly. He that should begin the play, Master
Littlewit, the Proctor, has a stitch new fallen in his black
silk stocking; 'twill be drawn up ere you can tell twenty.
He plays one o' the Arches, that dwells about the Hos- 5
pital, and he has a very pretty part. But for the whole play,
will you ha' the truth on't? (I am looking, lest the poet
hear me, or his man, Master Brome, behind the arras) it is
like to be a very conceited scurvy one, in plain English.
When 't comes to the Fair once, you were e'en as good go 10
to Virginia for anything there is of Smithfield. He has not
hit the humours, he does not know 'em; he has not con-
vers'd with the Bartholomew-birds, as they say; he has

---

5. *Arches*] practitioners in the ecclesiastical Court of Arches ('kept in
[Bow] Church', 'the first in this Cittie builded . . . with Arches of stone',
Stow, i. 253–4), the court of appeal from the diocesan courts.

5–6. *the Hospital*] 'S. Bartlemew in Smithfield, an Hospitall of great
receipt and reliefe for the poore . . . endowed by the Citizens beneuolence'
(Stow, ii. 143).

8. *Brome*] Richard Brome (d. 1652) at first servant, then friend, and, as a
playwright, imitator of Jonson (whose verses 'To my old Faithfull Seruant
and . . . louing Friend: the Author' are prefixed to Brome's *The Northerne
Lasse*, 1632, H. & S. viii. 409).

arras] tapestry hanging.

9. *conceited*] fantastic, ingenious.

11. *Smithfield*] site of the Fair (see III. ii. 37–8 below, and note).

12. *humours*] oddities exhibited by particular classes of people (cf.
O.E.D., s.v.6c, 1566: '. . . the seuerall conceited humours of Bumpkin, the
huntsman, Bobbinall, the shepheard . . .') rather than the technical sense of
Jonson's 'humour' plays (cf. *E.M.O.*, Ind. 88–199).

ne'er a sword and buckler man in his Fair, nor a little
Davy, to take toll o' the bawds there, as in my time, nor a   15
Kindheart, if anybody's teeth should chance to ache in his
play. Nor a juggler with a well-educated ape to come over
the chain, for the King of England, and back again for the
Prince, and sit still on his arse for the Pope, and the King
of Spain! None o' these fine sights! Nor has he the canvas-   20
cut i' the night, for a hobby-horse-man to creep in to his
she-neighbour, and take his leap there! Nothing! No, an'
some writer (that I know) had had but the penning o' this
matter, he would ha' made you such a jig-a-jog i' the
booths, you should ha' thought an earthquake had been i'   25
the Fair! But these master-poets, they will ha' their own
absurd courses; they will be inform'd of nothing! He has,
sir-reverence, kick'd me three or four times about the
Tiring-house, I thank him, for but offering to put in, with
my experience. I'll be judg'd by you, gentlemen, now, but   30
for one conceit of mine! Would not a fine pump upon the
stage ha' done well, for a property now? And a punk set
under upon her head, with her stern upward, and ha'

14. sword] *F3;* sword, *F.*

---

14. *sword and buckler man*] 'West-Smith-field . . . was formerly
called *Ruffians-Hall*, where such men met casually and otherwise, to try
Masteries with Sword and Buckler' (Fuller, *The Worthies of England*, 1662,
ii. 199).

14–15. *little Davy*] apparently 'a bully on the town' (Dyce, *Remarks on
. . . Shakespeare*, London, 1844, p. 286, quoting Dekker, *Newes from Hell
. . .* , 1606, sig. B: 'At sword and buckler little Davy was no bodie to him');
cf. Black Davie 'who at sword and buckler would fight with any gentleman
or other for twelve pence' (*Tarltons Jests*, 1611, ed. W. C. Hazlitt, *Shakespeare Jest Books*, 1864, ii. 197).

16. *Kindheart*] 'he, that all the daies of his life hath beene famous for
drawing teeth' (Chettle, *Kind-harts Dreame*, 1592, dedication; Percy Soc.
v. 7).

21. *hobby-horse-man*] ? wencher.

28. *sir-reverence*] with all respect, with apologies (altered from *sa'* (i.e.
save) reverence).

29. *to put in*] to intervene; cf. *O.E.D.*, s.v.44h, 1656: 'Unless your
Majesty put in betwixt my misery, and my Creditors rage'.

31. *conceit*] (ingenious) notion.

been sous'd by my witty young masters o' the Inns o'
Court ? What think you o' this for a show, now ? He will   35
not hear o' this ! I am an ass ! I ! And yet I kept the stage
in Master Tarlton's time, I thank my stars. Ho ! an' that
man had liv'd to have play'd in *Bartholomew Fair*, you
should ha' seen him ha' come in, and ha' been cozened i'
the cloth-quarter, so finely ! And Adams, the rogue, ha'   40
leap'd and caper'd upon him, and ha' dealt his vermin
about, as though they had cost him nothing. And then a
substantial watch to ha' stolen in upon 'em, and taken
'em away, with mistaking words, as the fashion is, in the
stage-practice.   45

[*Enter*] BOOK-HOLDER, SCRIVENER, *to him.*

Book. How now ? what rare discourse are you fall'n upon ? ha!
    Ha' you found any familiars here, that you are so free ?
    What's the business ?
Stage. Nothing, but the understanding gentlemen o' the
    ground here ask'd my judgement.   50
Book. Your judgement, rascal ? For what ? Sweeping the
    stage ? Or gathering up the broken apples for the bears

---

34. *sous'd*] drenched with water.

34–5. *Inns o' Court*] 'Houses of students in the Common Lawe . . . , a
whole Universitie, as it were' (Stow, i. 76); properly four—Lincoln's Inn,
the Inner Temple, the Middle Temple, and Gray's Inn.

37. *Tarlton*] leading comedian of the Queen's men till his death in 1588
(Chambers, ii. 342).

40. *cloth-quarter*] along the north wall of St Bartholomew's church, com-
mercially the most important part of the fair; in point here because of one
of *Tarltons Jests* (1611), 'How fiddlers fiddled away Tarltons apparel'
(Hazlitt, *op. cit.*, ii. 207), as a result of which he was mocked at the Curtain
as one 'Who in his shirt heard musicke play, While all his clothes were
stolen away'.

Adams] John, also of the Queen's men (Chambers, ii. 296, 343).

41. *vermin*] C.S.A. suggests fleas disturbed in the trunk hose.

44. *mistaking words*] as, for instance, in *Much Ado*, III. iii.

45.1. *BOOK-HOLDER*] prompter.

49. *understanding*] with pun on 'standing under', i.e. below, in the pit.

50. *ground*] pit (of theatre).

52–3. *bears within*] The Hope Theatre (on the site of the old Bear Garden)
was built with a stage on trestles so that it could be removed for bear-
baiting one day in fourteen (see *Henslowe's Diary*, ed. Greg, 1908, ii. 67).

within? Away rogue, it's come to a fine degree in these spectacles when such a youth as you pretend to a judgement. [*Exit* STAGE-KEEPER.] And yet he may, i' the most 55 o' this matter i' faith: for the author hath writ it just to his meridian, and the scale of the grounded judgements here, his play-fellows in wit. Gentlemen; not for want of a prologue, but by way of a new one, I am sent out to you here, with a scrivener, and certain articles drawn out in haste 60 between our author, and you; which if you please to hear, and as they appear reasonable, to approve of, the play will follow presently. Read, scribe, gi' me the counterpane.

Scriv. Articles of Agreement, indented, between the spectators or hearers, at the Hope on the Bankside, in the 65 county of Surrey, on the one party; and the author of *Bartholomew Fair* in the said place and county, on the other party: the one and thirtieth day of October 1614 and in the twelfth year of the reign of our Sovereign Lord, James, by the grace of God King of England, France, and 70 Ireland; Defender of the Faith; and of Scotland the seven and fortieth.

INPRIMIS, It is covenanted and agreed, by and between the parties above-said, and the said spectators, and hearers, as well the curious and envious, as the favouring and 75 judicious, as also the grounded judgements and understandings do for themselves severally covenant and agree, to remain in the places their money or friends have put them in, with patience, for the space of two hours and an half, and somewhat more. In which time the author promiseth to present them, by us, with a new sufficient play called *Bartholomew Fair*, merry, and as full of noise as sport: made to delight all, and to offend none; provided they have either the wit or the honesty to think well of themselves. 85

---

55. *Exit* STAGE-KEEPER.] *G.*

57. *meridian*] point of culmination, full stretch of his (the stage-keeper's) faculties; see Introduction, p. xv.

63. *counterpane*] the opposite part of an indenture.

It is further agreed that every person here have his or
their free-will of censure, to like or dislike at their own
charge, the author having now departed with his right: it
shall be lawful for any man to judge his six pen'orth, his
twelve pen'orth, so to his eighteen pence, two shillings,   90
half a crown, to the value of his place: provided always his
place get not above his wit. And if he pay for half a dozen,
he may censure for all them too, so that he will undertake
that they shall be silent. He shall put in for censures here,
as they do for lots at the lottery: marry if he drop but six-   95
pence at the door, and will censure a crown's worth, it is
thought there is no conscience, or justice in that.

It is also agreed, that every man here exercise his own
judgement, and not censure by contagion, or upon trust,
from another's voice, or face, that sits by him, be he   100
never so first in the commission of wit: as also, that he be
fix'd and settled in his censure, that what he approves, or
not approves, today, he will do the same tomorrow, and
if tomorrow, the next day, and so the next week (if need
be): and not to be brought about by any that sits on the   105

---

87. *censure*] opinion, judgement, criticism (without adverse sense); cf.
O.E.D., s.v.3, 1624: 'Give me thy free and true censure'.

88. *charge*] expense, cost.
departed] parted.

89–91. *six pen'orth . . . half a crown*] very high prices when Overbury
about this time can speak of 'twelvepence . . . for the best room in a playhouse' (*Characters*, ed. Rimbault, 1856, p. 154); perhaps, as Chambers
suggests (ii. 534), for 'a new play at a new house'. For the bearing of this
passage on the supposed Jonsonian authorship of the address 'To the great
Variety of Readers' in the Shakespeare First Folio see Greg, *The Shakespeare First Folio*, 1955, p. 20.

92. *pay for half a dozen*] cf. *M.L.*, II, Chorus, 63: 'Your two shilling worth
[of censure] is allow'd you: but you will take your ten shilling worth, your
twenty shilling worth, and more'.

95. *lottery*] the lottery opened in 1612, under royal patronage, 'for the
present plantation of English Colonies in Virginia'.

99. *contagion*] corrupting contact (with his neighbour, i.e. taking over
the latter's opinion).

101. *commission of wit*] body of critics (a commission being a body with
delegated authority to conduct an investigation).

105. *brought about*] made to turn right round; cf. *3 Henry VI*, II. v. 27:

bench with him, though they indict and arraign plays
daily. He that will swear *Jeronimo* or *Andronicus* are the
best plays yet, shall pass unexcepted at, here, as a man
whose judgement shows it is constant, and hath stood
still, these five and twenty, or thirty years. Though it be   110
an ignorance, it is a virtuous and staid ignorance; and
next to truth, a confirm'd error does well; such a one the
author knows where to find him.

It is further covenanted, concluded and agreed, that
how great soever the expectation be, no person here is to   115
expect more than he knows, or better ware than a Fair
will afford: neither to look back to the sword-and-buck-
ler-age of Smithfield, but content himself with the present. Instead of a little Davy, to take toll o' the bawds,
the author doth promise a strutting Horse-courser, with   120
a leer Drunkard, two or three to attend him, in as good
equipage as you would wish. And then for Kindheart,
the tooth-drawer, a fine oily Pig-woman with her Tapster to bid you welcome, and a consort of Roarers for
music. A wise Justice of Peace *meditant*, instead of a jug-   125
gler with an ape. A civil cutpurse *searchant*. A sweet
Singer of new Ballads *allurant*: and as fresh an Hypocrite as ever was broach'd *rampant*. If there be never a
servant-monster i' the Fair, who can help it? he says;

'How many hours brings about the day;... days will finish up the year.'
  106. *bench*] (*a*) a form on the stage, usually occupied (*S.N.*, Ind. 16) by
'noblemen' and 'grave wits'; (*b*) a court of justice.
  107. Jeronimo ... Andronicus] Kyd's *Spanish Tragedy* and Shakespeare's *Titus Andronicus*. This would give for both plays dates between 1584
and 1589, though exaggeration of their age is likely in this context. Jonson
was twitted in *Satiromastix*, IV. i. 130, with having taken 'mad Ieronimoes
part' as a strolling player, and he had been paid by Henslowe (Diary, 25
September 1601 and 22 June 1602) for 'new adicyons for Jeronymo.'
  121. *leer*] looking obliquely; sly.
  122. *equipage*] retinue, following.
  129–133. *servant-monster* ... Tales, Tempests ... *dances*] open tilting at
Shakespeare's last plays, their marvels (Caliban is three times called
'servant-monster' in the first nine lines of *The Tempest*, III. ii, and
'monster' is re-echoed throughout the scene) and dances (like that of
'twelve Satyres' in *The Winter's Tale*, IV. iii. 354.1); cf. the similar terms in

nor a nest of antics? He is loth to make Nature afraid in 130
his plays, like those that beget *Tales, Tempests,* and such
like drolleries, to mix his head with other men's heels;
let the concupiscence of jigs and dances reign as strong as
it will amongst you: yet if the puppets will please anybody, they shall be entreated to come in. 135

In consideration of which, it is finally agreed by the
foresaid hearers and spectators that they neither in themselves conceal, nor suffer by them to be concealed, any
state-decipherer, or politic picklock of the scene, so
solemnly ridiculous as to search out who was meant by 140
the Ginger-bread-woman, who by the Hobby-horse-
man, who by the Costermonger, nay, who by their
wares; or that will pretend to affirm, on his own inspired
ignorance, what Mirror of Magistrates is meant by the
Justice, what great lady by the Pig-woman, what con- 145
ceal'd statesman by the Seller of Mousetraps, and so of
the rest. But that such person, or persons so found, be
left discovered to the mercy of the author, as a forfeiture

the address 'To the Reader' in the Quarto (1612) of *A.*: '... thou wert never
more fair in the way to be cos'ned (then in this Age) in *Poetry*, especially in
Playes: wherein now, the Concupiscence of Daunces, and Antickes so
raigneth, as to runne away from Nature, and be afraid of her, is the onely
point of art that tickles the *Spectators*.'

130. *nest*] group.

antics] clowns, clownish dances; cf. *Samson Agonistes*, 1325: 'Jugglers
and dancers, antics, mummers, mimics'.

132. *drolleries*] (comic) entertainments; in *Tempest*, III. iii. 21, the dumb-
show of 'several strange shapes' is called 'a living drollery'.

139. *politic*] shrewd in public affairs, cf. *Richard III*, II. iii. 20: 'politic
grave counsel'.

picklock] cf. *M.L.*, II, Chorus, 11–14: 'It is picking the Lock of the Scene;
not opening it the faire way with a Key. A *Play* though it apparell, and present vices in generall, flies from all particularities in persons.'

144. *Mirror of Magistrates*] As *mirror* can mean 'paragon', Jonson need
not have in mind, as H. & S. believe, 'Whetstone's *A Mirour for Magestrates
of Cyties*, 1584, in which the chief argument is that a careful magistrate must
disguise himself and frequent places of entertainment in order to discover
their real character.' He seems rather to be warning against identification of
his Justice with Sir Thomas Hayes (see Introduction, p. xx).

148. *discovered*] exposed to view, revealed.

to the stage, and your laughter, aforesaid; as also, such
as shall so desperately, or ambitiously, play the fool by 150
his place aforesaid, to challenge the author of scurrility
because the language somewhere savours of Smithfield,
the booth, and the pig-broth, or of profaneness because
a madman cries, 'God quit you', or 'bless you'. In witness whereof, as you have preposterously put to your 155
seals already (which is your money), you will now add
the other part of suffrage, your hands. The play shall
presently begin. And though the Fair be not kept in the
same region that some here, perhaps, would have it, yet
think that therein the author hath observ'd a special de- 160
corum, the place being as dirty as Smithfield, and as
stinking every whit.

Howsoever, he prays you to believe his ware is still the
same, else you will make him justly suspect that he that
is so loth to look on a baby, or an hobby-horse, here, 165
would be glad to take up a commodity of them, at any
laughter, or loss, in another place.   [*Exeunt.*]

---

151. *to challenge . . . of*] to accuse; *O.E.D.* quotes *Arcadia* (1590): 'To
be challenged of unkindness'.

154. *God quit you*] As the madman (Trouble-all) cries only 'quit you',
'save you', etc., H. & S. conjecture omission to conform with the Act of
Abuses, 1606; cf. Epilogue, 7–8.

155. *preposterously*] in reversed order, doing first what should be last.

157. *suffrage*] approval.

160–1. *decorum*] fitness, congruity; the criterion governing the co-ordi-
nation of means and ends in Renaissance literature.

161. *dirty*] Smithfield was not paved and drained till the following year
(see Howes in Stow, *Annales*, 1615, p. 1023).

162. *stinking*] cf. Dekker, *Satiromastix*, III. i. 227–30: 'Th'ast a breath as
sweet as the Rose, that growes by the Beare-garden, as sweete as the
proud'st heade a Garlike in *England*.'

166. *commodity*] a quantity, 'lot'. It was a common swindle for part of a
loan to be granted in (often worthless) commodities. An agent of the lender
would buy them up for a fraction of their supposed 'value' though the
borrower would have to repay this in full. Hence he is saying, 'If you do not
laugh, the author will suspect it is because you are in debt.' Cf. Prologue,
l. 10.

Act I

Scene I

[*Enter*] LITTLEWIT.

[*Lit.*] A pretty conceit, and worth the finding! I ha' such luck
to spin out these fine things still, and like a silk-worm, out
of myself. Here's Master Bartholomew Cokes, of Harrow
o' th' Hill, i' th' county of Middlesex, esquire, takes forth
his licence to marry Mistress Grace Wellborn of the said   5
place and county: and when does he take it forth? Today!
The four and twentieth of August! Bartholomew day!
Bartholomew upon Bartholomew! There's the device!
Who would have mark'd such a leap-frog chance now? A
very less than ames-ace, on two dice! Well, go thy ways,   10
John Littlewit, Proctor John Littlewit: one o' the pretty
wits o' Paul's, the Littlewit of London (so thou art call'd)

O.I. LITTLEWIT.] LITTLE-VVIT. ⎰ *To him* ⎱ VVIN. *F*.

2–3. *spin . . . myself*] clearly taken by Jonson as a feeble witticism, cf. the
use of it by Peni-boy, the heir of *S.N.* (I. ii. 104 ff.), with the foolish comment, 'I think this suite Has made me wittier, then I was'.

8. *device*] ingenious contrivance.

9. *leap-frog chance*] one in which it does not matter which is uppermost.

9–10. *A very less*] There is no absolute need to assume the disappearance
of a word (G.) or a clause (H. & S.): *very* = 'truly', 'indeed' and *chance* is
understood from the previous clause.

10. *ames-ace*] double ace (*ambas as*), the lowest possible throw on two
dice.

12. *Paul's*] 'It was then the fashion of those times, and did so continue
till these, for the principall Gentry, Lords, Courtiers and men of all pro-
fessions not merely Mechanick, to meet in *Pauls Church* by eleven, and walk
in the middle Ile till twelve, and after dinner from three, to six, during
which time some discoursed of Businesse, others of Newes' (Osborn, *Historical Memoires on the Reigns of Queen Elizabeth and King James*, 1658,
pp. 64–5).

and something beside. When a quirk, or a quiblin does
'scape thee, and thou dost not watch, and apprehend it,
and bring it afore the constable of conceit (there now, I   15
speak quib too), let 'em carry thee out o' the archdcacon's
court into his kitchen, and make a Jack of thee, instead of a
John. (There I am again, la!)

[Enter] to him WIN.

Win, good morrow, Win. Aye marry, Win! Now you look
finely indeed, Win! This cap does convince! You'd not   20
ha' worn it, Win, nor ha' had it velvet, but a rough country beaver, with a copper-band, like the coney-skin
woman of Budge-row? Sweet Win, let me kiss it! And her
fine high shoes, like the Spanish lady! Good Win, go a
little, I would fain see thee pace, pretty Win! By this fine   25
cap, I could never leave kissing on't.

Win.   Come, indeed la, you are such a fool, still!

Lit.   No, but half a one, Win, you are the tother half: man and
wife make one fool, Win. (Good!) Is there the proctor, or
doctor indeed, i' the diocese, that ever had the fortune to   30
win him such a Win! (There I am again!) I do feel conceits
coming upon me, more than I am able to turn tongue to.
A pox o' these pretenders to wit, your Three Cranes,

---

13. *quirk*] conceit, quip.
quiblin] pun, quibble.

15. *conceit*] wit.

16. *quib*] affectedly, punningly.

17. *Jack*] (*a*) labourer, servant (not before 19th century in *O.E.D.* but cf.
III. iv. 67), (*b*) leather jug.

20. *convince*] overcome.

22. *beaver*] a hat of beaver's fur.

23. *Budge-row*] 'a street so called of Budge Furre [lambskin with the wool
dressed outwards], and of Skinners dwelling there' (Stow, i. 250).

24. *the Spanish lady*] 'There is A certaine *Lady*, here aboute the Towne,
An *English* widdow, who hath lately trauell'd, But shee's called the
Spaniard; 'cause she came Latest from thence: and keepes the *Spanish*
habit' (*D.A.*, II. viii. 25–9); cf. 'he wears *Cioppinos* [high shoes]: and they
doe so In Spaine' (*ibid.*, III. iv. 13–14).

33. *Three Cranes*] in 'the three Cranes lane, so called not onely of a signe
of three Cranes at a Tauerne door, but rather of three strong cranes of

D

Mitre and Mermaid men! Not a corn of true salt, nor a
grain of right mustard amongst them all. They may stand   35
for places or so, again' the next witfall, and pay twopence
in a quart more for their canary than other men. But gi'
me the man can start up a justice of wit out of six-shillings
beer, and give the law to all the poets, and poet-suckers, i'
town, because they are the players' gossips! 'Slid, other   40
men have wives as fine as the players, and as well dress'd.
Come hither, Win.

Act I. Scene II.

[Enter to them] WINWIFE.

[*Winw.*] Why, how now, Master Littlewit! Measuring of lips
or moulding of kisses ? Which is it ?

I. ii. 0.1. WINWIFE.] WIN-WIFE. LITTLEVVIT. WIN. *F.*

Timber placed on the Vintrie wharfe by the Thames side, to crane vp wines
there' (Stow, i. 239).

34. *Mitre*] in Fleet Street (formerly in Bread Street, Cheapside); recommended (though only by Puntarvalo) in *E.M.O.*: 'No better place then the
Mitre' (III. iii. 73), 'Your Miter is your best house' (III. vi. 161). H. &. S in a
note to the former passage quote Middleton's praise of its 'neat attendance,
diligent boys', in which it 'far excels' the Mermaid (*Your fine Gallants*,
1607-8, ed. Bullen, II. i. 220), and its catering: 'a true feast, a right Mitre
supper' (*A Mad World*, 1608, v. i. 77-8).

Mermaid] between Bread Street and Friday Street in Cheapside, the
place of the 'many meetings' which Beaumont celebrates in his *Letter to
Ben. Johnson* (ed. Waller, x. 200): '. . . what things have we seen, Done at the
Mermaid! heard words that have been So nimble, and so full of subtil
flame, As if that everyone from whence they came, Had meant to put
his whole wit in a jest, And had resolved to live a fool the rest Of his dull
life . . .'

36. *again*'] against, in anticipation of; cf. II. iv. 12.

witfall] the letting fall of a jest or repartee.

38-9. *six-shillings beer*] small beer at 6s. a barrel.

39. *poet-suckers*] sucking poets; cf. *rabbitsucker*, young rabbit.

40. *gossips*] friends. The antithesis seems to be between those who are
mere poets and those who are friends with the players; 'they', that is,
refers to the 'man' of l. 38 and has been attracted into the plural by the
phrase preceding.

Lit. Troth, I am a little taken with my Win's dressing here!
Does't not fine, Master Winwife? How do you apprehend,
sir? She would not ha' worn this habit. I challenge all   5
Cheapside to show such another—Moorfields, Pimlico
path, or the Exchange, in a summer evening—with a lace
to boot, as this has. Dear Win, let Master Winwife kiss
you. He comes a-wooing to our mother, Win, and may be
our father perhaps, Win. There's no harm in him, Win.   10

Winw. None i' the earth, Master Littlewit.

Lit. I envy no man my delicates, sir.

Winw. Alas, you ha' the garden where they grow still! A wife
here with a strawberry-breath, cherry-lips, apricot-
cheeks, and a soft velvet head, like a melicotton.   15

Lit. Good i' faith! Now dullness upon me, that I had not that
before him, that I should not light on't as well as he!
Velvet head!

Winw. But my taste, Master Littlewit, tends to fruit of a later
kind: the sober matron, your wife's mother.   20

Lit. Aye! we know you are a suitor, sir. Win and I both wish
you well: by this licence here, would you had her, that
your two names were as fast in it, as here are a couple. Win
would fain have a fine young father i' law with a feather,

---

4. fine,] *F3;* fine *F.*   12. man] *F3;* man, *F.*

---

4. *apprehend*] think, understand.

6. *Cheapside*] 'Mercers, and Haberdashers vsed to keepe their shoppes in West Cheape' (Stow, i. 81).

Moorfields] 'this Fenne or More', outside the north-eastern part of the city wall, had been by Stow's time 'made main and hard ground' (ii. 77). It was laid out in walks in 1606.

Pimlico] a Hoxton (I. iii. 60 n.) house noted for cakes and ale; cf. Glapthorne, *Wit in a Constable*, 1640, II. i (1874, i. 182): 'Nan . . . with Whom he used to goe to *Pimblico*, And spend ten groats in Cakes and Christian Ale'.

7. *Exchange*] probably the New Exchange on the south side of the Strand which was opened by James I in 1609 and had by now come to rival the Old Exchange in Cornhill as a fashionable resort for ladies.

lace] stripe; cf. Purchas, *Pilgrimage*, 1614, p. 558: 'The Zebra . . . all overlaid with partie coloured Laces, and guards, from head to Taile'.

8. *to boot*] in addition.

12. *delicates*] luxuries, delights.

15. *melicotton*] a peach grafted on a quince.

that her mother might hood it, and chain it, with Mistress   25
Overdo. But you do not take the right course, Master
Winwife.

Winw. No? Master Littlewit, why?

Lit. You are not mad enough.

Winw. How? Is madness a right course?   30

Lit. I say nothing, but I wink upon Win. You have a friend,
one Master Quarlous, comes here sometimes?

Winw. Why? he makes no love to her, does he?

Lit. Not a tokenworth that ever I saw, I assure you, but—

Winw. What?   35

Lit. He is the more madcap o' the two. You do not apprehend
me.

Win. You have a hot coal i' your mouth now, you cannot hold.

Lit. Let me out with it, dear Win.

Win. I'll tell him myself.   40

Lit. Do, and take all the thanks, and much good do thy pretty
heart, Win.

Win. Sir, my mother has had her nativity-water cast lately by
the cunning men in Cow-lane, and they ha' told her her
fortune, and do ensure her she shall never have happy   45
hour, unless she marry within this sen'night, and when it
is, it must be a madman, they say.

Lit. Aye, but it must be a gentleman madman.

Win. Yes, so the tother man of Moorfields says.

Winw. But does she believe 'em?   50

32. one Master Quarlous,] *G;* one (Master *Quarlous*) *F.*   41. good do] *W;*
do good *F.*

---

25. *hood...it*] walk proud of her husband's (marks of) office; cf. IV. iv.
152.

34. *tokenworth*] the smallest amount; a token was a piece of metal issued
by tradesmen to remedy the scarcity of small coin (cf. II. iv. 4).

43. *water cast*] properly of urine tested to diagnose a disease; here of a
horoscope (nativity).

44. *Cow-lane*] (the present King Street) curved round from West Smithfield to Snow Hill.

45. *ensure*] assure, tell confidently.

Lit. Yes, and has been at Bedlam twice since, every day, to enquire if any gentleman be there, or to come there, mad!

Winw. Why, this is a confederacy, a mere piece of practice
   upon her, by these impostors!

Lit. I tell her so; or else say I that they mean some young mad-   55
   cap-gentleman (for the devil can equivocate, as well as a
   shopkeeper) and therefore would I advise you to be a little
   madder than Master Quarlous, hereafter.

Winw. Where is she? Stirring yet?

Lit. Stirring! Yes, and studying an old elder, come from Ban-   60
   bury, a suitor that puts in here at meal-tide, to praise the
   painful brethren, or pray that the sweet singers may be
   restor'd; says a grace as long as his breath lasts him!
   Sometime the spirit is so strong with him, it gets quite out
   of him, and then my mother, or Win, are fain to fetch it   65
   again with malmsey, or *aqua cœlestis*.

Win. Yes indeed, we have such a tedious life with him for his
   diet, and his clothes too; he breaks his buttons, and cracks
   seams at every saying he sobs out.

Lit. He cannot abide my vocation, he says.   70

Win. No, he told my mother a Proctor was a claw of the Beast,
   and that she had little less than committed abomination in
   marrying me so as she has done.

Lit. Every line, he says, that a Proctor writes, when it comes to

---

51. *Bedlam*] the hospital of St Mary of Bethlehem in Bishopsgate, used
as a mad-house and visited as one of the sights of London.

62. *painful*] assiduous, diligent.

sweet singers] from the phrase applied in the Geneva Bible to David
(2 Samuel, xxiii. 1; *A.V.* 'sweet psalmist') and later to the Puritans; cf.
O.E.D., s.v. *singer*, a 1704: 'Quakers, Muggletonians, Sweet-singers of
Israel', and T. Brown, *Works*, 1715, iv. 241, where they are present with
'six Fifth-Monarchy-Men' at the marriage of a Muggletonian widow in
1693; cf. v. ii. 63–4 and note.

66. aqua cœlestis] made from wine by distillation.

74–6. *Proctor . . . Antichrist*] '. . . wicked Angels are the Bishops, Deanes
. . . besides his other Proctors, Protectors, Pursuivants, Pariters . . . all
which (brethren) are abhominations in the eyes of the Lord, and their very
names stink in his nostrils' (from a 'Sermon preached . . . by one of the
Elders' in *The Brownists Conventicle*, 1641, p. 7).

be read in the Bishop's court, is a long black hair, kemb'd   75
out of the tail of Antichrist.

Winw. When came this proselyte?

Lit. Some three days since.

Act I. Scene III.

[Enter to them] QUARLOUS.

[*Quar.*] O sir, ha' you ta'en soil, here? It's well a man may
reach you after three hours running, yet! What an un-
merciful companion art thou, to quit thy lodging at such
ungentlemanly hours! None but a scatter'd covey of
fiddlers, or one of these rag-rakers in dunghills, or some   5
marrow-bone man at most, would have been up when
thou wert gone abroad, by all description. I pray thee what
ailest thou, thou canst not sleep? Hast thou thorns i' thy
eyelids, or thistles i' thy bed?

Winw. I cannot tell: it seems you had neither i' your feet, that 10
took this pain to find me.

Quar. No, an' I had, all the lyam-hounds o' the City should
have drawn after you by the scent rather. Master John
Littlewit! God save you, sir. 'Twas a hot night with some
of us, last night, John: shall we pluck a hair o' the same   15
wolf today, Proctor John?

I. iii. 0.1. QUARLOUS.] QVARLOVS, IOHN, VVIN, WIN-VVIFE. *F.*   4. ungentle-
manly] *F3;* vngentle manly *F.*   13. rather.] *F3;* rather, *F.*

---

75. *kemb'd*] combed, the proper form from the verb, now displaced by
that from the substantive *comb*, but surviving in *kempt* and *unkempt*.

I. iii. 1. *ta'en soil*] taken refuge; cf. N. Cox, *Gentleman's Recreation*, 1677,
i. 78:'The last Refuge of a Hart sorely hunted is the Water (which, according to Art, is termed the Soil).'

5. *rag-rakers*] cf. *A.*, I. i. 33–4: 'the seuerall rags You had rak'd, and
pick'd from dung-hills, before day'.

12. *lyam-hounds*] leash-hounds, i.e. blood-hounds.

15–16. *hair . . . wolf*] 'Our Ale-knights often say, Giue us a haire of the
dog that last bit us' (Cotgrave, s.v. *Beste*). It was supposed 'that the hair of
a Dog will cure the Bite he gives' (Kelly, *Scottish Proverbs*, 1721).

Lit. Do you remember, Master Quarlous, what we discours'd
  on last night?

Quar. Not I, John: nothing that I either discourse or do, at
  those times I forfeit all to forgetfulness.   20

Lit. No? not concerning Win? Look you: there she is, and
  dress'd as I told you she should be: hark you, sir, had you
  forgot?

Quar. By this head, I'll beware how I keep you company,
  John, when I am drunk, and you have this dangerous   25
  memory! That's certain.

Winw. Why, sir?

Quar. Why? We were all a little stain'd last night, sprinkled
  with a cup or two, and I agreed with Proctor John here to
  come and do somewhat with Win (I know not what 'twas)   30
  today; and he puts me in mind on't, now; he says he was
  coming to fetch me: before truth, if you have that fearful
  quality, John, to remember, when you are sober, John,
  what you promise drunk, John, I shall take heed of you,
  John. For this once, I am content to wink at you; where's 35
  your wife? Come hither, Win.   *He kisseth her.*

Win. Why, John! do you see this, John? Look you! help me,
  John.

Lit. O Win, fie, what do you mean, Win? Be womanly, Win;
  make an outcry to your mother, Win? Master Quarlous is   40
  an honest gentleman, and our worshipful good friend,
  Win: and he is Master Winwife's friend, too: and Master
  Winwife comes a suitor to your mother, Win, as I told you

17. remember,] *F3;* remember *F.*   21. Win?] *1716;* Win, *F.*   25. I am
drunk] *F3;* I drunke *F.*   27. *Winw.] This ed.;* IOH. *F.*   42. friend] *F3;*
friends *F.*   43. mother,] *F3;* mother *F.*

25–6. *drunk . . . memory*] cf. Martial, *Ep.,* 1. xxvii. 5–7: 'et non sobria
verba subnotasti exemplo nimium periculoso. μισῶ μνάμονα συμπόταν,
Procille.'; 'and you took secret note of my unsober remark—a precedent
too dangerous! "I hate a messmate with a memory," Procillus' (W. C. A.
Ker).

27. Winw.] From 'Proctor John here' (l. 29) it is clear that Winwife
breaks in, not Littlewit. I owe this observation to Professor C. Leech.

28. *stain'd*] tipsy.

before, Win, and may perhaps be our father, Win: they'll
do you no harm, Win, they are both our worshipful good   45
friends. Master Quarlous! You must know Master Quarlous, Win; you must not quarrel with Master Quarlous,
Win.

Quar. No, we'll kiss again and fall in.

Lit. Yes, do, good Win.   50

Win. I' faith you are a fool, John.

Lit. A fool-John she calls me, do you mark that, gentlemen?
Pretty littlewit of velvet! A fool-John!

Quar. She may call you an apple-John, if you use this.

Winw. Pray thee forbear, for my respect somewhat.   55

Quar. Hoy-day! How respective you are become o' the sudden! I fear this family will turn you reformed too; pray
you come about again. Because she is in possibility to be
your daughter-in-law, and may ask you blessing hereafter, when she courts it to Tottenham to eat cream—   60
well, I will forbear, sir; but i' faith, would thou wouldst
leave thy exercise of widow-hunting once, this drawing
after an old reverend smock by the splay-foot! There
cannot be an ancient tripe or trillibub i' the town, but thou

44. Win:] *F3;* Win, *F.*   50. do,] *F3;* doe *F.*   60. cream—] *This ed.;*
creame. *F.*   62. once,] *This ed.;* once! *F.*   63. splay-foot!] *G;* splay-
foote: *F.*

---

49. *fall in*] become reconciled; cf. *Troilus and Cressida*, III. i. 114:
'Falling in, after falling out, may make them three.'

54. *apple-John*] a kind of apple eaten when shrivelled after two years'
keeping; cf. *2 Henry IV*, II. iv. 2–5. G. suggested a quibble on *apple-
squire*, pander.

56. *respective*] attentive (to matters of respect or courtesy?).

58. *come about*] come round (to my opinion).

60. *Tottenham*] either the village about five miles north of London, or,
more probably, Tottenham Court, the old manor house in Tottenham
Court Road; cf. Wither, *Britain's Remembrancer*, 1628, Canto 4 (Spenser
Soc., 1880, i. 242): 'Some, to the next adjoyning *Hamlets* going; And *Hogs-
done*, *Islington*, and *Tothnam Court*, For Cakes and Creame, had then no
small resort.'

62–3. *drawing after*] tracking by the scent (in hunting).

64. *tripe or trillibub*] 'the entrails, also a jeering appellation for a fat man'
(Grose).

art straight nosing it; and 'tis a fine occupation thou'lt   65
confine thyself to, when thou hast got one—scrubbing a
piece of buff, as if thou hadst the perpetuity of Pannyer-
alley to stink in, or perhaps, worse, currying a carcass that
thou hast bound thyself to alive. I'll be sworn, some of
them, that thou art or hast been a suitor to, are so old as   70
no chaste or married pleasure can ever become 'em: the
honest instrument of procreation has, forty years since,
left to belong to 'em; thou must visit 'em, as thou wouldst
do a tomb, with a torch, or three handfuls of link, flaming
hot, and so thou mayst hap to make 'em feel thee, and   75
after, come to inherit according to thy inches. A sweet
course for a man to waste the brand of life for, to be still
raking himself a fortune in an old woman's embers; we
shall ha' thee, after thou hast been but a month married to
one of 'em, look like the quartan ague and the black jaun-   80
dice met in a face, and walk as if thou hadst borrow'd legs
of a spinner, and voice of a cricket. I would endure to hear

dislikes marriage

---

67. *buff*] ox-hide leather, colloquial for the bare skin; cf. 'stripped to the buff'.

67–8. *Pannyer-alley*] 'is another passage out of *pater noster row*, and is called of such a signe, Panyar Alley, which commeth out into the North ouer against S. Martins lane [i.e. St Martin's le Grand]' (Stow, ii. 342); connected (as place of sale or manufacture?) with buff leather in Dekker and Webster, *Westward Hoe*, III. ii. 20: '. . . those Varlets that wear Pannier-alley on their baks (Sergeants) . . .'

68. *currying*] rubbing down (a horse, cf. II. v. 160), combing or tickling (a person).

70–5. *old . . . thee*] cf. Martial, *Ep.*, III. xciii *ad fin.*: 'intrare in istum sola fax potest cunnum.'

74. *link*] a torch made of tow and pitch, or the material of it.

76. *inherit . . . inches*] cf. Juvenal, *Sat.*, i. 40–1: 'Unciolam Proculeius habet sed Gillo deuncem, Partes quisque suas ad mensuram inguinis heres'; [each lover will have his share from a rich old woman] 'Proculeius a twelfth part, Gillo eleven parts, each in proportion to his services' (G. G. Ramsay).

80. *quartan ague*] a fever in which a paroxysm occurs every fourth day.

80–1. *jaundice*] caused by obstruction of the bile and called black, yellow, etc. according to the resulting colour of the skin.

82. *spinner*] spider.

fifteen sermons a week 'fore her, and such coarse and loud
ones as some of 'em must be; I would e'en desire of Fate, I
might dwell in a drum, and take in my sustenance with   85
an old broken tobacco-pipe and a straw. Dost thou ever
think to bring thine ears or stomach to the patience of a
dry grace, as long as thy tablecloth, and dron'd out by thy
son here, that might be thy father, till all the meat o' thy
board has forgot it was that day i' the kitchen? Or to   90
brook the noise made, in a question of predestination,
by the good labourers and painful eaters assembled together, put to 'em by the matron, your spouse, who
moderates with a cup of wine, ever and anon, and a sentence out of Knox between? Or the perpetual spitting,   95
before and after a sober drawn exhortation of six hours,
whose better part was the hum-ha-hum? Or to hear
prayers groan'd out, over thy iron-chests, as if they were
charms to break 'em? And all this, for the hope of two
apostle-spoons, to suffer! And a cup to eat a caudle in!   100
For that will be thy legacy. She'll ha' convey'd her state,
safe enough from thee, an' she be a right widow.

83. 'fore] *This ed.;* for *F.*

---

83. *'fore*] in preference to. This rather than *F* 'for' seems required by the
sense here. For the form cf. III. v. 138.

88. *dry*] plain, unattractive; ? thirsty (of those waiting to begin the meal).
See Appendix II.

grace] cf. Subtle to Ananias and Tribulation: 'Nor shall you need to . . .
shorten so your eares, against the hearing Of the next wire-drawne [drawn-
out] grace' (*A.*, III. ii. 86–8).

94. *moderates*] arbitrates.

94–5. *sentence*] opinion on the question.

97. *hum-ha-hum*] cf. 'leaue off to make Long-winded exercises: or suck
vp Your ha, and hum, in a tune' (*A.*, III. ii. 53–5).

100. *apostle-spoons*] silver, with the handles ending in figures of the
Apostles, the usual present of sponsors at baptisms, but, as H. & S. notice,
unlikely possessions for a Puritan.

caudle] a warm concoction given to invalids: cf. *O.E.D.*, 1612: 'A comfortable Caudle made with some Wine, Spices, Sugar, and the yolk of an
egge'.

101. *convey'd her state*] made her estate over to another; cf. *S.W.*, II. ii.
141–3: '. . . made a conuayance of her virginity aforehand, as your wise

Winw. Alas, I am quite off that scent now.

Quar. How so?

Winw. Put off by a brother of Banbury, one that, they say, is   105
come here and governs all, already.

Quar. What do you call him? I knew divers of those Ban-
burians when I was in Oxford.

Winw. Master Littlewit can tell us.

Lit. Sir! Good Win, go in, and if Master Bartholomew Cokes   110
his man come for the licence (the little old fellow), let
him speak with me; what say you, gentlemen? [*Exit* WIN.]

Winw. What call you the reverend elder you told me of?
your Banbury man.

Lit. Rabbi Busy, sir, he is more than an elder, he is a prophet,   115
sir.

Quar. O, I know him! A baker, is he not?

Lit. He was a baker, sir, but he does dream now, and see
visions; he has given over his trade.

Quar. I remember that too: out of a scruple he took, that (in   120
spic'd conscience) those cakes he made were serv'd to
bridales, maypoles, morrises, and such profane feasts
and meetings; his Christian name is Zeal-of-the-land.

Lit. Yes, sir, Zeal-of-the-land Busy.

Winw. How, what a name's there!   125

Lit. O, they have all such names, sir; he was witness for Win
here (they will not be call'd godfathers), and nam'd her
Win-the-fight; you thought her name had been Wini-
fred, did you not?

Winw. I did indeed.   130

Lit. He would ha' thought himself a stark reprobate, if it had.

---

widdowes doe of their states, before they marry, in trust to some friend'.

121. *spic'd*] over-scrupulous; cf. the speech of Sejanus beginning 'Be
thou dumb, scrupulous priest' and concluding 'Your pure, and spiced conscience' (v. 190–201).

122. *bridales*] wedding feasts.

maypoles] 'this stinking Ydol, rather' (Stubbes, *Anatomie of Abuses*,
1583, ed. Furnivall, i. 149).

morrises] morris-dances.

Quar. Aye, for there was a blue-starch-woman o' the name,
at the same time. A notable hypocritical vermin it is; I
know him. One that stands upon his face more than his
faith, at all times; ever in seditious motion, and reproving   135
for vain-glory; of a most lunatic conscience, and spleen,
and affects the violence of singularity in all he does;
(he has undone a grocer here, in Newgate-market, that
broke with him, trusted him with currants, as arrant a
zeal as he, that's by the way;) by his profession, he will   140
ever be i' the state of innocence, though, and childhood;
derides all antiquity; defies any other learning than inspiration; and what discretion soever years should afford
him, it is all prevented in his original ignorance; ha' not

---

132. *blue-starch-woman*] laundress (*a*) connected with luxury of dress;
cf. Greene, *Connycatching*, 1592, p. 16: 'Rufs of the largest size, quarter
and halfe deep, gloried richly with blew starch'; (*b*) of reputedly easy
virtue.

134. *stands upon*] trusts to, depends on.
face] effrontery; or outward appearance; cf. *C.*, II. 375–7: 'Let [the
Consul] whom we name . . . Be more with faith, then face endu'd.'

135. *seditious*] factious, turbulent; cf. Nashe, *Saffron Walden* (McKerrow, iii. 68): 'he is verie seditious and mutinous in conuersation, picking
quarrels with euerie man that will not magnifie and applaud him'.

138. *Newgate-market*] 'first of corne and meale, and then of other victuals' (Stow, i. 343); halfway along the south side of Newgate Street.

140. *profession*] (declaration of) religious faith.

141. *ever . . . innocence*] cf. Giles Widdowes detailing 'the specificall kinds
of Puritan': 'The Perfectist is he whose purenes is *continuata perseuerandi
actio sanctificans*; neuer to sinne after baptism. . . The Anabaptist is he,
whose purenes is a supposed birth without original sin' (*The Schysmaticall
Puritan*, Oxford, 1630, sig. B2).

childhood] (*a*) as a 'child of God'; (*b*) cf. *The Brownists Conventicle*, 1641,
p. 2: 'A young Lubber of that Sect [the Anabaptists] . . . being brought as a
witnesse to take his oath in Court, & the Judge by accident asking of what
age he was ? who answered him, that he was 3 yeares old. Three yeares old
(replyed the Judge) & no more ? how can that possibly be, seeing thou art of
that full growth & bignesse ? Who answered him [a]gain Verily I reckon
mine age from the time since I was last baptised'.

142–4. *learning . . . ignorance*] cf. O[liver] O[rmerod], *The Picture of a
Puritaine*, 1605, sigs. K4, C1: 'Our Sectaries despise all Gentile and Prophane learning . . . thinking themselves to haue all knowledge, when they
are ignorant, and had need to be catechized.'

144. *prevented*] anticipated, forestalled.

to do with him: for he is a fellow of a most arrogant and　145
invincible dullness, I assure you; who is this?

Act I. Scene IV.

[Enter to them] WASP, [WIN].

[*Wasp.*] By your leave, gentlemen, with all my heart to you,
and God you good morrow; Master Littlewit, my business is to you. Is this licence ready?

Lit. Here, I ha' it for you, in my hand, Master Humphrey.

Wasp. That's well, nay, never open, or read it to me, it's　5
labour in vain, you know. I am no clerk, I scorn to be
sav'd by my book, i' faith I'll hang first; fold it up o' your
word and gi' it me; what must you ha' for't?

Lit. We'll talk of that anon, Master Humphrey.

Wasp. Now, or not at all, good Master Proctor, I am for no　10
anon's, I assure you.

Lit. Sweet Win, bid Solomon send me the little black box
within, in my study.

Wasp. Aye, quickly, good mistress, I pray you: for I have
both eggs o' the spit, and iron i' the fire, say what you　15
must have, good Master Littlewit.　　　　　　　[*Exit* WIN.]

Lit. Why, you know the price, Master Numps.

Wasp. I know? I know nothing. Aye, what tell you me of
knowing, now I am in haste? Sir, I do not know, and I
will not know, and I scorn to know, and yet (now I think　20
on't) I will, and do know, as well as another; you must

I. iv. 0.1. WASP,] WASPE. IOHN. WIN-WIFE. QVARLOVS. *F.*　　19. knowing,
now . . . haste?] *This ed.;* knowing? (now . . . hast) *F.*

I. iv. 2. *God you*] God give you.
7. *sav'd by . . . book*] exempted from the penalty for a crime, as J. himself
was, after killing Gabriel Spencer (H. & S., i. 18), by pleading benefit of
clergy, i.e. showing ability to read; cf. the taunts in *Satiromastix*: 'Art not
famous enough yet, my mad *Horastratus*, for killing a Player . . . ?' (IV. ii.
60–1); '. . . saue thy selfe and read' (IV. i. 136); cf. III. v. 265.

　　　have a mark for your thing here, and eightpence for the
　　　box; I could ha' sav'd twopence i' that, an' I had bought it
　　　myself, but here's fourteen shillings for you. Good Lord!
　　　how long your little wife stays! Pray God, Solomon, your　　25
　　　clerk, be not looking i' the wrong box, Master Proctor.

Lit. Good i' faith! no, I warrant you, Solomon is wiser than so,
　　　sir.

Wasp. Fie, fie, fie, by your leave, Master Littlewit, this is
　　　scurvy, idle, foolish and abominable, with all my heart; I　　30
　　　do not like it.

Winw. Do you hear? Jack Littlewit, what business does thy
　　　pretty head think this fellow may have, that he keeps such
　　　a coil with?

Quar. More than buying of ginger-bread i' the Cloister, here　　35
　　　(for that we allow him), or a gilt pouch i' the Fair?

Lit. Master Quarlous, do not mistake him: he is his master's
　　　both-hands, I assure you.

Quar. What? to pull on his boots, a-mornings, or his stock-
　　　ings, does he?　　　　　　　　　　　　　　　　　　　　40

Lit. Sir, if you have a mind to mock him, mock him softly, and
　　　look t' other way: for if he apprehend you flout him once,
　　　he will fly at you presently. A terrible testy old fellow, and
　　　his name is Wasp too.

Quar. Pretty insect! make much on him.　　　　　　　　　45

Wasp. A plague o' this box, and the pox too, and on him that
　　　made it, and her that went for't, and all that should ha'
　　　sought it, sent it, or brought it! Do you see, sir?

Lit. Nay, good Master Wasp.

Wasp. Good Master Hornet, turd i' your teeth, hold you your　　50
　　　tongue; do not I know you? Your father was a 'pothecary,
　　　and sold glisters, more than he gave, I wusse: and turd i'

---

22. *mark*] 13s. 4d.
33–4. *keeps . . . a coil*] makes a fuss.
38. *both-hands*] factotum.
52. *glisters*] clysters, 'a noble remedye to dryue out superfluitees of the
guttes' (*O.E.D.*, 1543).
I wusse] properly *iwusse* (O.E. *gewis*), truly, indeed.

your little wife's teeth too; here she comes; 'twill make
her spit, as fine as she is, for all her velvet-custard on her
head, sir.   55

[*Re-enter* WIN.]

Lit. O! be civil, Master Numps.

Wasp. Why, say I have a humour not to be civil; how then?
Who shall compel me? You?

Lit. Here is the box, now.

Wasp. Why a pox o' your box, once again: let your little wife 60
stale in it, an' she will. Sir, I would have you to understand, and these gentlemen too, if they please—

Winw. With all our hearts. Sir.

Wasp. That I have a charge. Gentlemen.

Lit. They do apprehend, sir.   65

Wasp. Pardon me, sir, neither they nor you can apprehend
me, yet. (You are an ass.) I have a young master, he is now
upon his making and marring; the whole care of his well-
doing is now mine. His foolish schoolmasters have done
nothing but run up and down the country with him, to   70
beg puddings, and cake-bread, of his tenants, and almost
spoiled him; he has learn'd nothing, but to sing catches,
and repeat *Rattle bladder rattle*, and *O, Madge*. I dare not
let him walk alone, for fear of learning of vile tunes, which
he will sing at supper, and in the sermon-times! If he   75
meet but a carman i' the street, and I find him not talk to
keep him off on him, he will whistle him, and all his tunes

54. spit,] *1716;* spit *F.*

---

54. *velvet-custard*] cf. Petruchio of Katherine's cap 'moulded on a por-
ringer, A velvet dish' (*Taming of the Shrew*, IV. iii. 64–5, 82). A custard was
an open pie (of meat or fruit covered with a thickened preparation of broth
or milk).

61. *stale*] urinate (of horses or cattle).

71. *puddings*] sausages.

76. *carman*] cf. Falstaff of Shallow: ' 'A came ever in the rearward of the
fashion, and sung those tunes to the overscutch'd huswifes [whores] that he
heard the carmen whistle' (*2 Henry IV*, III. ii. 343–5).

over, at night in his sleep! He has a head full of bees! I am
fain now, for this little time I am absent, to leave him in
charge with a gentlewoman; 'tis true, she is a Justice of 80
Peace his wife, and a gentlewoman o' the hood, and his
natural sister: but what may happen, under a woman's
government, there's the doubt. Gentlemen, you do not
know him: he is another manner of piece than you think
for! but nineteen year old, and yet he is taller than either 85
of you, by the head, God bless him.

Quar. Well, methinks, this is a fine fellow!

Winw. He has made his master a finer by this description, I
should think.

Quar. 'Faith, much about one; it's cross and pile, whether for 90
a new farthing.

Wasp. I'll tell you, gentlemen—

Lit. Will't please you drink, Master Wasp?

Wasp. Why, I ha' not talk'd so long to be dry, sir, you see no
dust or cobwebs come out o' my mouth: do you? You'd 95
ha' me gone, would you?

Lit. No, but you were in haste e'en now, Master Numps.

Wasp. What an' I were? so I am still, and yet I will stay too;
meddle you with your match, your Win, there, she has as
little wit as her husband it seems: I have others to talk to. 100

Lit. She's my match indeed, and as little wit as I, good!

Wasp. We ha' been but a day and a half in town, gentlemen,
'tis true; and yesterday i' the afternoon, we walk'd London, to show the city to the gentlewoman he shall marry,
Mistress Grace; but, afore I will endure such another 105
half day, with him, I'll be drawn with a good gib-cat

---

78. *bees*] fantasies, whims.
81. *hood*] the mark of her husband's dignity as Justice.
84. *piece*] individual.
90. *one*] the same.
cross and pile] across and with the nap or pile of, for instance, a piece of
velvet; hence heads or tails, a toss-up.
whether] whichever of the two.
106. *gib-cat*] Gilbert-cat, i.e. tom-cat; *to draw through the water with a cat*
is to tie the victim and a cat to opposite ends of a rope thrown across a pond,

through the great pond at home, as his uncle Hodge
was! Why, we could not meet that heathen thing, all day,
but stay'd him: he would name you all the signs over, as
he went, aloud: and where he spied a parrot, or a mon-   110
key, there he was pitch'd, with all the little-long-coats
about him, male and female; no getting him away! I
thought he would ha' run mad o' the black boy in Bucklersbury, that takes the scurvy, roguy tobacco, there.
Lit. You say true, Master Numps: there's such a one indeed.   115
Wasp. It's no matter whether there be or no, what's that to
you?
Quar. He will not allow of John's reading at any hand.

Act I. Scene V.

[Enter to them] COKES, Mistress OVERDO, GRACE.

[Cok.] O Numps! are you here, Numps? Look where I am,
Numps! And Mistress Grace, too! Nay, do not look
angerly, Numps: my sister is here, and all, I do not come
without her.
Wasp. What the mischief, do you come with her? Or she with   5
you?

I. V. O.I. COKES, . . . GRACE.] COKES. Mistris OVER-DOO. WASPE. GRACE. QVAR-
LOVS. WIN-WIFE. IOHN. WIN. *F.*

---

after making a bet that the cat will pull him through it—the pulling being
actually done by those who are to 'lead' the cat.
    111. *little-long-coats*] children (in petticoats).
    113–14. *Bucklersbury*] keeps its name (and forms with Walbrook and the
Poultry a triangle which is cut by Victoria Street) but not its trade. In
Stow (i. 260), 'This whole streete called Buckles bury on both sides
throughout is possessed of Grocers and Apothecaries'. The latter sold
tobacco; cf. Dekker and Webster, *Westward Hoe*, I. ii. 39–41: 'Go into
Bucklersbury and fetch me two ounces of preserved *Melounes*, looke there
be no Tobacco taken in the shoppe when he weighes it.'
    118. *reading*] comment, interpretation.

    I. v. 3. *angerly*] with anger; cf. *Macbeth*, III. v. 1.

    E

Cok. We came all to seek you, Numps.

Wasp. To seek me? Why, did you all think I was lost? Or run
away with your fourteen shillings worth of small ware
here? Or that I had chang'd it i' the Fair, for hobby-   10
horses? 'Sprecious—to seek me!

Mrs. Over. Nay, good Master Numps, do you show discretion, though he be exorbitant, as Master Overdo says,
an't be but for conservation of the peace.

Wasp. Marry gip, goody she-Justice, Mistress French-hood!   15
Turd i' your teeth; and turd i' your French-hood's teeth,
too, to do you service, do you see? Must you quote your
Adam to me! You think you are Madam Regent still, Mistress Overdo, when I am in place? No such matter, I
assure you; your reign is out, when I am in, dame.   20

Mrs. Over. I am content to be in abeyance, sir, and be govern'd
by you; so should he too, if he did well; but 'twill be expected you should also govern your passions.

Wasp. Will't so forsooth? Good Lord! how sharp you are!
With being at Bedlam yesterday? Whetstone has set an   25
edge upon you, has he?

Mrs. Over. Nay, if you know not what belongs to your dignity: I do, yet, to mine.

Wasp. Very well, then.

10–11. *hobbyhorses*] (*a*) toy horses; (*b*) wenches.

11. *'Sprecious*] by God's precious blood.

13. *exorbitant*] abnormal; after the use in Roman law of *exorbitans* (from
exorbitare to go out of the track); cf. Overdo's use of 'enormous' and
'enormity'.

15. *Marry gip*] confusion of (*a*) *by Mary Gipcy* by St Mary of Egypt, (*b*)
gip gee-up, get out.

French-hood] with 'front band depressed over forehead and raised in
folds or loops over temples' (*O.E.D.*).

18. *Regent*] (*a*) governor, director (in the absence of her husband); (*b*) one
presiding over disputes (in the Schools at Oxford and Cambridge).

21. *abeyance*] in law, the position of waiting for or being without a
claimant or owner.

25. *Whetstone*] ? name of a keeper at Bedlam 'with quibble on a
whetstone's sharpening other instruments, though unable itself to cut'
(H. & S.).

Cok. Is this the licence, Numps? For love's sake, let me see't.   30
   I never saw a licence.

Wasp. Did you not so? Why, you shall not see't, then.

Cok. An' you love me, good Numps.

Wasp. Sir, I love you, and yet I do not love you, i' these fool-
   eries; set your heart at rest; there's nothing in't but hard   35
   words: and what would you see't for?

Cok. I would see the length and the breadth on't, that's all;
   and I will see't now, so I will.

Wasp. You sha' not see it, here.

Cok. Then I'll see't at home, and I'll look upo' the case here.   40

Wasp. Why, do so; a man must give way to him a little in
   trifles:—Gentlemen. These are errors, diseases of youth:
   which he will mend, when he comes to judgement, and
   knowledge of matters. I pray you conceive so, and I thank
   you. And I pray you pardon him, and I thank you again.   45

Quar. Well, this dry nurse, I say still, is a delicate man.

Winw. And I am for the cosset, his charge! Did you ever see a
   fellow's face more accuse him for an ass?

Quar. Accuse him? It confesses him one without accusing.
   What pity 'tis yonder wench should marry such a cokes!   50

Winw. 'Tis true.

Quar. She seems to be discreet, and as sober as she is handsome.

Winw. Aye, and if you mark her, what a restrain'd scorn she
   casts upon all his behaviour, and speeches!   55

Cok. Well, Numps, I am now for another piece of business
   more, the Fair, Numps, and then—

Wasp. Bless me! deliver me, help, hold me! the Fair!

Cok. Nay, never fidge up and down, Numps, and vex itself. I
   am resolute Bartholomew, in this; I'll make no suit on't to   60

---

46. *delicate*] courteous; critical; but here probably merely a term of
general (ironic) approbation, 'I say still' linking it with 'fine fellow' in I.
iv. 87.

47. *cosset*] pet-lamb, spoilt child.

59. *fidge*] pace restlessly.

you; 'twas all the end of my journey, indeed, to shew Mistress Grace my Fair: I call't my Fair, because of Bartholomew: you know my name is Bartholomew, and Bartholomew Fair.

Lit. That was mine afore, gentlemen: this morning. I had that   65
i' faith, upon his licence, believe me, there he comes after me.

Quar. Come, John, this ambitious wit of yours, I am afraid,
will do you no good i' the end.

Lit. No? Why sir?   70

Quar. You grow so insolent with it, and overdoing, John, that
if you look not to it, and tie it up, it will bring you to some
obscure place in time, and there 'twill leave you.

Winw. Do not trust it too much, John; be more sparing, and
use it but now and then; a wit is a dangerous thing, in   75
this age; do not overbuy it.

Lit. Think you so, gentlemen? I'll take heed on't, hereafter.

Win. Yes, do, John.

Cok. A pretty little soul, this same Mistress Littlewit! would I
might marry her.   80

Grace. [*Aside*] So would I, or anybody else, so I might 'scape
you.

Cok. Numps, I will see it, Numps, 'tis decreed: never be
melancholy for the matter.

Wasp. Why, see it, sir, see it, do see it! Who hinders you? Why   85
do you not go see it? 'Slid, see it.

Cok. The Fair, Numps, the Fair.

Wasp. Would the Fair and all the drums and rattles in't were
i' your belly for me; they are already i' your brain: he that
had the means to travel your head, now, should meet finer   90
sights than any are i' the Fair and make a finer voyage on't,
to see it all hung with cockle-shells, pebbles, fine wheat-
straws, and here and there a chicken's feather, and a cob-
web.

---

76. *overbuy*] pay too much for.
86. *'Slid*] by God's (eye-)lid.

Quar. Good faith, he looks, methinks, an' you mark him, like　95
　　one that were made to catch flies, with his Sir Cranion
　　legs.

Winw. And his Numps, to flap 'em away.

Wasp. God be wi' you, sir, there's your bee in a box, and
　　much good do't you.　　　　　　　　　　　　　　　　　100

Cok. Why, your friend, and Bartholomew; an' you be so con-
　　tumacious.

Quar. What mean you, Numps?

Wasp. I'll not be guilty, I, gentlemen.

Mrs. Over. You will not let him go, brother, and lose him?　105

Cok. Who can hold that will away? I had rather lose him than
　　the Fair, I wusse.

Wasp. You do not know the inconvenience, gentlemen, you
　　persuade to: nor what trouble I have with him in these
　　humours. If he go to the Fair, he will buy of everything　110
　　to a baby there; and household-stuff for that too. If a leg
　　or an arm on him did not grow on, he would lose it i' the
　　press. Pray heaven I bring him off with one stone! And
　　then he is such a ravener after fruit! You will not believe
　　what a coil I had, t'other day, to compound a business　115
　　between a Cather'ne-pear-woman and him, about
　　snatching! 'Tis intolerable, gentlemen!

Winw. O! but you must not leave him, now, to these hazards,
　　Numps.

Wasp. Nay, he knows too well I will not leave him, and that　120
　　makes him presume: well, sir, will you go now? If you
　　have such an itch i' your feet to foot it to the Fair, why do

---

96. *Sir Cranion*] cf. *crane-fly*, daddy-long-legs; edd. quote Drayton,
Nimphidia, 133–6, of the Fairy Queen's chariot: 'Foure nimble Gnats the
Horses were, ... Flye Cranion her Chariottere".

101–2. *contumacious*] insubordinate.

106. *Who ... away*] a proverb 'spoken when our Friends will not be prevail'd upon to tarry with us' (Kelly, *Scottish Proverbs*, 1721). G. quotes it
from Dunbar.

115. *coil*] fuss.

116. *Cather'ne-pear*] Catherine pear, small and early; cf. IV. ii. 46.

you stop; am I your tarriers? Go, will you go? Sir, why
do you not go?

Cok. O Numps! have I brought you about? Come, Mistress   125
Grace, and sister, I am resolute Bat, i' faith, still.

Grace. Truly, I have no such fancy to the Fair; nor ambition
to see it; there's none goes thither of any quality or
fashion.

Cok. O Lord, sir! You shall pardon me, Mistress Grace, we   130
are enough of ourselves to make it a fashion: and for
qualities, let Numps alone, he'll find qualities.

[*Exeunt* COKES, WASP, GRACE, Mistress OVERDO.]

Quar. What a rogue in apprehension is this! to understand
her language no better.

Winw. Aye, and offer to marry to her? Well, I will leave the   135
chase of my widow, for today, and directly to the Fair.
These flies cannot, this hot season, but engender us excellent creeping sport.

Quar. A man that has but a spoonful of brain would think so.
Farewell, John.   [*Exeunt* QUARLOUS, WINWIFE.]   140

Lit. Win, you see, 'tis in fashion, to go to the Fair, Win: we
must to the Fair too, you and I, Win. I have an affair i'
the Fair, Win, a puppet-play of mine own making—say
nothing—that I writ for the motion-man, which you
must see, Win.   145

Win. I would I might, John, but my mother will never con-
sent to such a 'profane motion', she will call it.

Lit. Tut, we'll have a device, a dainty one; (now, Wit, help at
a pinch, good Wit come, come, good Wit, an't be thy
will). I have it, Win, I have it i' faith, and 'tis a fine one.   150
Win, long to eat of a pig, sweet Win, i' the Fair; do you

123. your tarriers] *F;* o' your tarriers *G.*

---

123. *tarriers*] obstructors, delayers.
128, 132. *quality*] (*a*) rank in society; (*b*) feature of a man's character.
133. *apprehension*] understanding.
138. *creeping*] ? stealthy.
144. *motion-man*] puppet-master.

see? I' the heart o' the Fair; not at Pie-corner. Your
mother will do anything, Win, to satisfy your longing,
you know; pray thee long, presently, and be sick o' the
sudden, good Win. I'll go in and tell her; cut thy lace i'   155
the meantime, and play the hypocrite, sweet Win.

Win. No, I'll not make me unready for it. I can be hypocrite
enough, though I were never so strait-lac'd.

Lit. You say true, you have been bred i' the family, and
brought up to't. Our mother is a most elect hypocrite,   160
and has maintain'd us all this seven year with it, like
gentlefolks.

Win. Aye, let her alone, John, she is not a wise wilful widow
for nothing, nor a sanctified sister for a song. And let me
alone too, I ha' somewhat o' the mother in me, you shall   165
see, fetch her, fetch her, ah, ah.   [*Exit* LITTLEWIT.]

Act I. Scene VI.

[*Enter to her*] PURECRAFT, LITTLEWIT.

[*Pure.*] Now, the blaze of the beauteous discipline fright
away this evil from our house! How now, Win-the-fight,
child: how do you? Sweet child, speak to me.

I. vi. o. 1. PURECRAFT, LITTLEWIT.] PVRECRAFT. WIN. IOHN. BVSY. SALOMON. *F.*
1. discipline] *G;* discipline, *F.*

___

152. *Pie-corner*] 'a place so called of such a signe [magpie], sometimes a
fayre Inne for receipte of trauellers, but now diuided into tenementes'
(Stow, ii. 22), at the Smithfield end of Giltspur Street. It was here that
Face first met Subtle (*A.,* I. i. 25).

157. *make . . . unready*] undress.

158. *strait-lac'd*] (*a*) with stays or bodice tightly laced; (*b*) precise in
morality.

161. *this seven year*] cf. v. ii. 52.

165. *mother*] (quibblingly) hysteria.

I. vi. 1. *beauteous discipline*] cf. Tribulation Wholesome: 'And stand vp for
the *beauteous discipline*, Against the menstruous cloth, and ragg of Rome'
(*A.,* III. i. 32–3).

Win. Yes, forsooth.

Pure. Look up, sweet Win-the-fight, and suffer not the enemy   5
    to enter you at this door; remember that your education
    has been with the purest; what polluted one was it, that
    nam'd first the unclean beast, pig, to you, child?

Win. Uh, uh.

Lit. Not I, o' my sincerity, mother: she long'd above three   10
    hours, ere she would let me know it; who was it, Win?

Win. A profane black thing with a beard, John.

Pure. O! resist it, Win-the-fight, it is the Tempter, the wicked
    Tempter, you may know it by the fleshly motion of pig, be
    strong against it, and its foul temptations, in these as-   15
    saults, whereby it broacheth flesh and blood, as it were, on
    the weaker side, and pray against its carnal provocations,
    good child, sweet child, pray.

Lit. Good mother, I pray you, that she may eat some pig, and
    her belly full, too; and do not you cast away your own   20
    child, and perhaps one of mine, with your tale of the
    Tempter: how do you, Win? Are you not sick?

Win. Yes, a great deal, John (uh, uh).

Pure. What shall we do? Call our zealous brother Busy hither,
    for his faithful fortification in this charge of the adversary;   25
    child, my dear child, you shall eat pig, be comforted, my
    sweet child.   [*Exit* LITTLEWIT.]

Win. Aye, but i' the Fair, mother.

Pure. I mean i' the Fair, if it can be anyway made, or found
    lawful; where is our brother Busy? Will he not come?   30
    Look up, child.

[*Re-enter* LITTLEWIT.]

Lit. Presently, mother, as soon as he has cleans'd his beard. I
    found him, fast by the teeth i' the cold turkey-pie, i' the
    cupboard, with a great white loaf on his left hand, and a
    glass of malmsey on his right.   35

---

14. *motion*] prompting, urging.

Pure. Slander not the brethren, wicked one.

Lit. Here he is now, purified, mother.   *adjective usage*

[*Enter*] BUSY.

Pure. O brother Busy! your help here to edify, and raise us
up in a scruple; my daughter Win-the-fight is visited
with a natural disease of women; call'd, 'A longing to eat   40
pig'.

Lit. Aye sir, a Bartholomew pig: and in the Fair.

Pure. And I would be satisfied from you, religiously-wise,
whether a widow of the sanctified assembly, or a widow's
daughter, may commit the act, without offence to the   45
weaker sisters.

Busy. Verily, for the disease of longing, it is a disease, a carnal
disease, or appetite, incident to women: and as it is carnal,
and incident, it is natural, very natural. Now pig, it is a
meat, and a meat that is nourishing, and may be long'd for,   50
and so consequently eaten; it may be eaten; very exceeding well eaten: but in the Fair, and as a Bartholomew-pig,
it cannot be eaten, for the very calling it a Bartholomew-
pig, and to eat it so, is a spice of idolatry, and you make the
Fair no better than one of the high places. This, I take it,   55
is the state of the question. A high place.

Lit. Aye, but in state of necessity: place should give place,
Master Busy. (I have a conceit left, yet.)

Pure. Good brother, Zeal-of-the-land, think to make it as
lawful as you can.   60

Lit. Yes sir, and as soon as you can: for it must be, sir; you see
the danger my little wife is in, sir.

Pure. Truly, I do love my child dearly, and I would not have

47–53. *for the disease . . . it cannot be eaten*] cf. the repetitive pseudo-
rhetoric of Dickens's Mr Chadband (*Bleak House*, ch. 19).

54. *spice*] species, kind.

55. *high places*] Hebrew *Bamoth*, where the Israelites worshipped idols
(e.g. Leviticus, xxvi. 30: 'And I will destroy your high places, and cut down
your images, and cast your carcases upon the carcases of your idols'); cf.
III. vi. 89.

  her miscarry, or hazard her first fruits, if it might be otherwise.   65

Busy. Surely, it may be otherwise, but it is subject to construction, subject, and hath a face of offence with the
  weak, a great face, a foul face, but that face may have a veil
  put over it, and be shadowed, as it were—it may be eaten,
  and in the Fair, I take it, in a booth, the tents of the wick- 70
  ed: the place is not much, not very much, we may be religious in midst of the profane, so it be eaten with a
  reformed mouth, with sobriety, and humbleness; not
  gorg'd in with gluttony, or greediness; there's the fear:
  for, should she go there, as taking pride in the place, or 75
  delight in the unclean dressing, to feed the vanity of the
  eye, or the lust of the palate, it were not well, it were not
  fit, it were abominable, and not good.

Lit. Nay, I knew that afore, and told her on't; but courage,
  Win, we'll be humble enough; we'll seek out the home- 80
  liest booth i' the Fair, that's certain; rather than fail, we'll
  eat it o' the ground.

Pure. Aye, and I'll go with you myself, Win-the-fight, and my
  brother, Zeal-of-the-land, shall go with us too, for our
  better consolation.   85

Win. Uh, uh.

Lit. Aye, and Solomon too, Win; the more the merrier, Win;
  [*Aside to Win*] we'll leave Rabbi Busy in a booth. Solomon, my cloak.

       [*Enter*] SOLOMON.

Sol. Here, sir.   90

Busy. In the way of comfort to the weak, I will go, and eat. I
  will eat exceedingly, and prophesy; there may be a good

---

81. certain;] *1716;* certaine, *F.*

---

  67. *face*] outward appearance.
  74. *fear*] thing to be feared.
  92. *eat . . . prophesy*] cf. *The Brownists Conventicle*, 1641, p. 5: '. . . let us
fall too, and feed exceedingly, that after our full repast, wee may the better
prophesie' (Appendix II).

use made of it, too, now I think on't: by the public eating
of swine's flesh, to profess our hate and loathing of Judaism, whereof the brethren stand taxed. I will therefore   95
eat, yea, I will eat exceedingly.

Lit. Good, i' faith, I will eat heartily too, because I will be no
Jew; I could never away with that stiffnecked generation.
And truly, I hope my little one will be like me, that cries
for pig so, i' the mother's belly.   100

Busy. Very likely, exceeding likely, very exceeding likely. [*Exeunt.*]

94–5. *Judaism . . . taxed*] from their attention to the Old Testament.
  98. *away with*] agree with; cf. *2 Henry IV*, III. ii. 216–18: '. . . she never
could away with me . . . she could not abide Master Shallow.'

Act II

Scene I

[*Enter*] JUSTICE OVERDO.

[*Jus.*] Well, in Justice' name, and the King's, and for the Commonwealth! defy all the world, Adam Overdo, for a disguise, and all story; for thou hast fitted thyself, I swear:
fain would I meet the Lynceus now, that eagle's eye, that
piercing Epidaurian serpent (as my Quintus Horace calls   5
him), that could discover a Justice of Peace (and lately of
the Quorum) under this covering. They may have seen
many a fool in the habit of a Justice; but never till now, a
Justice in the habit of a fool. Thus we must do, though,
that wake for the public good: and thus hath the wise   10
magistrate done in all ages. There is a doing of right out of
wrong, if the way be found. Never shall I enough commend a worthy worshipful man, sometime a capital member of this city, for his high wisdom in this point, who
would take you, now the habit of a porter; now of a car-   15
man; now of the dog-killer, in this month of August; and
in the winter, of a seller of tinder-boxes; and what would
he do in all these shapes? Marry go you into every ale-
house, and down into every cellar; measure the length of

1–2. *Commonwealth*] the general good.

3. *fitted*] furnished.

4. *Lynceus*] one of the Argonauts, renowned for keen sight; cf. Nashe,
Pierce Pennilesse, 1592 (McKerrow, i. 226): '*Linceus* eyes, that see through
stone walles'.

5. *Horace*] in *Sat.*, I. iii. 26–7.

7. *Quorum*] those J.P.s of learning and ability whose presence was
necessary to constitute a bench.

13. *a worthy worshipful man*] Introduction, p. xx above.
capital] chief.

puddings, take the gauge of black pots and cans, aye, and   20
custards, with a stick; and their circumference, with a
thread; weigh the loaves of bread on his middle-finger;
then would he send for 'em, home; give the puddings to
the poor, the bread to the hungry, the custards to his
children; break the pots, and burn the cans, himself; he   25
would not trust his corrupt officers; he would do't himself. Would all men in authority would follow this worthy
precedent! For (alas) as we are public persons, what do
we know? Nay, what can we know? We hear with other
men's ears; we see with other men's eyes; a foolish con-   30
stable, or a sleepy watchman, is all our information: he
slanders a gentleman, by the virtue of his place (as he calls
it), and we, by the vice of ours, must believe him: as, a
while gone, they made me, yea me, to mistake an honest
zealous pursuivant, for a seminary; and a proper young   35
Bachelor of Music, for a bawd. This we are subject to,
that live in high place: all our intelligence is idle, and
most of our intelligencers knaves; and, by your leave,
ourselves thought little better, if not arrant fools, for be-
lieving 'em. I, Adam Overdo, am resolv'd therefore to   40
spare spy-money hereafter, and make mine own discoveries. Many are the yearly enormities of this Fair, in
whose courts of Pie-powders I have had the honour during the three days sometimes to sit as judge. But this is the
special day for detection of those foresaid enormities.   45
Here is my black book for the purpose, this the cloud that
hides me: under this cover I shall see, and not be seen.
On, Junius Brutus. And as I began, so I'll end: in Justice'
name, and the King's; and for the Commonwealth!

30. eyes;] *HS;* eyes ? *F.*   48. On,] *W;* On *F.*

---

35. *pursuivant*] a state messenger with power to execute warrants for
arrest, seizure, search, etc.
   seminary] seminary-priest (trained abroad for the English mission).
37. *intelligence*] information.   *idle*] without foundation.
45. *enormities*] irregularities, wickednesses.
48. *Junius Brutus*] Like Overdo he took a disguise as a man of dull wits

Act II. Scene II.

[*Enter*] LEATHERHEAD, TRASH, *Passengers.*

[*Lea.*] The Fair's pestilence dead, methinks; people come not
abroad, today, what ever the matter is. Do you hear, Sister
Trash, Lady o' the Basket? Sit farther with your ginger-
bread-progeny there, and hinder not the prospect of my
shop, or I'll ha' it proclaim'd i' the Fair, what stuff they   5
are made on.

Trash. Why, what stuff are they made on, Brother Leatherhead? Nothing but what's wholesome, I assure you.

Lea. Yes, stale bread, rotten eggs, musty ginger, and dead
honey, you know.   10

Jus. [*Aside*] Aye! have I met with enormity so soon?

Lea. I shall mar your market, old Joan.

Trash. Mar my market, thou too-proud pedlar? Do thy
worst; I defy thee, aye, and thy stable of hobby-horses. I
pay for my ground, as well as thou dost; an' thou wrong'st   15
me, for all thou art parcel-poet, and an inginer, I'll find a
friend shall right me, and make a ballad of thee, and thy
cattel all over. Are you puff'd up with the pride of your
wares? Your arsedine?

II. ii. O.I. LEATHERHEAD, . . . *Passengers.*] LEATHERHEAD. TRASH. IVSTICE.
VRS'LA. MOONE-CALFE. NIGHTINGALE. *Costermonger. Passengers. F.*   15.
dost;] *This ed.;* dost, F.   16. me,] *1716;* mee *F.*   inginer,] *G;* Inginer.
F.

(to escape death at the hands of Tarquinius Superbus, last of the kings).
After the expulsion of the Tarquinii he became one of the first two consuls.
His reputation as an inflexible judge comes from his sentencing his own
sons to death for their part in the conspiracy to restore the Tarquinii
(Livy, II. v).

II. ii. I. *pestilence*] 'plaguily'.
9. *dead*] having lost its flavour.
16. *parcel-poet*] part poet.
inginer] designer, inventor.
18. *cattel*] property.
19. *arsedine*] imitation gold-leaf (of copper and zinc) used for ornament-
ing toys.

Lea. Go to, old Joan, I'll talk with you anon; and take you   20
 down too afore Justice Overdo, he is the man must charm
 you; I'll ha' you i' the Pie-powders.

Trash. Charm me? I'll meet thee face to face, afore his worship, when thou dar'st: and though I be a little crooked o'
 my body, I'll be found as upright in my dealing as any   25
 woman in Smithfield; aye, charm me!

Jus. [*Aside*] I am glad to hear my name is their terror, yet; this
 is doing of Justice.

Lea. What do you lack? What is't you buy? What do you
 lack? Rattles, drums, halberts, horses, babies o' the best?   30
 Fiddles o' th' finest?

Enter Costermonger, NIGHTINGALE.

Cost. Buy any pears, pears, fine, very fine pears!

Trash. Buy any ginger-bread, gilt ginger-bread!

Nigh.   *Hey, now the Fair's a filling!*
    O, for a tune to startle   35
    The birds o' the booths here billing
    Yearly with old Saint Bartle!
    The drunkards they are wading,
    The punks and chapmen trading;
    Who'd see the Fair without his lading?   40
 Buy any ballads; new ballads?

[*Enter*] URSULA.

26. Smithfield; aye,] Smithfield; I, *F3;* Smithfield, I, *F.*   27. yet;] *This ed.;* yet, F.   31.1. *Enter Costermonger,* NIGHTINGALE] *G; Enter Cost. F.* 36. billing] HS; billing: F.

20–1. take . . . down] humiliate.
 21. charm] subdue; cf. *C.R.,* I. i. 52: 'Charme your skipping tongue, or I'le—.'
 22. *Pie-powders*] a summary court held at fairs to administer justice among itinerant dealers and others temporarily present (*O.E.D.*); Anglo-French *piepouldrous,* dusty-footed, itinerant.
 30. *halberts, horses*] toy soldiers, with halberts, or else mounted.
 33. *gilt*] Gold leaf was used to decorate gingerbread (hence Trash's jibe at Leatherhead's 'arsedine').
 40. lading] freight.

Urs. Fie upon't: who would wear out their youth and prime
thus, in roasting of pigs, that had any cooler vocation?
Hell's a kind of cold cellar to't, a very fine vault, o' my
conscience! What, Mooncalf!   45

Moon. [*within*] Here, Mistress.

Nigh. How now, Urs'la? In a heat, in a heat?

Urs. My chair, you false faucet you; and my morning's
draught, quickly, a bottle of ale to quench me, rascal. I am
all fire, and fat, Nightingale; I shall e'en melt away to the   50
first woman, a rib, again, I am afraid. I do water the
ground in knots as I go, like a great garden-pot; you may
follow me by the S's I make.

Nigh. Alas, good Urs; was 'Zekiel here this morning?

Urs. 'Zekiel? what 'Zekiel?   55

Nigh. 'Zekiel Edgworth, the civil cutpurse, you know him
well enough; he that talks bawdy to you still: I call him
my secretary.

Urs. He promis'd to be here this morning, I remember.

Nigh. When he comes, bid him stay: I'll be back again pre-   60
sently.

Urs. Best take your morning's dew in your belly, Nightingale.

MOONCALF *brings in the chair.*

Come, sir, set it here; did not I bid you should get this
chair let out o' the sides, for me, that my hips might play?
You'll never think of anything, till your dame be rump-   65
gall'd; 'tis well, changeling: because it can take in your
grasshopper's thighs, you care for no more. Now, you
look as you had been i' the corner o' the booth, flaying

45. What, Mooncalf!] *G;* what *Moone-calfe. F.*   62. Nightingale.] *G;*
Nightingale, F.   62.1. MOONCALF . . . *chair.*] *F margin, ll. 63–5.*

---

48. *faucet*] tap for drawing liquor from a barrel.
52. *knots*] figures formed of criss-crossing lines; cf. *S.N.*, II. iii. 15–16:
'You might haue followed me like a watering pot, And seene the knots I
made along the street.'
58. *secretary*] one entrusted with another's secrets.
66. *gall'd*] chafed.
    changeling] a stupid or ugly child supposed to have been left by the fairies
in exchange for a better.

　　　your breech with a candle's end, and set fire o' the Fair.
　　　Fill, stot: fill.　　　　　　　　　　　　　　　　　　70
Jus. [*Aside*] This pig-woman do I know, and I will put her in,
　　　for my second enormity; she hath been before me, punk,
　　　pinnace and bawd, any time these two and twenty years,
　　　upon record i' the Pie-powders.
Urs. Fill again, you unlucky vermin.　　　　　　　　　　75
Moon. 'Pray you be not angry, mistress, I'll ha' it widen'd
　　　anon.
Urs. No, no, I shall e'en dwindle away to't, ere the Fair be
　　　done, you think, now you ha' heated me ? A poor vex'd
　　　thing I am, I feel myself dropping already, as fast as I can:　80
　　　two stone o' suet a day is my proportion: I can but hold
　　　life and soul together, with this (here's to you, Nightin-
　　　gale) and a whiff of tobacco, at most. Where's my pipe
　　　now ? Not fill'd ? Thou arrant incubee.
Nigh. Nay, Urs'la, thou'lt gall between the tongue and the　85
　　　teeth, with fretting, now.
Urs. How can I hope that ever he'll discharge his place of
　　　trust—tapster, a man of reckoning under me—that
　　　remembers nothing I say to him ?　　　[*Exit* NIGHTINGALE.]
　　　But look to't, sirrah, you were best; threepence a pipeful,　90
　　　I will ha' made of all my whole half-pound of tobacco, and
　　　a quarter of a pound of coltsfoot mix'd with it too, to eke
　　　it out. I that have dealt so long in the fire, will not be to
　　　seek in smoke, now. Then, six and twenty shillings a

92. eke] *G;* itch *F;* eech *F3.*

　　　70. *stot*] a stupid, clumsy person; applied to women in Chaucer (*Canter-
bury Tales,* D 1630) and to men in 19th-century dialect.
　　　73. *pinnace*] from the context apparently a go-between; more usually a
prostitute, cf. Dekker and Webster, *Northward Hoe,* v. i, where a woman is
recommended to Fetherstone as a 'pretty . . . little Pinnas' (428) and he
concludes, 'Ile . . . board your Pynnis while 'tis hotte' (444).
　　　84. *incubee*] incubus, ? the child resulting from intercourse with such a
demon; cf. *O.E.D.*, 1674: 'A sort of incubus brats, the infamous progenies
of the lying spirit'.
　　　88. *reckoning*] (*a*) distinction, consideration, cf. *O.E.D.*, s.v.8, 1598:
'Such beasts . . . are . . . not meete for any man of reckoning to eate'; (*b*)
adding up charges for drink (cf. ll. 100–1).

barrel I will advance o' my beer, and fifty shillings a hun-   95
dred o' my bottle-ale; I ha' told you the ways how to
raise it. Froth your cans well i' the filling, at length,
rogue, and jog your bottles o' the buttock, sirrah, then
skink out the first glass, ever, and drink with all com-
panies, though you be sure to be drunk; you'll mis-   100
reckon the better, and be less asham'd on't. But your
true trick, rascal, must be, to be ever busy, and mis-take
away the bottles and cans, in haste, before they be half
drunk off, and never hear anybody call (if they should
chance to mark you), till you ha' brought fresh, and be   105
able to forswear 'em. Give me a drink of ale.

Jus. [*Aside*] This is the very womb and bed of enormity!
gross, as herself! This must all down for enormity, all,
every whit on't.   *One knocks.*

Urs. Look who's there, sirrah! Five shillings a pig is my   110
price, at least; if it be a sow-pig, sixpence more: if she be
a great-bellied wife, and long for't, sixpence more for
that.

Jus. [*Aside*] *O tempora ! O mores !* I would not ha' lost my discovery of this one grievance, for my place, and worship o'   115
the bench. How is the poor subject abus'd, here! Well, I
will fall in with her, and with her Mooncalf, and win out
wonders of enormity. [*To* URSULA] By thy leave, goodly
woman, and the fatness of the Fair: oily as the King's
constable's lamp, and shining as his shoeing-horn! Hath   120
thy ale virtue, or thy beer strength? that the tongue
of man may be tickled? and his palate pleas'd in the
morning? Let thy pretty nephew here go search and
see.

---

109. *One knocks.*] F margin, *l. 110.*   110. Look] *1716;* Looke, *F.*
116. bench.] *1716; Bench, F.*

---

95. *advance*] raise.
99. *skink*] pour.
114. O . . . mores!] Cicero, *In Catilinam,* I. i. 2: 'What an age! What manners!'; cf. *C.,* iv. 190.
115. *worship*] honour; good name.

Urs. What new roarer is this?   125

Moon. O Lord! do you not know him, mistress, 'tis mad
Arthur of Bradley, that makes the orations. Brave master,
old Arthur of Bradley, how do you? Welcome to the
Fair; when shall we hear you again, to handle your matters? With your back again' a booth, ha? I ha' been one   130
o' your little disciples, i' my days!

Jus. Let me drink, boy, with my love, thy Aunt, here; that I
may be eloquent: but of thy best, lest it be bitter in my
mouth, and my words fall foul on the Fair.

Urs. Why dost thou not fetch him drink? And offer him to   135
sit?

Moon. Is't ale, or beer, Master Arthur?

Jus. Thy best, pretty stripling, thy best; the same thy dove
drinketh, and thou drawest on holy days.

Urs. Bring him a sixpenny bottle of ale; they say, a fool's   140
handsel is lucky.

Jus. Bring both, child. Ale for Arthur, and beer for Bradley.
Ale for thine Aunt, boy.   [*Exit* MOONCALF.]
[*Aside*] My disguise takes to the very wish and reach of it.
I shall, by the benefit of this, discover enough, and more   145
—and yet get off with the reputation of what I would
be: a certain middling thing, between a fool and a madman.

137. beer,] *1716*; Beere? *F.*

---

127. *Arthur of Bradley*] For the ballad 'O Brave Arthur of Bradley' see
Ritson's *Robin Hood*, 1795, ii. 210—though it is irrelevant to Overdo's
case.

132. *Aunt*] old woman.

138. *dove*] darling.

141. *handsel*] the first money taken (as earnest of what is to follow).

Act II. Scene III.

[*Enter*] KNOCKEM {*to them.*

[*Kno.*] What! my little lean Urs'la! my she-bear! art thou
alive yet? With thy litter of pigs, to grunt out another
Bartholomew Fair? Ha!

Urs. Yes, and to amble afoot, when the Fair is done, to hear
you groan out of a cart, up the heavy hill.   5

Kno. Of Holborn, Urs'la, meanst thou so? For what? For
what, pretty Urs?

Urs. For cutting halfpenny purses, or stealing little penny
dogs, out o' the Fair.

Kno. O! good words, good words, Urs.   10

Jus. [*Aside*] Another special enormity. A cutpurse of the
sword! the boot, and the feather! Those are his marks.

[*Re-enter* MOONCALF.]

Urs. You are one of those horse-leeches that gave out I was
dead, in Turnbull-street, of a surfeit of bottle-ale, and
tripes?   15

Kno. No, 'twas better meat, Urs: cow's udders, cow's udders!

Urs. Well, I shall be meet with your mumbling mouth one
day.

Kno. What? Thou'lt poison me with a newt in a bottle of ale,
wilt thou? Or a spider in a tobacco-pipe, Urs? Come,   20
there's no malice in these fat folks, I never fear thee, an' I

II. iii. 8. purses,] *1716;* purses: *F.*

II. iii. 5. *heavy hill*] Holborn Hill, part of the route from Newgate (near
the Old Bailey) to the gallows at Tyburn (near the junction of Oxford Street
and the Edgware Road); cf. S. Rowlands, *Knave of Hearts,* 1612, p. 48:
'. . . those that ride up Holbourne-hill And at the Gallowes make their
Will'; and Appendix I, paragraph 4.

13. *horse-leeches*] farriers; bloodsuckers; figuratively, rapacious, insati-
able persons; cf. Sylvester's *Du Bartas,* ed. 4, 1613, p. 624: 'Thou life of
Strife, thou Horse-leach sent from Hell' (*O.E.D.*).

17. *meet*] even, quits.

21. *fat folks*] cf. *Julius Caesar,* I. ii. 191–4.

can 'scape thy lean Mooncalf here. Let's drink it out, good
Urs, and no vapours!   [*Exit* URSULA.]

Jus. Dost thou hear, boy? (There's for thy ale, and the remnant for thee.) Speak in thy faith of a faucet, now; is this   25
goodly person before us here, this vapours, a knight of the
knife?

Moon. What mean you by that, Master Arthur?

Jus. I mean a child of the horn-thumb, a babe of booty, boy; a
cutpurse.   30

Moon. O Lord, sir! far from it. This is Master Dan. Knockem: Jordan the ranger of Turnbull. He is a horse-courser,
sir.

Jus. Thy dainty dame, though, call'd him cutpurse.

Moon. Like enough, sir, she'll do forty such things in an hour   35
(an' you listen to her) for her recreation, if the toy take her
i' the greasy kerchief: it makes her fat, you see. She bat-
tens with it.

Jus. [*Aside*] Here might I ha' been deceiv'd, now, and ha' put
a fool's blot upon myself, if I had not play'd an after-game   40
o' discretion.

URSULA *comes in again dropping.*

Kno. Alas, poor Urs, this's an ill season for thee.
Urs. Hang yourself, hackney-man.

---

37. fat,] *1716;* fat *F.*   39. now,] *F3;* now: *F.*   41.1. URSULA . . .
dropping.] *F margin, ll. 42–4.*

---

23. *vapours*] ? fantastic notions, foolish bragging. The nonsensical mis-
use of the word (see, e.g., II. v. 53) is peculiar to Knockem and noticed by
several characters—the Justice in l. 26, Quarlous, II. v. 142–3, Ursula, III.
ii. 105.

29. *horn-thumb*] the cutpurse's thimble to protect his thumb from the
edge of the knife; cf. the essentials for the trade in Preston, *King Cambyses*,
1570, sig. F, 'a horne on your thumb, A quick eye, a sharp knife, at hand a
receiver' (G.).

32. *Jordan*] chamber-pot; applied derisively to a person even in Lang-
land (*Piers Plowman* B, xiii. 83).

36. *toy*] whim.

40. *after-game*] a second game played to reverse the issue of the first.

Kno. How ? How ? Urs, vapours! Motion breed vapours ?

Urs. Vapours ? Never tusk nor twirl your dibble, good Jordan,   45
   I know what you'll take to a very drop. Though you be
   captain o' the roarers, and fight well at the case of piss-
   pots, you shall not fright me with your lion-chop, sir, nor
   your tusks; you angry ? You are hungry: come, a pig's
   head will stop your mouth, and stay your stomach, at all   50
   times.

Kno. Thou art such another mad merry Urs still! Troth I do
   make conscience of vexing thee now i' the dog-days, this
   hot weather, for fear of found'ring thee i' the body; and
   melting down a pillar of the Fair. Pray thee take thy chair   55
   again, and keep state; and let's have a fresh bottle of ale,
   and a pipe of tobacco; and no vapours. I'll ha' this belly o'
   thine taken up, and thy grass scour'd, wench; look! here's
   Ezekiel Edgworth; a fine boy of his inches as any is i' the
   Fair! has still money in his purse, and will pay all, with a   60
   kind heart; and good vapours.

49. tusks;] *F3;* tuskes, *F.*

---

44. *Motion*] exertion.
   45. *tusk*] to form into a tuft; cf. *Ep.*, cvii. 29–30: 'Nay, now you puffe,
tuske, and draw vp your chin.' The noun (l. 49) seems to mean a tuft of hair
or moustache; cf. S. Rowley, *The Noble Spanish Soldier*, 1634 (ed. Bullen,
O.E. Plays, 1882, II. i. 11–12): 'Had my Barbour . . . poak'd out My Tuskes
more stiffe than are a Cats muschatoes' (H. & S.).
   dibble] trowel, spade-beard (affected by swashbucklers; H. & S. cf.
Greene, *A Quip for an Upstart Courtier*, 1592, D3v–D4: 'whether he will
haue his peak cut short & sharpe, amiable like an *Inamorato* or broad pen-
dant like a spade, to be terrible lyke a warrior and a Soldado').
   48. *lion-chop*] lion-jaw.
   54. *found'ring . . . body*] cf. Markham, p. 122: 'Of foundring in the body,
being a surfaite [eruptive disease] got either by Meate, Drinke, or Labour'.
   56. *keep state*] observe the pomp and ceremony due to your dignity; cf.
C.R., II. iii. 182–4: 'The worst in her is want of keeping state, and too much
descending into inferior and base offices'.
   58. *taken up*] reduced; cf. Markham, *Cavalarice*, 1607, V, ch. iv, of a horse
whose belly is 'taken vp well within his ribbes' by fasting (H. & S.).
   scour'd] cleared out, purged.

Act II. Scene IV.

[*Enter*] *to them* EDGWORTH, NIGHTINGALE, *Corn-cutter,*
Tinderbox-man, Passengers.

[*Edg.*] That I will, indeed, willingly, Master Knockem; fetch
    some ale, and tobacco.   [*Exit* MOONCALF.]

Lea. What do you lack, gentlemen? Maid: see a fine hobby-
    horse for your young master: cost you but a token a week
    his provender.   5

Corn. Ha' you any corns i' your feet and toes?

Tin. Buy a mousetrap, a mousetrap, or a tormentor for a flea.

Trash. Buy some ginger-bread.

Nigh. Ballads, ballads! fine new ballads:
    Hear for your love, and buy for your money!   10
    A delicate ballad o' *The Ferret and the Coney*!
    A Preservative again' the Punks' Evil!
    Another of *Goose-green Starch, and the Devil*!
    A Dozen of Divine Points, and *The Godly Garters*!

II. iv. 1. Knockem;] *1716; Knockhum, F.*

II. iv. 7. *tormentor*] trap; *O.E.D.* quotes the *Cries of Rome* appended to
T. Heywood, *Rape of Lucrece,* 1609: 'Buy a very fine Mouse-trap, or a tormentor for your Fleaes'.

13. Goose-green] yellowish green; Harrison (*Description of England,*
1577, Bk. II, ch. vii, ed. Furnivall, 1877, p. 172) names 'gooseturd greene'
among 'a sort of hewes deuised for the nonce, wherewith to please phan-
tasticall heads'.

and the Devil] H. & S. quote from Stubbes, *Anatomie of Abuses,* 1583
(ed. Furnivall, i. 71–2), the story of a woman who, unable to get anyone to
starch and set her ruff to her satisfaction, 'fell to sweare . . . , wishing the
Deuill might take her, when she weare any of those Neckerchers againe'.
The Devil, in the guise of a young man, set the ruff 'to her greate contenta-
tion' and then in kissing her 'writhe her necke in sonder, so she died
miserably'.

14. Dozen . . . Points] twelve moral maxims, 'a knotte of peerlesse
points', 'sent by a gentlewoman to her lover' (Percy Soc. xxvii. 79, from
Sloane MS. 1896).

Godly Garters] entered on 20 October 1578 a 'ballate intituled *A paire of
garters for yonge menne to weare yat serue the LORD GOD and Lyve in his
feare*' (S.R., Arber, ii. 339).

    The Fairing of Good Counsel, of an ell and three quarters! 15
    What is't you buy?
      The Windmill blown down by the witch's fart!
      Or *Saint George, that O! did break the dragon's heart!*

        [*Re-enter* MOONCALF.]

Edg. Master Nightingale, come hither, leave your mart a
    little.   20
Nigh. O my secretary! What says my secretary?
Jus. Child o' the bottles, what's he? What's he?
Moon. A civil young gentleman, Master Arthur, that keeps
    company with the roarers, and disburses all, still. He has
    ever money in his purse; he pays for them, and they roar   25
    for him: one does good offices for another. They call him
    the secretary, but he serves nobody. A great friend of the
    ballad-man's—they are never asunder.
Jus. What pity 'tis so civil a young man should haunt this de-
    bauch'd company! Here's the bane of the youth of our   30
    time apparent. A proper penman, I see't in his counte-
    nance; he has a good clerk's look with him, and I warrant
    him a quick hand.
Moon. A very quick hand, sir.   [*Exit.*]
Edg. All the purses and purchase I give you to-day by con-   35
    veyance, bring hither to Urs'la's presently. Here we will
    meet at night in her lodge, and share. Look you choose
    good places for your standing i' the Fair, when you sing,
    Nightingale.

      This they whisper, that OVERDO *hears it not.*

22. What's] *F3;* what *F.*   39.1. *This . . . not.*] *F margin, ll. 36–40.*

---

15. *ell*] forty-five inches; referring (with exaggeration) to the length of the
paper?
    21. *secretary*] here with emphasis on the sense of transacting business for
another; cf. II. ii. 58.
    35. *purchase*] booty.
    35–6. *conveyance*] transference; cunning contrivance, sleight of hand; cf.
III. v. 170, *O.E.D.*, 1615: 'He hath a sleight of hand, or cleanly conveiance,
which threaten silver spoones'.

Urs. Aye, near the fullest passages; and shift 'em often.   40

Edg. And i' your singing, you must use your hawk's eye
    nimbly, and fly the purse to a mark still—where 'tis worn
    and o' which side—that you may gi' me the sign with your
    beak, or hang your head that way i' the tune.

Urs. Enough, talk no more on't: your friendship, masters, is   45
    not now to begin. Drink your draught of indenture, your
    sup of covenant, and away: the Fair fills apace, company
    begins to come in, and I ha' ne'er a pig ready, yet.

Kno. Well said! Fill the cups, and light the tobacco: let's give
    fire i' th' works, and noble vapours.   50

Edg. And shall we ha' smocks, Urs'la, and good whimsies, ha?

Urs. Come, you are i' your bawdy vein! The best the Fair will
    afford, 'Zekiel, if bawd Whit keep his word.

[Re-enter MOONCALF.]

How do the pigs, Mooncalf?

Moon. Very passionate, mistress, one on 'em has wept out an   55
    eye. Master Arthur o' Bradley is melancholy, here, no-
    body talks to him. Will you any tobacco, Master Arthur?

Jus. No, boy, let my meditations alone.

Moon. He's studying for an oration, now.

Jus. [*Aside*] If I can, with this day's travel, and all my policy,   60
    but rescue this youth, here, out of the hands of the lewd

---

    42. *fly . . . to a mark*] 'generally said of a Goshawk, when, having "putin"
a covey of partridges, she takes stand, marking the spot where they dis-
appeared from view, until the falconer arrives to put them out to her' (J. E.
Harting, *Bibliotheca Accipitraria*, 1881, Glossary).

    44. *beak*] nose.

    45–6. *friendship . . . begin*] *Canterbury Tales*, A 427–8; cf. *M.L.*, III. v. 21–
3: 'Doctors, learned men, And their Apothecaries, who are not now, (As
Chaucer sayes) their friendship to begin'. Speght's Chaucer (1598) has the
more nearly correct reading 'new'.

    46. *draught of indenture*] from the drinking which went with the making
of agreements; 'to make indentures' was even cant for 'to get drunk'.

    51. *smocks, whimsies*] wenches.

    55. *passionate*] sorrowful; cf. *King John*, II. i. 544: 'She is sad and passion-
ate'.

    55–6. *wept out an eye*] a sign that a roasting pig is nearly ready.

    60. *policy*] shrewdness.

man, and the strange woman, I will sit down at night, and
say with my friend Ovid, *Jamque opus exegi, quod nec Jovis
ira, nec ignis, &c.*

Kno. Here, 'Zekiel; here's a health to Urs'la, and a kind   65
vapour: thou hast money i' thy purse still; and store!
How dost thou come by it? Pray thee vapour thy friends
some in a courteous vapour.

Edg. Half I have, Master Dan. Knockem, is always at your
service.   70

Jus. [*Aside*] Ha, sweet nature! What goshawk would prey
upon such a lamb?

Kno. Let's see what 'tis, 'Zekiel! Count it, come, fill him to
pledge me.

Act II. Scene V.

[*Enter*] WINWIFE, QUARLOUS, {*to them.*

[*Winw.*] We are here before 'em, methinks.

Quar. All the better, we shall see 'em come in now.

Lea. What do you lack, gentlemen, what is't you lack? A fine
horse? A lion? A bull? A bear? A dog, or a cat? An excellent fine Bartholomew-bird? Or an instrument? What   5
is't you lack?

Quar. 'Slid! here's Orpheus among the beasts, with his fiddle,
and all!

Trash. Will you buy any comfortable bread, gentlemen?

62. woman,] *F3;* woman. *F.*   66. vapour:] *F3;* vapour, *F.*   73. see]
1716; see, *F.*

---

62. *strange woman*] harlot; cf. A.V. 1 Kings xi. 1: 'But king Solomon
loved many strange women'.

63–4. Jamque . . . &c.] 'Jamque . . . ignis, nec poterit ferrum nec edax
abolere vetustas', Ovid, *Met.*, xv. 871–2; 'And now my work is done, which
neither the wrath of Jove, nor fire, nor sword, nor the gnawing tooth of time
shall ever be able to undo' (F. J. Miller).

66. *store*] plenty.

II. v. 9. *comfortable*] sustaining, refreshing.

Quar. And Ceres selling her daughter's picture, in ginger- 10
work!

Winw. That these people should be so ignorant to think us
chapmen for 'em! Do we look as if we would buy ginger-
bread? Or hobby-horses?

Quar. Why, they know no better ware than they have, nor 15
better customers than come. And our very being here
makes us fit to be demanded, as well as others. Would
Cokes would come! There were a true customer for 'em.

Kno. How much is't? Thirty shillings? Who's yonder! Ned
Winwife? And Tom Quarlous, I think! Yes. (Gi' me it all, 20
gi' me it all.) Master Winwife! Master Quarlous! Will you
take a pipe of tobacco with us? (Do not discredit me now,
'Zekiel.)

Winw. Do not see him! He is the roaring horse-courser, pray
thee let's avoid him: turn down this way. 25

Quar. 'Slud, I'll see him, and roar with him too, an' he roar'd
as loud as Neptune; pray thee go with me.

Winw. You may draw me to as likely an inconvenience, when
you please, as this.

Quar. Go to then, come along, we ha' nothing to do, man, but 30
to see sights now.

Kno. Welcome Master Quarlous, and Master Winwife! Will
you take any froth, and smoke with us?

Quar. Yes, sir, but you'll pardon us if we knew not of so much
familiarity between us afore. 35

Kno. As what, sir?

Quar. To be so lightly invited to smoke, and froth.

Kno. A good vapour! Will you sit down, sir? This is old
Urs'la's mansion, how like you her bower? Here you may
ha' your punk and your pig in state, sir, both piping hot. 40

Quar. I had rather ha' my punk cold, sir.

---

13. *chapmen*] customers.
24. *roaring*] riotous.
26. *'Slud*] by God's blood; cf. IV. iii. 6.
39. *bower*] cf. III. ii. 55.

Jus. [*Aside*] There's for me; punk! and pig!

Urs. What, Mooncalf? You rogue.   *She calls within.*

Moon. By and by, the bottle is almost off, mistress; here,
    Master Arthur.   45

Urs. I'll part you and your play-fellow there i' the guarded
    coat, an' you sunder not the sooner.   [*Exit.*]

Kno. Master Winwife, you are proud, methinks; you do not
    talk, nor drink; are you proud?

Winw. Not of the company I am in, sir, nor the place, I assure   50
    you.

Kno. You do not except at the company! Do you? Are you in
    vapours, sir?

Moon. Nay, good Master Dan. Knockem, respect my mis-
    tress' bower, as you call it; for the honour of our booth,   55
    none o' your vapours here.

She comes out with a fire-brand.

Urs. Why, you thin lean polecat you, an' they have a mind to
    be i' their vapours, must you hinder 'em? What did you
    know, vermin, if they would ha' lost a cloak, or such a
    trifle? Must you be drawing the air of pacification here,   60
    while I am tormented, within, i' the fire, you weasel?

Moon. Good mistress, 'twas in the behalf of your booth's
    credit that I spoke.

Urs. Why? Would my booth ha' broke, if they had fall'n out
    in't, sir? Or would their heat ha' fir'd it? In, you rogue,   65
    and wipe the pigs, and mend the fire, that they fall not, or
    I'll both baste and roast you, till your eyes drop out, like

---

43. *She . . . within.*] *F margin, ll. 43–4.*   44. off, mistress;] *F3;* off Mistresse, *F.*   56.1. *She . . . fire-brand.*] *F margin, ll. 58–61.*   65. in't,] *F3;*
in't? *F.*

---

46. *guarded*] having 'guards' or trimmings (of braid, etc.); cf. note to
I. ii. 7 (*lace*).

64. *broke*] gone bankrupt; cf. *Richard the Second*, II. i. 258: 'The King's
grown bankrupt like a broken man'.

67. *baste*] (*a*) moisten roasting meat with fat to keep it from burning;
(*b*) thrash. *Roast* has the same secondary meaning.

'em. (Leave the bottle behind you, and be curst a while.)

[*Exit* MOONCALF.]

Quar. Body o' the Fair! what's this? Mother o' the bawds?

Kno. No, she's mother o' the pigs, sir, mother o' the pigs!   70

Winw. Mother o' the Furies, I think, by her firebrand.

Quar. Nay, she is too fat to be a Fury, sure some walking sow of tallow!

Winw. An inspir'd vessel of kitchen-stuff! *She drinks this while.*

Quar. She'll make excellent gear for the coach-makers, here in   75
Smithfield, to anoint wheels and axle-trees with.

Urs. Aye, aye, gamesters, mock a plain plump soft wench o'
the suburbs, do, because she's juicy and wholesome: you
must ha' your thin pinch'd ware, pent up i' the compass
of a dog-collar (or 'twill not do), that looks like a long   80
lac'd conger, set upright, and a green feather, like fennel,
i' the jowl on't.

Kno. Well said, Urs, my good Urs; to 'em, Urs.

Quar. Is she your quagmire, Dan. Knockem? Is this your
bog?   85

Nigh. We shall have a quarrel presently.

Kno. How? Bog? Quagmire? Foul vapours! Hum'h!

Quar. Yes, he that would venture for't, I assure him, might

72. sure] *F3;* sure, *F.*   74. *She . . . while.*] *F margin, ll. 74–6.*

---

68. *a while*] cf. *Measure for Measure,* v. i. 354–5: 'show your sheep-biting face and be hang'd an hour!'

74. *inspir'd*] (*a*) inflated; (*b*) infused with divine power.

vessel] a person filled with some quality; a Biblical and Puritan phrase; cf. Hinde's *Life* of the puritan Bruen, 1641, ii. 6: 'a vessell of Honour'.

78. *suburbs*] persistently associated with licentiousness in the 17th century; cf. Nashe, *Christ's Teares,* 1593 (McKerrow, ii. 148): 'London, what are thy Suburbes but licensed Stewes?'

81. *lac'd*] streaked; cf. I. ii. 7 and n., and *Macbeth,* II. iii. 119: 'His silver skin laced with his golden blood.'

conger] sea-eel; as a term of abuse for a man cf. *2 Henry IV,* II. iv. 57: 'Hang yourself you muddy conger, hang yourself!'

82. *jowl*] fish-head.

84–5. *quagmire . . . bog*] cf. Cunningham's note (Appendix, p. 550): 'Every dealer in unsound horses has a prepared corner of his yard in which the "screws" may stand up to their knees in wet clay.'

sink into her, and be drown'd a week, ere any friend he
had could find where he were.   90

Winw. And then he would be a fortnight weighing up again.

Quar. 'Twere like falling into a whole shire of butter: they
had need be a team of Dutchmen, should draw him out.

Kno. Answer 'em, Urs; where's thy Bartholomew-wit,
now ? Urs, thy Bartholomew-wit ?   95

Urs. Hang 'em, rotten, roguy cheaters, I hope to see 'em
plagu'd one day (pox'd they are already, I am sure) with
lean playhouse poultry, that has the bony rump sticking
out like the ace of spades or the point of a partizan, that
every rib of 'em is like the tooth of a saw; and will so   100
grate 'em with their hips and shoulders, as (take 'em
altogether) they were as good lie with a hurdle.

Quar. Out upon her, how she drips! She's able to give a man
the sweating sickness with looking on her.

Urs. Marry look off, with a patch o' your face; and a dozen i'   105
your breech, though they be o' scarlet, sir. I ha' seen as
fine outsides, as either o' yours, bring lousy linings to the
brokers, ere now, twice a week!

Quar. Do you think there may be a fine new cucking-stool i'

---

91. *weighing up*] raising up (of a sunken ship).

93. *Dutchmen*] famous for their consumption of butter, 'the first and last
dish at the Table . . . and thereupon by strangers they are merrily called
Butter-mouthes' (Moryson, *Itinerary*, 1617, pt. iii, p. 97); cf. *V.*, I. i. 41–3:
'. . . some will swallow A melting heir, as glibly as your Dutch Will pills of
butter'; *E.M.I.*, III. iv. 42: '. . . they [fasting days] are of a Flemish breed . . .
for they rauen vp more butter, then all the dayes of the weeke, beside.'

98. *lean . . . poultry*] H. & S. quote Martial, *Ep.*, XI. c: 'Habere amicam
nolo, Flacce, subtilem. . . Quae clune nudo radat et genu pugnat, Cui serra
lumbis, cuspis eminet culo'; 'I don't wish to have, Flaccus, a mistress who
is thin . . . who rasps me with her skinny haunch and pricks me with her
knee, from whose spine protrudes a saw, from whose latter end a spear'
(W. C. A. Ker).

99. *partizan*] a long-handled spear with one or more lateral projecting
blades.

105–6. *patch . . . breech*] symptoms of the French pox.

108. *brokers*] dealers in second-hand clothes.

109. *cucking-stool*] properly a close stool; here one used for ducking
scolds.

the Fair, to be purchas'd? One large enough, I mean. I   110
know there is a pond of capacity for her.

Urs. For your mother, you rascal; out, you rogue, you
hedge-bird, you pimp, you pannier-man's bastard, you!

Quar. Ha, ha, ha.

Urs. Do you sneer, you dog's-head, you trendle-tail! You   115
look as you were begotten a'top of a cart in harvest-time,
when the whelp was hot and eager. Go, snuff after your
brother's bitch, Mistress Commodity, that's the livery
you wear, 'twill be out at the elbows shortly. It's time
you went to't, for the tother remnant.   120

Kno. Peace, Urs, peace, Urs; they'll kill the poor whale, and
make oil of her. Pray thee go in.

Urs. I'll see 'em pox'd first, and pil'd, and double pil'd.

Winw. Let's away; her language grows greasier than her
pigs.   125

Urs. Does't so, snotty nose? Good Lord! are you snivelling?
You were engend'red on a she-beggar, in a barn, when
the bald thrasher, your sire, was scarce warm.

Winw. Pray thee, let's go.

Quar. No, faith; I'll stay the end of her, now: I know she   130
cannot last long; I find by her similes she wanes apace.

Urs. Does she so? I'll set you gone. Gi' me my pig-pan
hither a little. I'll scald you hence, an' you will not go. [*Exit.*]

Kno. Gentlemen, these are very strange vapours! And very
idle vapours! I assure you.   135

Quar. You are a very serious ass, we assure you.

Kno. Hum'h! Ass? And serious? Nay, then pardon me my

---

111. *a pond*] 'Horsepoole in *Westsmithfield*, was sometime a great water
... it is now much decaycd, the springs being stopped vp, and the land water
falling into the small bottome, remayning inclosed with Bricke, is but fowle:
and is called *Smithfield pond*' (Stow, i. 16, ii. 231).

113. *hedge-bird*] vagrant, footpad.
pannier-man] hawker.

115. *trendle-tail*] cur, dog with a curly tail.

118. *Commodity*] self-interest, gain.

123. *pil'd*] (*a*) deprived of hair; (*b*) afflicted with piles; (*c*) provided with a
pile or nap like velvet (*double*, with one pile higher than the other).

vapour. I have a foolish vapour, gentlemen: any man
that does vapour me the ass, Master Quarlous—

Quar. What then, Master Jordan?   140

Kno. I do vapour him the lie.

Quar. Faith, and to any man that vapours me the lie, I do
vapour that.   [*Strikes him.*]

Kno. Nay, then, vapours upon vapours.

Edg. Nigh. 'Ware the pan, the pan, the pan, she comes with   145
the pan, gentlemen. God bless the woman.

URSULA *comes in, with the scalding-pan. They fight. She falls with it.*

Urs. Oh!   [*Exeunt* QUARLOUS, WINWIFE.]

Trash. What's the matter?

Jus. Goodly woman!

Moon. Mistress!   150

Urs. Curse of hell, that ever I saw these fiends, oh! I ha'
scalded my leg, my leg, my leg, my leg. I ha' lost a limb in
the service! Run for some cream and salad oil, quickly!
Are you under-peering, you baboon? Rip off my hose,
an' you be men, men, men!   155

Moon. Run you for some cream, good mother Joan. I'll look
to your basket.   [*Exit* TRASH.]

Lea. Best sit up i' your chair, Urs'la. Help, gentlemen.

Kno. Be of good cheer, Urs; thou hast hind'red me the
currying of a couple of stallions here, that abus'd the   160
good race-bawd o' Smithfield; 'twas time for 'em to go.

Nigh. I'faith, when the pan came, they had made you run
else. (This had been a fine time for purchase, if you had
ventur'd.)

Edg. Not a whit, these fellows were too fine to carry money.   165

Kno. Nightingale, get some help to carry her leg out o' the

---

139. me] *F3;* me, *F.*   143. *Strikes him.*] *G.*   146.1. URSULA . . . *it.*] *F*
margin, ll. 144–50.

---

160. *currying*] 'dressing down', beating.
161. *race-bawd*] on the model of *race-mare*, mare for breeding.
163. *purchase*] robbery.

air; take off her shoes; body o' me, she has the mallanders, the scratches, the crown scab, and the quitter bone, i' the tother leg.

Urs. Oh! the pox, why do you put me in mind o' my leg, thus, 170
to make it prick and shoot? Would you ha' me i' the Hospital, afore my time?

Kno. Patience, Urs. Take a good heart, 'tis but a blister, as big as a windgall; I'll take it away with the white of an egg, a little honey, and hog's grease; ha' thy pasterns 175
well roll'd, and thou shalt pace again by tomorrow. I'll tend thy booth and look to thy affairs, the while: thou shalt sit i' thy chair, and give directions, and shine Ursa major.　　　　　[*Exeunt* KNOCKEM, MOONCALF, URSULA.]

Act II. Scene VI.

[*Enter*] COKES, WASP, Mistress OVERDO, GRACE.

[*Jus.*] These are the fruits of bottle-ale, and tobacco! the foam of the one, and the fumes of the other! Stay, young man, and despise not the wisdom of these few hairs, that are grown grey in care of thee.

Edg. Nightingale, stay a little. Indeed I'll hear some o' this! 5
Cok. Come, Numps, come, where are you? Welcome into the Fair, Mistress Grace.

II. vi. O.I. COKES, . . . GRACE.] IVSTICE. EDGEWORTH. NIGHTINGALE. COKES. WASPE. Mistris OVERDOO. GRACE. *F.*

167–9. *mallanders . . . quitter bone*] all diseases of legs and feet in horses, in order: a scabby eruption behind the knee, an irritation of the pastern, a sore in the coronet of the foot, and a dangerous ulcer there.

174. *windgall*] a soft tumour on either side of a horse's leg, just above the fetlock.

174–5. *white of an egg . . . grease*] cf. Markham (p. 366) for a similar remedy for the scratches: 'of hony halfe a pint, of hogges grease a quarterne, and three yolkes of egges . . .'

179. Exeunt. . . *Ursula.*] Ursula plainly subsides into her chair on the inner stage and the curtain is drawn to form the 'backside' of the booth.

G

Edg. 'Slight, he will call company, you shall see, and put us
into doings presently.

Jus. Thirst not after that frothy liquor, ale: for who knows,   10
when he openeth the stopple, what may be in the bottle?
Hath not a snail, a spider, yea, a newt been found there?
Thirst not after it, youth; thirst not after it.

Cok. This is a brave fellow, Numps, let's hear him.

Wasp. 'Sblood, how brave is he? In a guarded coat? You were   15
best truck with him; e'en strip, and truck presently, it will
become you. Why will you hear him? Because he is an ass,
and may be akin to the Cokeses?

Cok. O, good Numps!

Jus. Neither do thou lust after that tawny weed, tobacco.   20

Cok. Brave words!

Jus. Whose complexion is like the Indian's that vents it!

Cok. Are they not brave words, sister?

Jus. And who can tell if, before the gathering and making up
thereof, the alligator hath not piss'd thereon?   25

Wasp. 'Heart, let 'em be brave words, as brave as they will!
An' they were all the brave words in a country, how then?
Will you away yet? Ha' you enough on him? Mistress
Grace, come you away, I pray you, be not you accessary.
If you do lose your licence, or somewhat else, sir, with   30
list'ning to his fables, say Numps is a witch, with all my
heart, do, say so.

Cok. Avoid, i' your satin doublet, Numps.

Jus. The creeping venom of which subtle serpent, as some late
writers affirm, neither the cutting of the perilous plant,   35

17. you.] *G;* you, *F.*   him?] *G;* him, *F.*

---

16. *truck*] deal.
strip] move quickly. (A different verb from that meaning to denude; cf.
outstrip.)
22. *vents*] discharges.
31. *witch*] magician; cf. the invective exchange between Subtle and Face,
A., I. i. 107.
33. *Avoid*] be off.
34–5. *some late writers*] of whom the most famous was James I, *A Counter-
blaste to Tobacco* (1604).

nor the drying of it, nor the lighting, or burning, can any
way persway or assuage.

Cok. Good, i' faith! is't not, sister?

Jus. Hence it is, that the lungs of the tobacconist are rotted, the
liver spotted, the brain smok'd like the backside of the　40
pig-woman's booth, here, and the whole body within,
black as her pan you saw e'en now, without.

Cok. A fine similitude, that, sir! Did you see the pan?

Edg. Yes, sir.

Jus. Nay, the hole in the nose here, of some tobacco-takers, or　45
the third nostril (if I may so call it), which makes that they
can vent the tobacco out like the acc of clubs, or rather the
flower-de-lys, is caused from the tobacco, the mere
tobacco! when the poor innocent pox, having nothing to
do there, is miserably, and most unconscionably slander'd.　50

Cok. Who would ha' miss'd this, sister?

Mrs. Over. Not anybody, but Numps.

Cok. He does not understand.

Edg. Nor you feel.　　　　　　　　　　　*He picketh his purse.*

Cok. What would you have, sister, of a fellow that knows no-　55
thing but a basket-hilt, and an old fox in't? The best
music i' the Fair will not move a log.

Edg. In, to Urs'la, Nightingale, and carry her comfort: see it
told. This fellow was sent to us by fortune for our first
fairing.　　　　　　　　　　　　[*Exit* NIGHTINGALE.]　60

Jus. But what speak I of the diseases of the body, children of
the Fair?

Cok. That's to us, sister. Brave i' faith!

Jus. Hark, O you sons and daughters of Smithfield! and hear
what malady it doth the mind: it causeth swearing, it　65

---

54. *He . . . purse.*] F margin, ll. 55–6.

37. *persway*] (=*perswage*) lessen.
39. *tobacconist*] smoker.
42. *black*] cf. the smoker who is said in *E.M.I.*, III. v. 110 to have 'voyded
a bushel of soot . . . vpward and downward'.
56. *fox*] sword.

causeth swaggering, it causeth snuffling, and snarling, and
now and then a hurt.

Mrs. Over. He hath something of Master Overdo, methinks,
brother.

Cok. So me thought, sister, very much of my brother Overdo: 70
and 'tis when he speaks.

Jus. Look into any angle o' the town—the Straits, or the Bermudas—where the quarrelling lesson is read, and how do
they entertain the time, but with bottle-ale, and tobacco?
The lecturer is o' one side, and his pupils o' the other; but 75
the seconds are still bottle-ale, and tobacco, for which the
lecturer reads, and the novices pay. Thirty pound a week
in bottle-ale! forty in tobacco! and ten more in ale again.
Then for a suit to drink in, so much, and (that being
slaver'd) so much for another suit, and then a third suit, 80
and a fourth suit! and still the bottle-ale slavereth, and the
tobacco stinketh!

Wasp. Heart of a madman! are you rooted here? Will you
never away? What can any man find out in this bawling
fellow, to grow here for? He is a full handful higher, sin' 85
he heard him. Will you fix here? And set up a booth? Sir?

Jus. I will conclude briefly—

Wasp. Hold your peace, you roaring rascal, I'll run my head i'
your chops else. You were best build a booth, and entertain him, make your will, an' you say the word, and him 90
your heir! Heart, I never knew one taken with a mouth of
a peck, afore. By this light, I'll carry you away o' my back,
an' you will not come.

83. Will] *F3;* well *F.*   86. him.] *F3;* him, *F.*

72–3. *Straits . . . Bermudas*] '. . . a nest of obscure courts, alleys, and
avenues, . . . between the bottom of St. Martin's Lane, Half-moon, and
Chandos-street . . . the receptacle of fraudulent dealers, thieves, and prostitutes' (G.).

76. *seconds*] things which assist or support; cf. *O.E.D.*, 1632: '. . . gold
was my best second . . . my continuall vade Mecum.'

89. *chops*] jaws.

91–2. *of a peck*] of two gallons' capacity.

He gets him up on pick-pack.

Cok. Stay, Numps, stay, set me down: I ha' lost my purse,
  Numps, O my purse! One o' my fine purses is gone.   95
Mrs. Over. Is't indeed, brother?
Cok. Aye, as I am an honest man, would I were an arrant
  rogue, else! A plague of all roguy, damn'd cutpurses for
  me.
Wasp. Bless 'em with all my heart, with all my heart, do you   100
  see! Now, as I am no infidel, that I know of, I am glad
  on't. Aye I am; here's my witness! do you see, sir! I did
  not tell you of his fables, I? No, no, I am a dull malt-
  horse, I, I know nothing. Are you not justly serv'd i'
  your conscience now? Speak i' your conscience. Much   105
  good do you with all my heart, and his good heart that has
  it, with all my heart again.
Edg. [*Aside*] This fellow is very charitable; would he had a
  purse too! But I must not be too bold all at a time.
Cok. Nay, Numps, it is not my best purse.   110
Wasp. Not your best! Death! why should it be your worst?
  Why should it be any, indeed, at all? Answer me to that,
  gi' me a reason from you, why it should be any?
Cok. Nor my gold, Numps; I ha' that yet; look here else,
  sister.   115
Wasp. Why so, there's all the feeling he has!
Mrs. Over. I pray you, have a better care of that, brother.
Cok. Nay, so I will, I warrant you; let him catch this, that
  catch can. I would fain see him get this, look you here.
Wasp. So, so, so, so, so, so, so, so! Very good.   120
Cok. I would ha' him come again, now, and but offer at it.
  Sister, will you take notice of a good jest? I will put it just
  where th' other was, and if we ha' good luck, you shall see
  a delicate fine trap to catch the cutpurse, nibbling.
Edg. [*Aside*] Faith, and he'll try ere you be out o' the Fair.   125

93.1. *He . . . pick-pack.*] F margin, *ll. 92–4.*   94. Stay,] *F3;* Stay *F.*

103–4. *malt-horse*] dray-horse.

Cok. Come, Mistress Grace, prithee be not melancholy for
my mischance; sorrow wi' not keep it, sweetheart.
Grace. I do not think on't, sir.
Cok. 'Twas but a little scurvy white money, hang it: it may
hang the cutpurse, one day. I ha' gold left to gi' thee a   130
fairing, yet, as hard as the world goes: nothing angers
me, but that nobody here look'd like a cutpurse, unless
'twere Numps.
Wasp. How? I? I look like a cutpurse? Death! your sister's
a cutpurse! and your mother and father and all your kin   135
were cutpurses! And here is a rogue is the bawd o' the
cutpurses, whom I will beat to begin with.

They speak all together; and WASP *beats the* JUSTICE.

Jus. Hold thy hand, child of wrath, and heir of anger, make
it not Childermass day in thy fury, or the feast of the
French Bartholomew, parent of the Massacre.   140
Cok. Numps, Numps!
Mrs. Over. Good Master Humphrey.
Wasp. You are the Patrico! are you? the patriarch of the
cutpurses? You share, sir, they say, let them share this
with you. Are you i' your hot fit of preaching again? I'll   145
cool you.
Jus. Murther, murther, murther!   [*Exeunt.*]

137.1. *They* . . . JUSTICE.] *F margin, ll. 138–45.*   138–40. *Jus.* . . . Massacre.] *F right-hand column, ll. 141–5.*   141–5. *Cok.* . . . with] *F left-hand
column, ll. 138–40.*

129. *white money*] silver.
139. *Childermass*] Holy Innocents, 28 December.
140. *French Bartholomew*] the massacre of 24 August 1572.
143. *Patrico*] parson; cf. *S.N.*, IV. i. 45: 'the *Patrico* . . . Or *Arch-priest* o'
Canters . . . some *primate metropolitan* Rascall'.

Act III

Scene I

[*Enter*] WHIT, HAGGIS, BRISTLE, LEATHERHEAD, TRASH.

[*Whit.*] Nay, 'tish all gone, now! Dish 'tish, phen tou vilt not
   be phitin call, Mashter Offisher! Phat ish a man te better
   to lishen out noishes for tee an' tou art in an oder 'orld—
   being very shuffishient noishes and gallantsh too, one o'
   their brabblesh would have fed ush all dish fortnight; but   5
   tou art so bushy about beggersh still, tou hast no leishure
   to intend shentlemen, an't be.

Hag. Why, I told you, Davy Bristle.

Bri. Come, come, you told me a pudding, Toby Haggis; a
   matter of nothing; I am sure it came to nothing! You said,   10
   'Let's go to Urs'la's', indeed; but then you met the man
   with the monsters, and I could not get you from him. An
   old fool, not leave seeing yet?

Hag. Why, who would ha' thought anybody would ha' quar-
   rell'd so early? Or that the ale o' the Fair would ha' been   15
   up so soon?

Whit. Phy, phat a clock tost tou tink it ish, man?

Hag. I cannot tell.

Whit. Tou art a vishe vatchman, i' te mean teeme.

Hag. Why, should the watch go by the clock, or the clock by   20
   the watch, I pray?

Bri. One should go by another, if they did well.

Whit. Tou art right now! phen didst tou ever know or hear of
   a shuffishient vatchman but he did tell the clock, phat
   business soever he had?   25

1–7.] Elizabethan stage-Irish; cf. Captain Macmorris in *Henry V*.
5. *brabblesh*] (=*brabbles*) noisy quarrels.

Bri. Nay, that's most true, a sufficient watchman knows what o'clock it is.

Whit. Shleeping, or vaking! ash well as te clock himshelf, or te jack dat shtrikes him!

Bri. Let's enquire of Master Leatherhead, or Joan Trash here. 30
Master Leatherhead, do you hear, Master Leatherhead?

Whit. If it be a Ledderhead, tish a very tick Ledderhead, tat sho mush noish vill not piersh him.

Lea. I have a little business now; good friends, do not trouble me. 35

Whit. Phat? Because o' ty wrought neet-cap, and ty phelvet sherkin, man? Phy? I have sheen tee in ty ledder sherkin, ere now, mashter o' de hobby-horses, as bushy and as stately as tou sheem'st to be.

Trash. Why, what an' you have, Captain Whit? He has his 40
choice of jerkins, you may see by that, and his caps too, I assure you, when he pleases to be either sick, or employ'd.

Lea. God a mercy, Joan, answer for me.

Whit. Away, be not sheen i' my company; here be shentle-men, and men of vorship.   [*Exeunt* HAGGIS, BRISTLE.] 45

Act III. Scene II.

[*Enter to them*] QUARLOUS, WINWIFE.

[*Quar.*] We had wonderful ill luck to miss this prologue o' the purse, but the best is we shall have five Acts of him ere night: he'll be spectacle enough! I'll answer for't.

Whit. O Creesh! Duke Quarlous, how dosht tou? Tou dosht not know me, I fear? I am te vishesht man, but Justish 5
Overdo, in all Bartholomew Fair, now. Gi' me twelve-

---

34. friends,] *F3;* friends *F.*

III. ii. 0.1. QUARLOUS, WINWIFE.] QVARLOVS. WHIT. WIN-VVIFE. BVSY. IOHN.
PVRE-CRAFT. WIN. KNOKHVM. MOON-CALFE. VRSLA. *F.*

---

29. *jack*] figure which strikes the bell.

pence from tee, I vill help tee to a vife vorth forty marks
for't, an't be.

Quar. Away, rogue, pimp, away.

Whit. And she shall show tee as fine cut 'ork for't in her　10
shmock too, as tou cansht vish i' faith; vilt tou have her,
vorshipful Vinvife? I vill help tee to her, here, be an't be,
in te pig-quarter, gi' me ty twel'pence from tee.

Winw. Why, there's twel'pence; pray thee, wilt thou be gone?

Whit. Tou art a vorthy man, and a vorshipful man still.　15

Quar. Get you gone, rascal.

Whit. I do mean it, man. Prinsh Quarlous, if tou hasht need on
me, tou shalt find me here, at Urs'la's; I vill see phat ale
and punk ish i' te pigshty for tee, bless ty good vorship. [*Exit.*]

Quar. Look! who comes here! John Littlewit!　20

Winw. And his wife, and my widow, her mother: the whole
family.

Quar. 'Slight, you must gi' em all fairings, now!

Winw. Not I, I'll not see 'em.

Quar. They are going a-feasting. What school-master's that is　25
with 'em?

Winw. That's my rival, I believe, the baker!

[*Enter*] BUSY, PURECRAFT, LITTLEWIT, WIN.

Busy. So, walk on in the middle way, fore-right, turn neither
to the right hand, nor to the left: let not your eyes be
drawn aside with vanity, nor your ear with noises.　30

Quar. O, I know him by that start!

Lea. What do you lack? What do you buy, pretty Mistress! a
fine hobby-horse, to make your son a tilter? a drum to
make him a soldier? a fiddle, to make him a reveller?
What is't you lack? Little dogs for your daughters! or　35
babies, male, or female?

9. pimp,] *G;* pimp *F.*

---

10. *cut 'ork*] 'cut work', lace, open-work embroidery (as worn by
'high-class' prostitutes).
28. *fore-right*] straight ahead.
33. *tilter*] a jouster; a rider at the quintain.

Busy. Look not toward them, hearken not: the place is Smith-
    field, or the field of smiths, the grove of hobby-horses and
    trinkets, the wares are the wares of devils. And the whole
    Fair is the shop of Satan! They are hooks, and baits, very   40
    baits, that are hung out on every side, to catch you, and to
    hold you as it were, by the gills, and by the nostrils, as the
    fisher doth: therefore, you must not look, nor turn to-
    wards them—the heathen man could stop his ears with
    wax, against the harlot o' the sea: do you the like, with   45
    your fingers, against the bells of the Beast.
Winw. What flashes comes from him!
Quar. O, he has those of his oven! A notable hot baker 'twas,
    when he plied the peel: he is leading his flock into the
    Fair, now.   50
Winw. Rather driving 'em to the pens: for he will let 'em look
    upon nothing.

                    [*Enter*] KNOCKEM, WHIT.

Kno. Gentlewomen, the weather's hot! Whither walk you?
    Have a care o' your fine velvet caps; the Fair is dusty.
    Take a sweet delicate booth, with boughs, here, i' the   55
    way, and cool yourselves i' the shade: you and your
    friends. The best pig and bottle-ale i' the Fair, sir. Old
    Urs'la is cook, there you may read: the pig's head speaks
    it.

        LITTLEWIT *is gazing at the sign; which is the Pig's Head*
                with a large writing under it.

46. fingers,] *HS;* fingers *F.*   59.1–2. LITTLEWIT . . . it.] *F margin,*
ll. 54–62.

37–8. *Smithfield*] the early form (A.D. 1145) *Smethefelda* shows the name
to mean 'smoothfield'.

44–5. *heathen . . . wax*] Ulysses had himself lashed to the mast and the
ears of his *crew* stopped against the singing of the sirens.

47. *comes*] the so-called northern plural form (cf. III. v. 36) not infrequent
in Shakespeare; see example in note to Induction 105.

49. *peel*] a baker's shovel for handling loaves.

55. *delicate*] delightful.

Poor soul, she has had a stringhalt, the maryhinchco: but   60
she's prettily amended.

Whit. A delicate show-pig, little mistress, with shweet sauce,
and crackling, like de bay-leaf i' de fire, la! Tou shalt ha'
de clean side o' de table-clot and dy glass vash'd with
phatersh of Dame Annessh Cleare.   [*Exit.*]   65

Lit. This's fine, verily: 'Here be the best pigs: and she does
roast 'em as well as ever she did', the pig's head says.

Kno. Excellent, excellent, mistress, with fire o' juniper and
rosemary branches! The Oracle of the pig's head, that,
sir.   70

Pure. Son, were you not warn'd of the vanity of the eye? Have
you forgot the wholesome admonition, so soon?

Lit. Good mother, how shall we find a pig, if we do not look
about for't? Will it run off o' the spit into our mouths,
think you? as in Lubberland? and cry, 'We, we'?   75

Busy. No, but your mother, religiously wise, conceiveth it
may offer itself by other means to the sense, as by way of
steam, which I think it doth, here in this place. Huh, huh
—yes, it doth.

BUSY *scents after it like a hound.*

And it were a sin of obstinacy, great obstinacy, high and   80

79.1. BUSY . . . *hound.*] *F margin, ll. 78–81.*

---

60. *stringhalt*] Edd. quote Markham, p. 415: 'The string-halt, of some
cald the mary-hinchcho, is a sodaine twitching vp of the horses hinder
legges, as if hee did tread vpon needles, and were not able to indure his feet
vpon the ground.'

65. *Dame Annessh Cleare*] '. . . a spring . . . called by the name of a rich
London widow, called *Annis Clare*, who matching herself with a riotous
Courtier in the time of *Edward* the first, who vainely consumed all her
wealth, and leauing her in much pouertie, there she drowned herself . . .'
(R. Johnson, *The Pleasant Walkes of Moore-fields*, 1607, B2v, cit. Kings-
ford in Stow, ii. 273).

68. *juniper*] burnt to purify the air.

69. *rosemary*] esteemed for its fragrance, whether burnt or not.

75. *Lubberland*] land of loafers and all delights; cf. the 14th-century
poem *The Land of Cokaygne*, ll. 15 ff.: 'Þe gees irostid on þe spitte Fleez to
þat abbai, God hit wote, And grediþ, Gees al hote, al hote . . . þe leverokes—
þat beþ cuþ—Liʒtiþ adun to manis muþ . . .'

horrible obstinacy, to decline, or resist the good titillation
of the famelic sense, which is the smell. Therefore be bold
(huh, huh, huh), follow the scent. Enter the tents of the
unclean, for once, and satisfy your wife's frailty. Let your
frail wife be satisfied: your zealous mother, and my suf-   85
fering self, will also be satisfied.

Lit. Come, Win, as good winny here as go farther and see nothing.

Busy. We 'scape so much of the other vanities, by our early
ent'ring.   90

Pure. It is an edifying consideration.

Win. This is scurvy, that we must come into the Fair and not
look on't.

Lit. Win, have patience, Win, I'll tell you more anon.

Kno. Mooncalf, entertain within there; the best pig i' the   95
booth, a pork-like pig. These are Banbury-bloods, o' the
sincere stud, come a pig-hunting. Whit, wait, Whit, look
to your charge.

Busy. A pig prepare, presently, let a pig be prepared to us.

[*He leads off* LITTLEWIT, WIN, PURECRAFT.]

[*Enter*] MOONCALF, URSULA.

Moon. 'Slight, who be these?   100

Urs. Is this the good service, Jordan, you'd do me?

Kno. Why, Urs? Why, Urs? Thou'lt ha' vapours i' thy
leg again presently; pray thee go in, 't may turn to the
scratches else.

Urs. Hang your vapours, they are stale, and stink like you; 105
are these the guests o' the game you promis'd to fill my
pit withal, today?

Kno. Aye, what ail they, Urs?

Urs. Ail they? They are all sippers, sippers o' the city; they

---

82. *famelic*] exciting hunger.
87. *winny*] dwell.
97. *sincere*] (a) unadulterated, genuine; (b) morally uncorrupted, not
feigned.
stud] breed.

look as they would not drink off two penn'orth of bottle- 110
ale amongst 'em.

Moon. A body may read that i' their small printed ruffs.

Kno. Away, thou art a fool, Urs, and thy Mooncalf too, i'
your ignorant vapours, now! hence, good guests, I say
right hypocrites, good gluttons. In, and set a couple o' 115
pigs o' the board, and half a dozen of the biggest bottles
afore 'em, and call Whit. I do not love to hear innocents
abus'd: fine ambling hypocrites! and a stone-puritan,
with a sorrel head, and beard, good mouth'd gluttons:
two to a pig, away.　　　　　　　　[*Exit* MOONCALF.] 120

Urs. Are you sure they are such?

Kno. O' the right breed, thou shalt try 'em by the teeth, Urs.
Where's this Whit?

[*Re-enter* WHIT.]

Whit. *Behold, man, and see, what a worthy man am ee!*
With the fury of my sword, and the shaking of my beard, 125
I will make ten thousand men afeard.

Kno. Well said, brave Whit; in, and fear the ale out o' the
bottles into the bellies of the brethren, and the sisters;
drink to the cause, and pure vapours.

[*Exeunt* KNOCKEM, WHIT, URSULA.]

Quar. My roarer is turn'd tapster, methinks. Now were a 130
fine time for thee, Winwife, to lay aboard thy widow;
thou'lt never be master of a better season, or place; she
that will venture herself into the Fair, and a pig-box, will
admit any assault, be assur'd of that.

Winw. I love not enterprises of that suddenness, though. 135

128. sisters;] *This ed.;* sisters *F;* sisters, *HS.*

---

112. *small printed*] set not only 'in print', i.e. to a nicety, but in a small or
Geneva print; cf. J. in *Coryats Crudities*, H. & S., viii. 375: 'a . . . well
traueld scholar . . . by his starchd beard, and printed ruffe . . .'

118. *stone-puritan*] male puritan; cf. *stone-horse*, stallion.

119. *sorrel*] chestnut coloured (of horses).

131. *lay aboard*] literally, to place one's ship alongside another for attack.

Quar. I'll warrant thee, then, no wife out o' the widow's
hundred: if I had but as much title to her, as to have
breath'd once on that strait stomacher of hers, I would
now assure myself to carry her, yet, ere she went out of
Smithfield. Or she should carry me, which were the   140
fitter sight, I confess. But you are a modest undertaker,
by circumstances, and degrees; come, 'tis disease in thee,
not judgement: I should offer at all together. Look,
here's the poor fool again that was stung by the wasp,
erewhile.   145

Act III. Scene III.

[*Enter*] JUSTICE.

[*Jus.*] I will make no more orations, shall draw on these tragical conclusions. And I begin now to think that, by a spice
of collateral justice, Adam Overdo deserv'd this beating;
for I, the said Adam, was one cause (a by-cause) why the
purse was lost: and my wife's brother's purse too, which   5
they know not of yet. But I shall make very good mirth
with it, at supper (that will be the sport), and put my little
friend Master Humphrey Wasp's choler quite out of
countenance. When, sitting at the upper end o' my table,
as I use, and drinking to my brother Cokes and Mistress   10
Alice Overdo, as I will, my wife, for their good affection

III. iii. 0.1. JUSTICE.] IVSTICE. WIN-WIFE. QVARLOVS. *F.*   3. Overdo] *F3;*
Overdoo, F.

137. *hundred*] ? class, group, locality. The expression seems not to be
proverbial.
138. *stomacher*] a stiff ornamental covering for the abdomen filling in the
opening of the bodice.
139. *carry*] win.
141. *undertaker*] one who takes up a challenge.
143. *offer at*] make an attempt at or upon.

III. iii. 3. *collateral*] accompanying, concomitant.
4. *by-cause*] an incidental cause.

to old Bradley, I deliver to 'em it was I that was cudgell'd,
and show 'em the marks. To see what bad events may peep
out o' the tail of good purposes! The care I had of that
civil young man I took fancy to this morning (and have   15
not left it yet) drew me to that exhortation, which drew
the company, indeed, which drew the cutpurse; which
drew the money; which drew my brother Cokes his loss;
which drew on Wasp's anger; which drew on my beating:
a pretty gradation! And they shall ha' it i' their dish, i'   20
faith, at night for fruit: I love to be merry at my table. I
had thought once, at one special blow he ga' me, to have
revealed myself! But then (I thank thee, fortitude) I rememb'red that a wise man (and who is ever so great a part
o' the Commonwealth in himself) for no particular dis-   25
aster ought to abandon a public good design. The hus-
bandman ought not, for one unthankful year, to forsake
the plough; the shepherd ought not, for one scabb'd
sheep, to throw by his tar-box; the pilot ought not, for one
leak i' the poop, to quit the helm; nor the alderman ought   30
not, for one custard more, at a meal, to give up his cloak;
the constable ought not to break his staff, and forswear the
watch, for one roaring night; nor the piper o' the parish
(*ut parvis componere magna solebam*) to put up his pipes,
for one rainy Sunday. These are certain knocking con-   35
clusions; out of which I am resolv'd, come what come
can—come beating, come imprisonment, come infamy,
come banishment, nay, come the rack, come the hurdle,
welcome all—I will not discover who I am till my due
time; and yet still all shall be, as I said ever, in Justice'   40
name, and the King's, and for the Commonwealth!

Winw. What does he talk to himself, and act so seriously?
Poor fool!   [*Exit* JUSTICE.]

---

29. *tar-box*] used to hold tar-salve for sores in sheep.
31. *custard*] cf. *A.*, III. ii. 90: 'the *Alderman*, Whose daily custard you
deuoure'.
34. ut . . . solebam] 'sic . . .' in Virgil, *Ecl.*, i. 23.
42. *What*] why.

Quar. No matter what. Here's fresher argument, intend
that.   45

Act III. Scene IV.

[*Enter to them*] COKES, Mistress OVERDO, GRACE, WASP.

[*Cok.*] Come, Mistress Grace, come sister, here's more fine
sights yet, i' faith. God's lid, where's Numps?
Lea. What do you lack, gentlemen? What is't you buy? Fine
rattles! Drums? Babies? Little dogs? And birds for
ladies? What do you lack?   5
Cok. Good honest Numps, keep afore, I am so afraid thou'lt
lose somewhat: my heart was at my mouth when I miss'd
thee.
Wasp. You were best buy a whip i' your hand to drive me.
Cok. Nay, do not mistake, Numps, thou art so apt to mistake: 10
I would but watch the goods. Look you now, the treble
fiddle was e'en almost like to be lost.
Wasp. Pray you take heed you lose not yourself: your best way
were e'en get up and ride for more surety. Buy a token's
worth of great pins, to fasten yourself to my shoulder.   15
Lea. What do you lack, gentlemen? Fine purses, pouches,
pincases, pipes? What is't you lack? A pair o' smiths to
wake you i' the morning? Or a fine whistling bird?
Cok. Numps, here be finer things than any we ha' bought, by
odds! And more delicate horses, a great deal! Good   20
Numps, stay, and come hither.
Wasp. Will you scourse with him? You are in Smithfield, you
may fit yourself with a fine easy-going street-nag for your

III. iv. 0.1. COKES, . . . WASP.] COKES. LEATHERHEAD. WASPE. Mistresse OVER-
DOO. WIN-VVIFE. QVARLOVS. TRASH. GRACE. *F.*

44. *intend*] attend to.

III. iv. 17. *pair o' smiths*] ? two pieces of beaten metal to form a bell (by
hanging one up and striking it with the other).
22. *scourse*] swap, deal.

saddle again' Michaelmas term, do; has he ne'er a little
odd cart for you, to make a caroche on, i' the country,   25
with four pied hobby-horses? Why the measles, should
you stand here, with your train, cheaping of dogs, birds,   *practical*
and babies? You ha' no children to bestow 'em on? Ha'
you?

Cok. No, but again' I ha' children, Numps, that's all one.   30
Wasp. Do, do, do, do; how many shall you have, think you?
An' I were as you, I'd buy for all my tenants, too: they are
a kind o' civil savages, that will part with their children for
rattles, pipes, and knives. You were best buy a hatchet, or
two, and truck with 'em.   35
Cok. Good Numps, hold that little tongue o' thine, and save it
a labour. I am resolute Bat, thou know'st.
Wasp. A resolute fool you are, I know, and a very sufficient
coxcomb; with all my heart; nay, you have it, sir, an' you
be angry, turd i' your teeth, twice (if I said it not once   40
afore): and much good do you.
Winw. Was there ever such a self-affliction? And so imperti-
nent?
Quar. Alas! his care will go near to crack him: let's in, and
comfort him.   45
Wasp. Would I had been set i' the ground, all but the head on
me, and had my brains bowl'd at, or thresh'd out, when
first I underwent this plague of a charge!
Quar. How now, Numps! Almost tir'd i' your protectorship?
Overparted? Overparted?   50

---

25. *caroche*] a luxury carriage—cf. *Greenes Tu Quoque*, 1614: 'a coach
For country and caroch for London' (Dodsley, 1875, xi. 202)—hence
ironical here.

27. *cheaping*] buying, bargaining for.

33. *civil*] civilized.

46–7. *set ... thresh'd out*] Cunningham quoted *Merry Wives of Windsor*,
III. iv. 90–1: 'Alas! I had rather be set quick i' th' earth, And bowl'd to death
with turnips.'

50. *Overparted*] given too difficult a part; cf. Costard of Sir Nathaniel
in *Love's Labour's Lost*, v. ii. 584–6: 'He is a marvellous good neighbour ...
but for Alisander ... a little o'erparted.'

H

Wasp. Why, I cannot tell, sir; it may be I am; does't grieve
    you?

Quar. No, I swear does't not, Numps: to satisfy you.

Wasp. Numps? 'Sblood, you are fine and familiar! How long
    ha' we been acquainted, I pray you?   55

Quar. I think it may be rememb'red, Numps, that? 'Twas
    since morning sure.

Wasp. Why, I hope I know't well enough, sir; I did not ask to
    be told.

Quar. No? Why then?   60

Wasp. It's no matter why; you see with your eyes, now, what
    I said to you today? You'll believe me another time?

Quar. Are you removing the Fair, Numps?

Wasp. A pretty question! and a very civil one! Yes faith, I ha'
    my lading you see, or shall have anon; you may know   65
    whose beast I am by my burthen. If the pannier-man's
    jack were ever better known by his loins of mutton, I'll be
    flay'd and feed dogs for him, when his time comes.

Winw. How melancholy Mistress Grace is yonder! Pray thee
    let's go enter ourselves in grace, with her.   70

Cok. Those six horses, friend, I'll have—

Wasp. How!

Cok. And the three Jew's trumps; and half a dozen o' birds,
    and that drum (I have one drum already) and your smiths
    (I like that device o' your smiths, very pretty well) and   75
    four halberts—and (le' me see) that fine painted great
    lady, and her three women for state, I'll have.

Wasp. No, the shop; buy the whole shop, it will be best, the
    shop, the shop!

---

66. *pannier-man*] 'in the Inns of Court, is one whose office is to blow the
Horn for Dinner, and wait at the Barristers Table' (Blount, *Glossographia*,
1661); he also brought in provisions. Cf. II. v. 113.

67. *jack*] labourer, servant (not before 19th century in *O.E.D.*).

70. *grace*] favour.

73. *Jew's trumps*] Jew's harps.

77. *state*] splendour, 'solemn pomp, appearance of greatness' (Johnson).

Lea. If his worship please.   80
Wasp. Yes, and keep it during the Fair, bobchin.
Cok. Peace, Numps. Friend, do not meddle with him, an' you
    be wise, and would show your head above board: he will
    sting through your wrought nightcap, believe me. A set of
    these violins I would buy too, for a delicate young noise I   85
    have i' the country, that are every one a size less than an-
    other, just like your fiddles. I would fain have a fine
    young masque at my marriage, now I think on't: but I do
    want such a number o' things. And Numps will not help
    me now, and I dare not speak to him.   90
Trash. Will your worship buy any ginger-bread, very good
    bread, comfortable bread?
Cok. Ginger-bread! Yes, let's see.   *He runs to her shop.*
Wasp. There's the tother springe!
Lea. Is this well, goody Joan? To interrupt my market? In   95
    the midst? And call away my customers? Can you an-
    swer this, at the Pie-powders?
Trash. Why? If his mastership have a mind to buy, I hope
    my ware lies as open as another's; I may show my ware,
    as well as you yours.   100
Cok. Hold your peace; I'll content you both: I'll buy up his
    shop, and thy basket.
Wasp. Will you i' faith?
Lea. Why should you put him from it, friend?
Wasp. Cry you mercy! you'd be sold too, would you? What's   105
    the price on you? Jerkin, and all as you stand? Ha' you
    any qualities?

82. Numps.] *F3; Numps, F.*   93. *He . . . shop.] F margin, ll. 93–4.*

---

81. *bobchin*] fool (whose chin jerks up and down).
83. *above board*] in (sight of the) company; with quibble on *board* = tray
for his wares.
85. *delicate*] finely sensitive, 'fine'.
noise] band of musicians.
88. *masque*] a set of masquers; cf. *C.R.*, v. x. o.1: 'The Maskes ioyne, and
they dance'.
94. *springe*] snare (for birds).
107. *qualities*] accomplishments, attainments, cf. i. v. 128, 132 and Lyly,

Trash. Yes, good-man angry-man, you shall find he has
    qualities, if you cheapen him.

Wasp. Godso, you ha' the selling of him! What are they?   110
    Will they be bought for love, or money?

Trash. No indeed, sir.

Wasp. For what then? Victuals?

Trash. He scorns victuals, sir; he has bread and butter at
    home, thanks be to God! And yet he will do more for a   115
    good meal, if the toy take him i' the belly; marry then
    they must not set him at lower end; if they do, he'll go
    away, though he fast. But put him atop o' the table,
    where his place is, and he'll do you forty fine things. He
    has not been sent for, and sought out, for nothing, at   120
    your great city-suppers, to put down Coriat, and Cokely,
    and been laugh'd at for his labour; he'll play you all the
    puppets i' the town over, and the players, every com-
    pany, and his own company too; he spares nobody!

Cok. I' faith?   125

Trash. He was the first, sir, that ever baited the fellow i' the
    bear's skin, an't like your worship: no dog ever came
    near him, since. And for fine motions!

Cok. Is he good at those too? Can he set out a masque, trow?

Campaspe, v. i. 2–3: 'What can thy sons do? ... You shall see their qualities.
Dance, sirrah!'

109. *cheapen*] bargain or bid for, ask the price of.

110. *Godso*] sometimes *Catso*, from Italian *cazzo*, membrum virile.

121. *Coriat*] Thomas Coryate, the traveller (1577?–1617). Jonson had
contributed to the group of mock-commendatory verses added, at the command of Prince Henry (in whose household Coryate was jester) to Coryate's
account of his travels on foot in 1608, *Coryats Crudities*, 1611.

Cokely] a jester, cf. *Ep.*, cxxix. 16–17, *To Mime*: 'Thou dost out-zany
COKELY, POD; nay GVE: And thine own Coriat too.'

126–7. *baited ... skin*] From Samuel Rowlands, *Knave of Hearts*, 1612
(sig. F4, cit. H. & S.), it appears that it was an actor at the Fortune 'who
... Some Butchers (playing dogs) did well-nye kil. . .'; a 'ballad *The men
[sic] bayted in a beares skyn &c*' was entered in S.R. on 21 January 1612
(Arber, iii. 476).

128. *motions*] puppet-shows.

129. *trow?*] do you suppose?

Trash. O Lord, Master! sought to, far and near, for his inven-   130
tions: and he engrosses all, he makes all the puppets i'
the Fair.

Cok. Dost thou (in troth), old velvet Jerkin? Give me thy
hand.

Trash. Nay, sir, you shall see him in his velvet jerkin, and a   135
scarf, too, at night, when you hear him interpret Master
Littlewit's motion.

Cok. Speak no more, but shut up shop presently, friend. I'll
buy both it and thee too, to carry down with me, and her
hamper, beside. Thy shop shall furnish out the masque,   140
and hers the banquet: I cannot go less, to set out anything
with credit. What's the price, at a word, o' thy whole
shop, case and all as it stands?

Lea. Sir, it stands me in six and twenty shillings sevenpence
halfpenny, besides three shillings for my ground.   145

Cok. Well, thirty shillings will do all, then! And what comes
yours to?

Trash. Four shillings and elevenpence, sir, ground and all,
an't like your worship.

Cok. Yes, it does like my worship very well; poor woman,   150
that's five shillings more. What a masque shall I furnish
out for forty shillings (twenty pound Scotch)! And a
banquet of ginger-bread! There's a stately thing!
Numps! Sister! And my wedding gloves too! (That I
never thought on afore.) All my wedding gloves, ginger-   155
bread! O me! what a device will there be, to make 'em eat
their fingers' ends! And delicate brooches for the bride-
men! And all! And then I'll ha' this posy put to 'em:

147. to] *1716;* too *F.*

---

131. *engrosses*] monopolizes the trade.
141. *banquet*] dessert.
144. *stands . . . in*] costs; cf. Cosin, *Correspondence* (1625, Surtees Soc.,
i. 71): 'Boording and breakfest will stand him in 16^{li} per annum.'
152. *pound Scotch*] 1s. 8d. sterling in 1603.
158. *posy*] motto.

'For the best grace,' meaning Mistress Grace, my wedding posy.   160
Grace. I am beholden to you, sir, and to your Bartholomew-
wit.
Wasp. You do not mean this, do you? Is this your first purchase?
Cok. Yes, faith, and I do not think, Numps, but thou'lt say,   165
it was the wisest act, that ever I did in my wardship.
Wasp. Like enough! I shall say anything. I!

Act III. Scene V.

[*Enter to them*] JUSTICE, EDGWORTH, NIGHTINGALE.

[*Jus.*] [*Aside*] I cannot beget a project, with all my political
brain, yet; my project is how to fetch off this proper young
man from his debauch'd company: I have followed him all
the Fair over, and still I find him with this songster; and
I begin shrewdly to suspect their familiarity; and the   5
young man of a terrible taint, poetry! with which idle disease if he be infected, there's no hope of him, in a state-
course. *Actum est* of him for a commonwealths-man, if he
go to't in rhyme once.
Edg. [*To Nightingale*] Yonder he is buying o' ginger-bread: 10
set in quickly, before he part with too much on his money.
Nigh. *My masters and friends, and good people, draw near, &c.*
Cok. Ballads! hark, hark! Pray thee, fellow, stay a little; good
Numps, look to the goods. What ballads hast thou? Let
me see, let me see myself.   15

III. v. 13. little;] *1716;* little, *F.*

III. v. 1. *political*] sagacious, prudent, shrewd.
7–8. *state-course*] ? course of life concerned with public affairs or wel-
fare.
8. Actum . . . *him*] 'It's all up with him'.
commonwealths-man] good citizen.

He runs to the ballad-man.

Wasp. Why so! he's flown to another lime-bush; there he will
flutter as long more, till he ha' ne'er a feather left. Is there
a vexation like this, gentlemen? Will you believe me now,
hereafter? Shall I have credit with you?

Quar. Yes faith, shalt thou, Numps, an' thou art worthy on't,   20
for thou sweatest for't. I never saw a young pimp errant
and his squire better match'd.

Winw. Faith, the sister comes after 'em, well, too.

Grace. Nay, if you saw the Justice her husband, my guardian,
you were fitted for the mess; he is such a wise one his   25
way—

Winw. I wonder we see him not here.

Grace. O! he is too serious for this place, and yet better sport
than the other three, I assure you, gentlemen: where'er he
is, though 't be o' the bench.   30

Cok. How dost thou call it? *A caveat against cutpurses*! a good
jest, i' faith; I would fain see that demon, your cutpurse,
you talk of, that delicate-handed devil; they say he walks
hereabout: I would see him walk, now. Look you, sister,
here, here, let him come, sister, and welcome.   35

He shows his purse boastingly.

Ballad-man, does any cutpurses haunt hereabout? Pray
thee raise me one or two: begin and show me one.

Nigh. Sir, this is a spell against 'em, spick and span new; and
'tis made as 'twere in mine own person, and I sing it in
mine own defence. But 'twill cost a penny alone, if you   40
buy it.

15.1. *He...ballad-man.*] F margin, ll. *13–15.*   29. than] *HS;* then then *F.*
35.1. *He...boastingly.*] F margin, ll. *32–5.*

16. *lime-bush*] snare (bush smeared with birdlime; cf. *3 Henry VI*, v. vi.
13–14: 'The bird that hath been limed in a bush With trembling wings mis-
doubteth every bush'); cf. iv. iii. 103.

25. *mess*] each of the groups (usually of four) into which a banqueting
company was divided; cf. *E.M.I.*, i. iii. 70–3: 'Ile furnish our feast with one
gull more to'ard the messe. He writes to me of a brace, and here's one, that's
three: O, for a fourth...'

Cok. No matter for the price; thou dost not know me, I see; I
am an odd Bartholomew.

Mrs. Over. Has't a fine picture, brother?

Cok. O sister, do you remember the ballads over the nursery-   45
chimney at home o' my own pasting up? There be brave
pictures. Other manner of pictures, than these, friend.

Wasp. Yet these will serve to pick the pictures out o' your
pockets, you shall see.

Cok. So I heard 'em say. Pray thee mind him not, fellow: he'll   50
have an oar in everything.

Nigh. It was intended, sir, as if a purse should chance to be cut
in my presence, now, I may be blameless, though: as by
the sequel, will more plainly appear.

Cok. We shall find that i' the matter. Pray thee begin.   55

Nigh. To the tune of *Paggington's Pound*, sir.

Cok. Fa, la la la, la la la, fa la la la. Nay, I'll put thee in tune,
and all! Mine own country dance! Pray thee begin.

Nigh. It is a gentle admonition, you must know, sir, both to
the purse-cutter, and the purse-bearer.   60

Cok. Not a word more, out o' the tune, an' thou lov'st me: Fa,
la la la, la la la, fa la la la. Come, when?

Nigh.   *My masters and friends and good people draw near,*
            And look to your purses, for that I do say;

Cok. Ha, ha, this chimes! Good counsel at first dash.   65

Nigh.   *And though little money, in them you do bear,*
            It cost more to get, than to lose in a day.

Cok. Good!

Nigh.   *You oft have been told,*
                Both the young and the old;   70
            And bidden beware of the cutpurse so bold;

Cok. Well said! He were to blame that would not, i' faith.

---

68. *Cok.* Good!] *F right-hand column, l. 67.*   72. *Cok.* . . . . faith.] *F right-
hand column, ll. 70–4.*

---

48. *pictures*] the king's pictures, i.e. coins.
53. *though*] for all that, nevertheless.
56. *the tune of* Paggington's Pound] CLXXVIII in the Fitzwilliam Virginal
Book, ed. Maitland and Squire, 1949, ii. 234.

Nigh. *Then if you take heed not, free me from the curse,*
    Who both give you warning, for and the cutpurse.
    Youth, youth, thou hadst better been starv'd by thy nurse,
    Than live to be hanged for cutting a purse.   76

Cok. Good i' faith, how say you, Numps ? Is there any harm i'
    this ?

Nigh. *It hath been upbraided to men of my trade,*
    That oftentimes we are the cause of this crime.   80

Cok. The more coxcombs they that did it, I wusse.

Nigh. *Alack and for pity, why should it be said ?*
    As if they regarded or places, or time.
        Examples have been
        Of some that were seen,   85
    In Westminster Hall, yea the pleaders between,
    Then why should the judges be free from this curse,
    More than my poor self, for cutting the purse ?

Cok. God a mercy for that! Why should they be more free in-
    deed ?   90

Nigh. *Youth, youth, thou hadst better been starv'd by thy nurse,*
    Than live to be hanged for cutting a purse.

Cok. That again, good ballad-man, that again.

        He sings the burden with him.

    O rare! I would fain rub mine elbow now, but I dare not
    pull out my hand. On, I pray thee; he that made this   95
    ballad shall be poet to my masque.

Nigh. *At Worc'ster, 'tis known well, and even i' the jail,*
    A knight of good worship did there show his face,
    Against the foul sinners, in zeal for to rail,
    And lost (ipso facto) *his purse in the place.*   100

---

81. *Cok. . . . wusse.*] F *right-hand column, ll. 79–83.*   89–90. *Cok. . . .*
indeed ?] F *right-hand column, ll. 86–92.*   93.1. *He . . . him.*] F *margin,*
ll. 93–6.

---

74. for and] and moreover; cf. *Hamlet*, v. i. 100–1: 'A pick-axe and a
spade, a spade, For and a winding sheet' (H. & S.).

86. Westminster Hall] the great hall of the Palace, where the courts of
Common Law and of Chancery sat until the late 18th century.

94. *rub . . . elbow*] show pleasure; cf. *1 Henry IV*, v. i. 77.

Cok. Is it possible ?

Nigh.   *Nay, once from the seat*
              Of judgement so great,
      A judge there did lose a fair pouch of velvet.

Cok. I' faith?   105

Nigh. *O Lord for thy mercy, how wicked or worse*
      Are those that so venture their necks for a purse !
          Youth, youth, &c.

Cok.   *Youth, youth, &c.*

Pray thee stay a little, friend; yet o' thy conscience,   110
Numps, speak, is there any harm i' this ?

Wasp. To tell you true, 'tis too good for you, 'less you had
grace to follow it.

Jus. [*Aside.*] It doth discover enormity, I'll mark it more: I
ha' not lik'd a paltry piece of poetry so well, a good while.   115

Cok.   *Youth, youth, &c.*

Where's this youth, now ? A man must call upon him, for
his own good, and yet he will not appear: look here,
here's for him; handy-dandy, which hand will he have ?

              He shows his purse.

On, I pray thee, with the rest; I do hear of him, but I   120
cannot see him, this Master Youth, the cutpurse.

Nigh. *At plays and at sermons, and at the sessions,*
      'Tis daily their practice such booty to make:
      Yea, under the gallows, at executions,
      They stick not the stare-abouts' purses to take—   125
          Nay, one without grace,
          At a far better place,
      At court, and in Christmas, before the King's face.

---

101. *Cok.* Is it possible ?] *F right-hand column, ll. 100–2.*   105. *Cok.* I'
faith ?] *F right-hand column, l. 104.*   119.1. *He . . . purse.*] *F margin,
ll. 118–19.*   127. *a far*] *G conj., HS; a F.*

---

119. *handy-dandy*] a children's game of guessing which hand contains a
concealed object.

128. At . . . face] in 1611, as H. & S. show, citing the pamphlet entered in
S.R. on 7 January 1612, the day of the cutpurse's execution (Arber, iii. 474).

Cok. That was a fine fellow! I would have him, now.

Nigh. *Alack then for pity, must I bear the curse,*   130
  That only belongs to the cunning cutpurse?

Cok. But where's their cunning, now, when they should use
  it? They are all chain'd now, I warrant you.
      Youth, youth, thou hadst better, &c.
  The rat-catcher's charm, are all fools and asses to this?   135
  A pox on 'em, that they will not come! that a man should
  have such a desire to a thing, and want it.

Quar. 'Fore God, I'd give half the Fair, an' 'twere mine, for
  a cutpurse for him, to save his longing.

Cok. Look you, sister, here, here, where is't now? which   140
  pocket is't in, for a wager?

              He shows his purse again.

Wasp. I beseech you leave your wagers, and let him end his
  matter, an't may be.

Cok. O, are you edified, Numps?

Jus. [*Aside*] Indeed he does interrupt him, too much: 145
  there Numps spoke to purpose.

Cok. Sister, I am an ass, I cannot keep my purse.

              [*He shows it*] *again.*

  On, on; I pray thee, friend.

Winw. Will you see sport? look, there's a fellow gathers up to
  him, mark.   150

EDGWORTH *gets up to him and tickles him in the ear with a straw twice*
              to draw his hand out of his pocket.

Quar. Good, i' faith! O, he has lighted on the wrong pocket.

129. *Cok. . . . now.*] *F right-hand column, ll. 126–8.*   135. charm, . . . this?]
This ed.; charme, . . . this! *F;* charms . . . this! *1716.*   141.1. *He . . . again.*]
F margin, ll. 140–1.   147.1. *again.*] *F margin, l. 147.*   149–50. *Winw.*
. . . mark.] *F right-hand column, ll. 148–57.*   150.1–2. EDGWORTH . . .
pocket.] *F margin, ll. 155–64.*   151–2. *Quar.* . . . 'fore] *F right-hand
column, ll. 159–64.*

    135. *rat-catcher's charm*] in apposition to 'this': Cokes thinks of himself
as a kind of Pied Piper to the pickpockets; cf. *S.N.*, 4th Intermean, 54–5:
'Or the fine Madrigall-*man, in rime, to haue him out o' the Countrey like an*
Irish *rat.*'

Winw. He has it, 'fore God, he is a brave fellow; pity he
should be detected.

Nigh. *But O, you vile nation of cutpurses all,*
  Relent and repent, and amend and be sound,   155
  And know that you ought not, by honest men's fall,
  Advance your own fortunes, to die above ground,
    And though you go gay,
    In silks as you may,
  It is not the high way to heaven (as they say).   160
  Repent then, repent you, for better, for worse:
  And kiss not the gallows for cutting a purse.
  Youth, youth, thou hadst better been starv'd by thy
   nurse,
  Than live to be hanged for cutting a purse.

All. An excellent ballad! an excellent ballad!   165

Edg. Friend, let me ha' the first, let me ha' the first, I pray
you.

Cok. Pardon me, sir. First come, first serv'd; and I'll buy the
whole bundle too.

Winw. That conveyance was better than all, did you see't?   170
He has given the purse to the ballad-singer.

Quar. Has he?

Edg. Sir, I cry you mercy; I'll not hinder the poor man's profit: pray you, mistake me not.

Cok. Sir, I take you for an honest gentleman, if that be mis-   175
taking; I met you today afore: ha! hum'h! O God! my
purse is gone, my purse, my purse, &c.

Wasp. Come, do not make a stir, and cry yourself an ass
through the Fair afore your time.

Cok. Why, hast thou it, Numps? Good Numps, how came   180
you by it? I marvel!

Wasp. I pray you seek some other gamester to play the fool
with: you may lose it time enough, for all your Fair-wit.

Cok. By this good hand, glove and all, I ha' lost it already, if

---

152–3. God . . . detected.] *F, between ll. 164 and 165.*   175–6. gentleman,
. . . mistaking;] *G;* Gentleman; . . . mistaking, *F.*

thou hast it not: feel else, and Mistress Grace's handker-   185
chief, too, out o' the tother pocket.

Wasp. Why, 'tis well; very well, exceeding pretty, and well.

Edg. Are you sure you ha' lost it, sir?

Cok. O God! yes; as I am an honest man, I had it but e'en
now, at 'Youth, youth'.   190

Nigh. I hope you suspect not me, sir.

Edg. Thee? that were a jest indeed! Dost thou think the
gentleman is foolish? Where hadst thou hands, I pray
thee? Away, ass, away.   [*Exit* NIGHTINGALE.]

Jus. [*Aside*] I shall be beaten again, if I be spied.   195

Edg. Sir, I suspect an odd fellow, yonder, is stealing away.

Mrs. Over. Brother, it is the preaching fellow! You shall
suspect him. He was at your tother purse, you know!
Nay, stay, sir, and view the work you ha' done; an' you
be benefic'd at the gallows, and preach there, thank your   200
own handiwork.

Cok. Sir, you shall take no pride in your preferment: you
shall be silenc'd quickly.

Jus. What do you mean, sweet buds of gentility?

Cok. To ha' my pennyworths out on you: bud! No less than   205
two purses a day, serve you? I thought you a simple
fellow, when my man Numps beat you, i' the morning,
and pitied you—

Mrs. Over. So did I, I'll be sworn, brother; but now I see he
is a lewd, and pernicious enormity (as Master Overdo   210
calls him.)

Jus. [*Aside*] Mine own words turn'd upon me, like swords.

Cok. Cannot a man's purse be at quiet for you, i' the master's
pocket, but you must entice it forth, and debauch it?

                                        [JUSTICE *is carried off.*]

Wasp. Sir, sir, keep your debauch and your fine Bartholo-   215
mew-terms to yourself; and make as much on 'em as you

---

198. *suspect*] regard, take note of.

214. *entice . . . debauch*] almost synonymous at this time. (Hence he is
trounced for his 'fine [i.e. subtle] . . . terms'.)

please. But gi' me this from you, i' the meantime: I beseech you, see if I can look to this.

                              WASP *takes the licence from him.*

Cok. Why, Numps ?

Wasp. Why ? because you are an ass, sir, there's a reason the   220
shortest way, an' you will needs ha' it; now you ha' got
the trick of losing, you'd lose your breech, an't 'twere
loose. I know you, sir, come, deliver, you'll go and crack
the vermin you breed now, will you ? 'Tis very fine, will
you ha' the truth on't ? They are such retchless flies as   225
you are, that blow cutpurses abroad in every corner;
your foolish having of money makes 'em. An' there were
no wiser than I, sir, the trade should lie open for you, sir,
it should i' faith, sir. I would teach your wit to come to
your head, sir, as well as your land to come into your   230
hand, I assure you, sir.

Winw. Alack, good Numps.

Wasp. Nay, gentlemen, never pity me, I am not worth it:
Lord send me at home once, to Harrow o' the Hill again,
if I travel any more, call me Coriat; with all my heart.   235

                    [*Exeunt* WASP, COKES *and* MISTRESS OVERDO.]

Quar. Stay, sir, I must have a word with you in private. Do
you hear ?

Edg. With me, sir ? What's your pleasure, good sir ?

Quar. Do not deny it. You are a cutpurse, sir; this gentleman
here, and I, saw you, nor do we mean to detect you,   240
though we can sufficiently inform ourselves, toward the
danger of concealing you; but you must do us a piece of
service.

Edg. Good gentlemen, do not undo me; I am a civil young
man, and but a beginner, indeed.   245

Quar. Sir, your beginning shall bring on your ending, for us.
We are no catchpoles nor constables. That you are to

218.1. WASP . . . *him*.] F *margin, ll. 218–19.*

---

225. *retchless*] heedless.

undertake, is this: you saw the old fellow, with the black
box, here?

Edg. The little old governor, sir?   250

Quar. That same: I see, you have flown him to a mark already. I would ha' you get away that box from him, and
bring it us.

Edg. Would you ha' the box and all, sir? or only that, that is
in't? I'll get you that, and leave him the box to play with   255
still (which will be the harder o' the two), because I would
gain your worship's good opinion of me.

Winw. He says well, 'tis the greater mastery, and 'twill make
the more sport when 'tis miss'd.

Edg. Aye, and 'twill be the longer a-missing, to draw on the   260
sport.

Quar. But look you do it now, sirrah, and keep your word:
or—

Edg. Sir, if ever I break my word, with a gentleman, may I
never read word at my need. Where shall I find you?   265

Quar. Somewhere i' the Fair, hereabouts. Dispatch it
quickly. I would fain see the careful fool deluded! Of all
beasts, I love the serious ass: he that takes pains to be one,
and plays the fool, with the greatest diligence that can be.

Grace. Then you would not choose, sir, but love my guar-   270
dian, Justice Overdo, who is answerable to that description, in every hair of him.

Quar. So I have heard. But how came you, Mistress Wellborn, to be his ward, or have relation to him, at first?

Grace. Faith, through a common calamity, he bought me,   275
sir; and now he will marry me to his wife's brother, this
wise gentleman, that you see, or else I must pay value o'
my land.

---

268. ass:] *This ed.;* Asse. *F.*

---

250. *governor*] tutor.
265. *read word*] cf. I. iv. 7.
275. *bought me*] from the king, who had the right to sell the guardianship
and marriage of royal wards (minors who were heirs to tenants holding land
from him).

Quar. 'Slid, is there no device of disparagement, or so ? Talk
    with some crafty fellow, some picklock o' the Law!   280
    Would I had studied a year longer i' the Inns of Court,
    an't had been but i' your case.

Winw. [*Aside*] Aye, Master Quarlous, are you proffering ?

Grace. You'd bring but little aid, sir.

Winw. (I'll look to you i' faith, gamester.) An unfortunate   285
    foolish tribe you are fall'n into, lady, I wonder you can
    endure 'em.

Grace. Sir, they that cannot work their fetters off, must wear
    'em.

Winw. You see what care they have on you, to leave you thus.   290

Grace. Faith, the same they have of themselves, sir. I cannot
    greatly complain, if this were all the plea I had against
    'em.

Winw. 'Tis true! but will you please to withdraw with us a
    little, and make them think they have lost you. I hope   295
    our manners ha' been such hitherto, and our language,
    as will give you no cause to doubt yourself in our com-
    pany.

Grace. Sir, I will give myself no cause; I am so secure of mine
    own manners, as I suspect not yours.   300

Quar. Look where John Littlewit comes.

Winw. Away, I'll not be seen, by him.

Quar. No, you were not best, he'd tell his mother, the
    widow.

Winw. Heart, what do you mean ?   305

Quar. Cry you mercy, is the wind there ? Must not the
    widow be nam'd ?   [*Exeunt* GRACE, WINWIFE, QUARLOUS.]

299. myself] *F3;* my selfe, *F.*

---

    279. *disparagement*] marriage to someone of inferior rank: a guardian had
power to enforce only a marriage 'without disparagement or inequality'
(Blackstone).
    297. *to doubt yourself*] to fear.

Act III. Scene VI.

[Enter to them] LITTLEWIT, WIN.

[Lit.] Do you hear, Win, Win?

Win. What say you, John?

Lit. While they are paying the reckoning, Win, I'll tell you a
　　thing, Win: we shall never see any sights i' the Fair, Win,
　　except you long still, Win; good Win, sweet Win, long to　　5
　　see some hobby-horses, and some drums, and rattles, and
　　dogs, and fine devices, Win. The bull with the five legs,
　　Win; and the great hog: now you ha' begun with pig, you
　　may long for anything, Win, and so for my motion, Win.

Win. But we sha' not eat o' the bull and the hog, John, how　10
　　shall I long then?

Lit. O yes! Win, you may long to see, as well as to taste, Win:
　　how did the 'pothecary's wife, Win, that long'd to see the
　　anatomy, Win? Or the lady, Win, that desir'd to spit i' the
　　great lawyer's mouth, after an eloquent pleading? I as-　15
　　sure you they long'd, Win; good Win, go in, and long.

　　　　　　　　　　　　　　[Exeunt LITTLEWIT, WIN.]

Trash. I think we are rid of our new customer, brother
　　Leatherhead, we shall hear no more of him.

　　　　　　　　　　They plot to be gone.

Lea. All the better, let's pack up all, and be gone, before he
　　find us.　　　　　　　　　　　　　　　　　　　　　　20

Trash. Stay a little, yonder comes a company: it may be we
　　may take some more money.

　　　　　　　[Enter] KNOCKEM, BUSY.

Kno. Sir, I will take your counsel, and cut my hair, and
　　leave vapours: I see that tobacco, and bottle-ale, and

III. vi. O.I. LITTLEWIT, WIN.] IOHN. WIN. TRASH. LEATHERHEAD. KNOCKHVM.
BVSY. PVRECRAFT. *F.*　　1. hear,] *F3;* heare *F.*　　18.1. *They . . . gone.*] *F*
margin, ll. 18–19.

III. vi. 14. *anatomy*] skeleton.

I

pig, and Whit, and very Urs'la herself, is all vanity.   25
Busy. Only pig was not comprehended in my admonition, the
rest were. For long hair, it is an ensign of pride, a banner,
and the world is full of those banners,very full of banners.
And bottle-ale is a drink of Satan's, a diet-drink of
Satan's, devised to puff us up and make us swell in this   30
latter age of vanity, as the smoke of tobacco to keep us in
mist and error; but the fleshly woman (which you call
Urs'la) is above all to be avoided, having the marks upon
her, of the three enemies of man: the world, as being in
the Fair; the devil, as being in the fire; and the flesh, as   35
being herself.

[*Enter*] PURECRAFT.

Pure. Brother Zeal-of-the-land! what shall we do? My daugh-
ter, Win-the-fight, is fall'n into her fit of longing again.
Busy. For more pig? There is no more, is there?
Pure. To see some sights, i' the Fair.   40
Busy. Sister, let her fly the impurity of the place, swiftly, lest
she partake of the pitch thereof. Thou art the seat of the
Beast, O Smithfield, and I will leave thee. Idolatry peep-
eth out on every side of thee.
Kno. An excellent right hypocrite! now his belly is full, he   45
falls a-railing and kicking, the jade. A very good vapour!
I'll in, and joy Urs'la with telling how her pig works; two
and a half he eat to his share. And he has drunk a pailfull.
He eats with his eyes, as well as his teeth.   [*Exit.*]
Lea. What do you lack, gentlemen? What is't you buy?   50
Rattles, drums, babies—
Busy. Peace, with thy apocryphal wares, thou profane publi-
can: thy bells, thy dragons, and thy Toby's dogs. Thy
hobby-horse is an idol, a very idol, a fierce and rank idol;
and thou the Nebuchadnezzar, the proud Nebuchad-   55

---

29. *diet-drink*] medicine.
52. *apocryphal*] sham, 'imitation' (with a glancing reference to the Puritans' rejection of the Apocrypha); cf. *A.*, I. i. 127 and, in *S.N.*, I. v. 8, the
division of news 'Into *Authenticall* and *Apocryphall*'.

nezzar of the Fair, that sett'st it up, for children to fall
down to, and worship.

Lea. Cry you mercy, sir, will you buy a fiddle to fill up your
noise?

[Re-enter LITTLEWIT, WIN.]

Lit. Look, Win. Do, look o' God's name, and save your long-　60
ing. Here be fine sights.

Pure. Aye child, so you hate 'em, as our Brother Zeal does,
you may look on 'em.

Lea. Or what do you say to a drum, sir?

Busy. It is the broken belly of the Beast, and thy bellows there　65
are his lungs, and these pipes are his throat, those feathers
are of his tail, and thy rattles, the gnashing of his teeth.

Trash. And what's my ginger-bread? I pray you.

Busy. The provender that pricks him up. Hence with thy
basket of popery, thy nest of images: and whole legend of　70
ginger-work.

Lea. Sir, if you be not quiet the quicklier, I'll ha' you clapp'd
fairly by the heels, for disturbing the Fair.

Busy. The sin of the Fair provokes me, I cannot be silent.

Pure. Good brother Zeal!　　　　　　　　　　　　　　　75

Lea. Sir, I'll make you silent, believe it.

Lit. I'd give a shilling you could, i' faith, friend.

Lea. Sir, give me your shilling; I'll give you my shop, if I do
not, and I'll leave it in pawn with you, i' the meantime.

Lit. A match i' faith, but do it quickly, then.　　　　　　80

[Exit LEATHERHEAD.]

Busy. Hinder me not, woman.

He speaks to the widow.

I was mov'd in spirit, to be here, this day, in this Fair, this

59. noise?] *F3;* noise. *F.*　　64. drum,] *F3;* Drumme. *F.*　　77. shilling
you could,] *F3;* shilling, you could *F.*　　81.1. *He . . . widow.] F margin,*
ll. 82–4.

---

69. *pricks . . . up*] stimulates.
70. *images*] cf. Appendix I, paragraph 2.
legend] a collection of saints' lives.

wicked, and foul Fair—and fitter may it be called a foul,
than a Fair—to protest against the abuses of it, the foul
abuses of it, in regard of the afflicted saints, that are   85
troubled, very much troubled, exceedingly troubled,
with the opening of the merchandise of Babylon again, and
the peeping of popery upon the stalls, here, here, in the
high places. See you not Goldylocks, the purple strumpet,
there, in her yellow gown, and green sleeves ? The pro-   90
fane pipes, the tinkling timbrels ? A shop of relics!

Lit. Pray you forbear, I am put in trust with 'em.

Busy. And this idolatrous grove of images, this flasket of
idols! which I will pull down—   *Overthrows the ginger-bread.*

Trash. O my ware, my ware, God bless it.   95

Busy. In my zeal, and glory to be thus exercis'd.

LEATHERHEAD *enters with officers.*

Lea. Here he is, pray you lay hold on his zeal, we cannot
sell a whistle, for him, in tune. Stop his noise, first!

Busy. Thou canst not: 'tis a sanctified noise. I will make a
loud and most strong noise, till I have daunted the pro-   100
fane enemy. And for this cause—

Lea. Sir, here's no man afraid of you, or your cause. You
shall swear it, i' the stocks, sir.

Busy. I will thrust myself into the stocks, upon the pikes of
the land.   105

Lea. Carry him away.

Pure. What do you mean, wicked men ?

Busy. Let them alone; I fear them not.

        [*Exeunt officers, with* BUSY, *followed by* PURECRAFT.]

Lit. Was not this shilling well ventur'd, Win, for our liberty ?

---

83. be] *F3;* be a *F.*   94. *Overthrows the ginger-bread.*] *F margin, ll. 93–5.*
96.1. LEATHERHEAD . . . *officers.*] *F margin, ll. 99–101.*

---

89. *high places*] cf. I. vi. 55 and note.
93. *flasket*] 'a long shallow basket' (Johnson).
104. *thrust myself . . . upon the pikes . . .*] rush into dangers; cf. *O.E.D.*,
s.v. *pike*[5], 2b, 1576: '. . . a couragious harted man, of his own accorde, to
pushe vpon the pykes of death'.

Now we may go play, and see over the Fair, where we   110
list, ourselves; my mother is gone after him, and let her
e'en go, and loose us.

Win. Yes, John, but I know not what to do.

Lit. For what, Win?

Win. For a thing, I am asham'd to tell you, i' faith, and 'tis   115
too far to go home.

Lit. I pray thee be not asham'd, Win. Come, i' faith thou
shall not be asham'd; is it anything about the hobby-
horse-man? An't be, speak freely.

Win. Hang him, base bobchin, I scorn him; no, I have very   120
great what sha' call 'um, John.

Lit. O! is that all, Win? We'll go back to Captain Jordan; to
the pig-woman's, Win: he'll help us, or she with a drip-
ping pan, or an old kettle, or something. The poor
greasy soul loves you, Win, and after we'll visit the Fair   125
all over, Win, and see my puppet play, Win; you know
it's a fine matter, Win.   [*Exeunt* LITTLEWIT, WIN.]

Lea. Let's away; I counsell'd you to pack up afore, Joan.

Trash. A pox of his Bedlam purity. He has spoil'd half my
ware: but the best is, we lose nothing, if we miss our first   130
merchant.

Lea. It shall be hard for him to find, or know us, when we are
translated, Joan.   [*Exeunt.*]

---

131. *merchant*] customer.
133. *translated*] transformed, like Bottom (*Midsummer Night's Dream*,
III. i. 125).

Act IV

Scene I

[Enter] TROUBLE-ALL, BRISTLE, HAGGIS, COKES, JUSTICE.

[Tro.] My Masters, I do make no doubt but you are officers.

Bri. What then, sir?

Tro. And the King's loving, and obedient subjects.

Bri. Obedient, friend? Take heed what you speak, I advise
you: Oliver Bristle advises you. His loving subjects, we   5
grant you; but not his obedient, at this time, by your
leave; we know ourselves a little better than so; we are to
command, sir, and such as you are to be obedient. Here's
one of his obedient subjects going to the stocks, and we'll
make you such another, if you talk.   10

Tro. You are all wise enough i' your places, I know.

Bri. If you know it, sir, why do you bring it in question?

Tro. I question nothing, pardon me. I do only hope you have
warrant, for what you do, and so, quit you, and so, multiply you.   *He goes away again.*   15

Hag. What's he? Bring him up to the stocks there. Why bring
you him not up?

[TROUBLE-ALL] *comes again.*

Tro. If you have Justice Overdo's warrant, 'tis well: you are
safe; that is the warrant of warrants. I'll not give this but-
ton, for any man's warrant else.   20

0.1. TROUBLE-ALL, ... JUSTICE.] TROVBLE-ALL. BRISTLE. HAGGISE. COKES.
IVSTICE. POCHER. BVSY. PVRECRAFT. *F.*   7. ourselves] *F3;* ourselues, *F.*
15. *He ... again.*] *F margin, ll. 14–16.*   17.1. *comes again.*] *F margin, l. 18.*

---

5. *Oliver*] called Davy at III. i. 8.
14–15. *quit ... you*] God reward you and increase your family.

Bri. Like enough, sir; but let me tell you, an' you play away
    your buttons, thus, you will want 'em ere night, for any
    store I see about you: you might keep 'em, and save pins,
    I wusse.   [TROUBLE-ALL] *goes away.*

Jus. [*Aside*] What should he be, that doth so esteem, and ad- 25
    vance my warrant ? He seems a sober and discreet person!
    It is a comfort to a good conscience to be follow'd with a
    good fame, in his sufferings. The world will have a pretty
    taste by this, how I can bear adversity: and it will beget a
    kind of reverence toward me, hereafter, even from mine 30
    enemies, when they shall see I carry my calamity nobly,
    and that it doth neither break me, nor bend me.

Hag. Come, sir, here's a place for you to preach in. Will you
    put in your leg ?

They put him in the stocks.

Jus. That I will, cheerfully.   35
Bri. O' my conscience, a seminary! He kisses the stocks.
Cok. Well, my masters, I'll leave him with you; now I see him
    bestow'd, I'll go look for my goods, and Numps.
Hag. You may, sir, I warrant you; where's the tother bawler ?
    fetch him too, you shall find 'em both fast enough. 40
                            [*Exit* COKES.]

Jus. [*Aside*] In the midst of this tumult, I will yet be the author
    of mine own rest, and, not minding their fury, sit in the
    stocks in that calm as shall be able to trouble a triumph.

[TROUBLE-ALL] *comes again.*

Tro. Do you assure me upon your words ? May I undertake for
    you, if I be ask'd the question; that you have this warrant ? 45
Hag. What's this fellow, for God's sake ?
Tro. Do but show me Adam Overdo, and I am satisfied. *Goes out.*
Bri. He is a fellow that is distracted, they say; one Trouble-all:

24. *goes away.*] *F margin, l. 22.*   34.1. *They . . . stocks.*] *F margin, ll. 33–5.*
43.1. *comes again.*] *F margin, l. 44.*   47. *Goes out.*] *F margin, l. 47.*

23. *store*] supply.

he was an officer in the court of Pie-powders, here last
year, and put out on his place by Justice Overdo.   50

Jus. Ha!

Bri. Upon which he took an idle conceit, and's run mad
upon't. So that, ever since, he will do nothing but by Justice Overdo's warrant: he will not eat a crust, nor drink a
little, nor make him in his apparel ready. His wife, sir-   55
reverence, cannot get him make his water, or shift his
shirt, without his warrant.

Jus. [*Aside*] If this be true, this is my greatest disaster! How
am I bound to satisfy this poor man, that is, of so good a
nature to me, out of his wits, where there is no room left   60
for dissembling!

                  [TROUBLE-ALL] *comes in.*

Tro. If you cannot show me Adam Overdo, I am in doubt of
you: I am afraid you cannot answer it.   *Goes again.*

Hag. Before me, neighbour Bristle, (and now I think on't better) Justice Overdo is a very peremptory person.   65

Bri. O! are you advis'd of that? And a severe Justicer, by
your leave.

Jus. [*Aside*] Do I hear ill o' that side, too?

Bri. He will sit as upright o' the bench, an' you mark him, as a
candle i' the socket, and give light to the whole court in   70
every business.

Hag. But he will burn blue, and swell like a boil (God bless us)
an' he be angry.

Bri. Aye, and he will be angry too, when he list, that's more:

59. is,] *This ed.; is* F.   61.1. *comes in.*] F *margin, l. 61.*   63. answer]
corr. F; asweare *uncorr.* F.   Goes again.] F *margin, l. 63.*   74. he²] *This
ed.;* his F; him HS.

---

52. *idle*] foolish.
63. *answer*] justify, make defence against (a charge). The reading
asweare occurs only in the Trinity College (Cambridge) copy, of those
collated (? cf. O.E. *aswerian* 'to swear').
66. *advis'd*] aware.
72. *blue*] pale (of candles: an ill omen, it was thought); livid (of persons).
74. *list*] please; invariably used with the nominative in *B.F.*

and when he is angry, be it right or wrong, he has the law　75
on's side, ever. I mark that too.

Jus. [*Aside*] I will be more tender hereafter. I see compassion
may become a Justice, though it be a weakness, I confess;
and nearer a vice, than a virtue.

Hag. Well, take him out o' the stocks again, we'll go a sure　80
way to work, we'll ha' the ace of hearts of our side, if we
can.

> *They take the* JUSTICE *out.* [*Enter*] POCHER, BUSY,
> PURECRAFT.

Poch. Come, bring him away to his fellow, there. Master Busy,
we shall rule your legs, I hope, though we cannot rule your
tongue.　85

Busy. No, minister of darkness, no, thou canst not rule my
tongue; my tongue it is mine own, and with it I will both
knock, and mock down your Bartholomew-abomina-
tions, till you be made a hissing to the neighbour parishes,
round about.　90

Hag. Let him alone, we have devis'd better upon't.

Pure. And shall he not into the stocks then?

Bri. No, mistress, we'll have 'em both to Justice Overdo, and
let him do over 'em as is fitting. Then I, and my gossip
Haggis, and my beadle Pocher are discharg'd.　95

Pure. O, I thank you, blessed, honest men!

Bri. Nay, never thank us, but thank this madman that comes
here, he put it in our heads.

> [TROUBLE-ALL] *comes again.*

Pure. Is he mad? Now heaven increase his madness, and
bless it, and thank it: sir, your poor handmaid thanks　100
you.

Tro. Have you a warrant? An' you have a warrant, show it.

82.1. *They . . . out.*] *F margin. ll. 80–2.*　98.1. *comes again.*] *F margin,*
ll. 100–2.　100. it:] *F3;* it, *F.*

---

95. *discharg'd*] freed from responsibility.

Pure. Yes, I have a warrant out of the word, to give thanks for
removing any scorn intended to the brethren.

                            [*Exeunt all but* TROUBLE-ALL.]

Tro. It is Justice Overdo's warrant, that I look for: if you   105
have not that, keep your word, I'll keep mine. Quit ye,
and multiply ye.

Act IV. Scene II.

[*Enter to him, severally*] EDGWORTH, NIGHTINGALE, COKES,
Costermonger.

[*Edg.*] Come away, Nightingale, I pray thee.

Tro. Whither go you? Where's your warrant?

Edg. Warrant, for what, sir?

Tro. For what you go about; you know how fit it is; an' you
have no warrant, bless you, I'll pray for you, that's all I   5
can do.   *Goes out.*

Edg. What means he?

Nigh. A madman that haunts the Fair, do you not know him?
It's marvel he has not more followers after his ragged
heels.   10

Edg. Beshrew him, he startled me: I thought he had known of
our plot. Guilt's a terrible thing! Ha' you prepar'd the
costermonger?

Nigh. Yes, and agreed for his basket of pears; he is at the corner here, ready. And your prize, he comes down, sailing,   15
that way, all alone; without his protector: he is rid of him,
it seems.

Edg. Aye, I know; I should ha' follow'd his Protectorship for
a feat I am to do upon him; but this offer'd itself so i' the

---

IV. ii. 0.1. EDGWORTH, . . . *Costermonger.*] EDGVVORTH. TROVBLE-ALL.
NIGHTINGALE. COKES. COSTARDMONGER. *F.*   6. *Goes out*] *F margin,*
l. 6.

---

103. *the word*] the Bible.

way, I could not let it 'scape: here he comes, whistle; be   20
this sport call'd 'Dorring the Dottrell.'

Nigh. Wh, wh, wh, wh, &c.   NIGHTINGALE *whistles.*

Cok. By this light, I cannot find my ginger-bread-wife, nor
my hobby-horse-man, in all the Fair, now, to ha' my
money again. And I do not know the way out on't, to go   25
home for more, do you hear, friend, you that whistle?
What tune is that you whistle?

Nigh. A new tune, I am practising, sir.

Cok. Dost thou know where I dwell, I pray thee? Nay, on
with thy tune, I ha' no such haste for an answer: I'll prac-   30
tise with thee.

Cost. Buy any pears, very fine pears, pears fine.

NIGHTINGALE *sets his foot afore him,*
and he falls with his basket.

Cok. Godso! a muss, a muss, a muss, a muss.

Cost. Good gentleman, my ware, my ware, I am a poor man.
Good sir, my ware.   35

Nigh. Let me hold your sword, sir, it troubles you.

Cok. Do, and my cloak, an' thou wilt; and my hat, too.

COKES *falls a-scrambling whilst they run away with his things.*

Edg. A delicate great boy! methinks, he out-scrambles 'em all.
I cannot persuade myself, but he goes to grammar-school
yet; and plays the truant, today.   40

Nigh. Would he had another purse to cut, 'Zekiel.

Edg. Purse? a man might cut out his kidneys, I think; and he
never feel 'em, he is so earnest at the sport.

---

20. whistle;] *F3;* whistle, *F.*   22. NIGHTINGALE *whistles.*] *F margin, ll. 20-*
1.   32.1-2. NIGHTINGALE ... *basket.*] *F margin, ll. 31-5.*   37.1. COKES
... *things.*] *F margin, ll. 36-41.*

---

21. *Dorring the Dottrel*] fooling the simpleton (properly a kind of
plover, easily taken; cf. l. 60 below, and Drayton, *Panegyric Verses* in
Coryats Crudities, 1611: 'As men take Dottrels so hast thou ta'en us'). Professor Leech has pointed out to me that there is an antimasque involving
dotterels and their catchers in Shirley's *The Triumph of Peace,* 1633.

33. *muss*] a scramble.

Nigh. His soul is half-way out on's body, at the game.

Edg. Away, Nightingale: that way.   45

    [NIGHTINGALE *runs off with his sword, cloak, and hat.*]

Cok. I think I am furnish'd for Cather'ne pears, for one under-
meal: gi' me my cloak.

Cost. Good gentleman, give me my ware.

Cok. Where's the fellow, I ga' my cloak to? My cloak? and my
hat? ha! God's lid, is he gone? Thieves, thieves, help me   50
to cry, gentlemen.   *He runs out.*

Edg. Away, costermonger, come to us to Urs'la's. [*Exit
Costermonger.*] Talk of him to have a soul? 'Heart, if he
have any more than a thing given him instead of salt, only
to keep him from stinking, I'll be hang'd afore my time,   55
presently: where should it be, trow? In his blood? He has
not so much to'ard it in his whole body as will maintain a
good flea; and if he take this course, he will not ha' so
much land left as to rear a calf within this twelvemonth.
Was there ever green plover so pull'd! That his little   60
overseer had been here now, and been but tall enough, to
see him steal pears, in exchange for his beaver-hat and his
cloak thus! I must go find him out, next, for his black box,
and his patent (it seems) he has of his place; which I think
the gentleman would have a reversion of, that spoke to me   65
for it so earnestly.   [*Exit.*]

He [COKES] *comes again.*

Cok. Would I might lose my doublet, and hose too, as I am an
honest man, and never stir, if I think there be anything
but thieving, and coz'ning, i' this whole Fair. Bartholomew-fair, quoth he; an' ever any Bartholomew had that   70

45.1. NIGHTINGALE . . . *hat.*] *G.*   51. *He runs out.*] F *margin, l. 50.*
56. presently:] *F3;* presently, *F.*   66.1. *He comes again.*] F *margin,*
ll. 67–8.

46–7. *under-meal*] afternoon meal; *under* or *undern,* originally mid-
morning (i.e. 9 a.m.), could even by the late 15th century mean mid-after-
noon.

64. *patent*] a document conferring an office.

luck in't that I have had, I'll be martyr'd for him, and in
Smithfield, too.

Throws away his pears.

I ha' paid for my pears, a rot on 'em, I'll keep 'em no
longer; you were choke-pears to me; I had been better ha'
gone to mum-chance for you, I wusse. Methinks the Fair   75
should not have us'd me thus, an' 'twere but for my
name's sake; I would not ha' us'd a dog o' the name, so.
O, Numps will triumph, now!

TROUBLE-ALL *comes again.*

Friend, do you know who I am? Or where I lie? I do not
myself, I'll be sworn. Do but carry me home, and I'll   80
please thee, I ha' money enough there; I ha' lost myself,
and my cloak and my hat; and my fine sword, and my sister, and Numps, and Mistress Grace (a gentlewoman that
I should ha' married), and a cut-work handkerchief she
ga' me, and two purses, today. And my bargain o' hobby-   85
horses and ginger-bread, which grieves me worst of all.

Tro. By whose warrant, sir, have you done all this?

Cok. Warrant? thou art a wise fellow, indeed—as if a man
need a warrant to lose anything with.

Tro. Yes, Justice Overdo's warrant, a man may get and lose   90
with, I'll stand to't.

Cok. Justice Overdo? Dost thou know him? I lie there, he is
my brother-in-law, he married my sister: pray thee show
me the way, dost thou know the house?

Tro. Sir, show me your warrant; I know nothing without a   95
warrant, pardon me.

Cok. Why, I warrant thee, come along: thou shalt see I have

72.1. *Throws . . . pears.*] *F margin, ll. 71–4.*   78.1. TROUBLE-ALL *comes
again.*] *F margin, ll. 86–7.*

---

74. *choke-pears*] coarse pears used for perry.
75. *mum-chance*] a dicing game.
80. *carry*] lead, escort.
92. *lie*] lodge.

     wrought pillows there, and cambric sheets, and sweet
     bags, too. Pray thee guide me to the house.

Tro. Sir, I'll tell you; go you thither yourself, first, alone;   100
     tell your worshipful brother your mind: and but bring
     me three lines of his hand, or his clerk's, with 'Adam
     Overdo' underneath; here I'll stay you; I'll obey you,
     and I'll guide you presently.

Cok. [*Aside*] 'Slid, this is an ass, I ha' found him; pox upon   105
     me, what do I talking to such a dull fool? [*To him*] Fare-
     well, you are a very coxcomb, do you hear?

Tro. I think I am; if Justice Overdo sign to it, I am, and so
     we are all; he'll quit us all, multiply us all.   [*Exeunt.*]

Act IV. Scene III.

          [*Enter*] GRACE. QUARLOUS, WINWIFE *enter*
               with their swords drawn.

[*Grace.*] Gentlemen, this is no way that you take: you do but
     breed one another trouble, and offence, and give me no
     contentment at all. I am no she that affects to be quar-
     rell'd for, or have my name or fortune made the question
     of men's swords.   5

Quar. 'Slood, we love you.

Grace. If you both love me, as you pretend, your own reason
     will tell you but one can enjoy me; and to that point, there
     leads a directer line than by my infamy, which must fol-
     low if you fight. 'Tis true, I have profess'd it to you in-   10

108. am;] *F3;* am, *F.*

IV. iii. 0.1. GRACE. QUARLOUS, WINWIFE] GRACE. QVARLOVS. VVINWIFE.
TROVBLE-ALL. EDGVVORTH. *F.*   0.1–2. enter . . . drawn.] *They enter with
their swords drawne. F margin.*

_____

     98. *wrought*] embroidered.
     105. *found*] detected.

     IV. iii. 3. *affects*] likes; cf. l. 35 below.

genuously that, rather than to be yok'd with this bride-
groom is appointed me, I would take up any husband,
almost upon any trust. Though subtlety would say to me
(I know) he is a fool, and has an estate, and I might govern
him, and enjoy a friend beside. But these are not my   15
aims; I must have a husband I must love, or I cannot live
with him. I shall ill make one of these politic wives!

Winw. Why, if you can like either of us, lady, say which is he,
and the other shall swear instantly to desist.

Quar. Content, I accord to that willingly.   20

Grace. Sure you think me a woman of an extreme levity,
gentlemen, or a strange fancy, that (meeting you by
chance in such a place as this, both at one instant, and not
yet of two hours' acquaintance, neither of you deserving,
afore the other, of me) I should so forsake my modesty   25
(though I might affect one more particularly) as to say,
'This is he', and name him.

Quar. Why, wherefore should you not? What should hinder
you?

Grace. If you would not give it to my modesty, allow it yet to   30
my wit; give me so much of woman, and cunning, as not
to betray myself impertinently. How can I judge of you,
so far as to a choice, without knowing you more? You are
both equal and alike to me, yet; and so indifferently
affected by me, as each of you might be the man, if the   35
other were away. For you are reasonable creatures, you
have understanding, and discourse. And if fate send me
an understanding husband, I have no fear at all, but mine
own manners shall make him a good one.

Quar. Would I were put forth to making for you, then.   40

---

15. *friend*] lover.

17. *politic*] cunning, scheming.

36. *For*] because; cf. *Othello*, III. iv. 159–60: 'They are not ever jealous
for the cause, But jealous for they are jealous.'

37. *discourse*] rationality.

40. *put forth*] sent out.

to making] for training (used, for instance, of a falcon).

Grace. It may be you are, you know not what's toward you:
    will you consent to a motion of mine, gentlemen?

Winw. Whatever it be, we'll presume reasonableness, coming
    from you.

Quar. And fitness, too.   45

Grace. I saw one of you buy a pair of tables, e'en now.

Winw. Yes, here they be, and maiden ones too, unwritten in.

Grace. The fitter for what they may be employed in. You shall
    write, either of you, here, a word, or a name, what you like
    best; but of two, or three syllables at most: and the next   50
    person that comes this way (because destiny has a high
    hand in business of this nature) I'll demand, which of the
    two words he or she doth approve; and according to that
    sentence, fix my resolution, and affection, without change.

Quar. Agreed, my word is conceived already.   55

Winw. And mine shall not be long creating after.

Grace. But you shall promise, gentlemen, not to be curious to
    know, which of you it is, is taken; but give me leave to
    conceal that till you have brought me, either home, or
    where I may safely tender myself.   60

Winw. Why, that's but equal.

Quar. We are pleas'd.

Grace. Because I will bind both your endeavours to work to-
    gether, friendly, and jointly, each to the other's fortune,
    and have myself fitted with some means to make him that   65
    is forsaken a part of amends.

Quar. These conditions are very courteous. Well, my word is
    out of the *Arcadia*, then: 'Argalus'.

Winw. And mine out of the play, 'Palemon'.

58. is, is taken] *HS;* is, taken *F.*

---

41. *toward*] in store for.
42. *motion*] suggestion.
46. *tables*] writing tablets.
60. *tender*] take care of.
61. *equal*] fair, equitable.
68. *Argalus*] cousin to King Basilius's queen and lover of Parthenia
(*Arcadia*, 1590, Bk I, chpp. 5–8 ff., ed. Feuillerat, 1912, i. 31, etc.).
69. *the play*] most probably *The Two Noble Kinsmen*, 1613.

TROUBLE-ALL *comes again.*

Tro. Have you any warrant for this, gentlemen?   70
Quar. Winw. Ha!
Tro. There must be a warrant had, believe it.
Winw. For what?
Tro. For whatsoever it is, anything indeed, no matter what.
Quar. 'Slight, here's a fine ragged prophet, dropp'd down i'   75
    the nick!
Tro. Heaven quit you, gentlemen.
Quar. Nay, stay a little: good lady, put him to the question.
Grace. You are content, then?
Winw. Quar. Yes yes.   80
Grace. Sir, here are two names written—
Tro. Is Justice Overdo, one?
Grace. How, sir? I pray you read 'em to yourself—it is for a
    wager between these gentlemen—and with a stroke or any
    difference, mark which you approve best.   85
Tro. They may be both worshipful names for ought I know,
    mistress, but Adam Overdo had been worth three of 'em,
    I assure you, in this place; that's in plain English.
Grace. This man amazes me! I pray you, like one of 'em, sir.
Tro. I do like him there, that has the best warrant. Mistress, to   90
    save your longing, (and multiply him) it may be this.
    [*Marks the book.*] But I am aye still for Justice Overdo,
    that's my conscience. And quit you.   [*Exit.*]
Winw. Is't done, lady?
Grace. Aye, and strangely, as ever I saw! What fellow is this,   95
    trow?
Quar. No matter what, a fortune-teller we ha' made him.
    Which is't, which is't?
Grace. Nay, did you not promise, not to enquire?

[*Enter*] EDGWORTH.

69.1. TROUBLE-ALL *comes again.*] *F margin, ll. 70–1.*   78. little:] *F3;* little,
F.   82. Justice] *F3; Iudice F.*   90. warrant.] *HS;* warrant, *F.*   91.
(and multiply] *HS;* and (multiply *F.*   98. is't?] *F3;* is't. *F.*

85. *difference*] distinguishing mark.

Quar. 'Slid, I forgot that, pray you pardon me. Look, here's   100
    our Mercury come: the licence arrives i' the finest time,
    too! 'Tis but scraping out Cokes his name, and 'tis done.
Winw. How now, lime-twig? Hast thou touch'd?
Edg. Not yet, sir; except you would go with me, and see't,
    it's not worth speaking on. The act is nothing, without a   105
    witness. Yonder he is, your man with the box fall'n into
    the finest company, and so transported with vapours;
    they ha' got in a northern clothier, and one Puppy, a
    western man, that's come to wrestle before my Lord
    Mayor anon, and Captain Whit, and one Val Cutting,   110
    that helps Captain Jordan to roar, a circling boy: with
    whom your Numps is so taken, that you may strip him of
    his clothes, if you will. I'll undertake to geld him for
    you; if you had but a surgeon, ready, to sear him. And
    Mistress Justice, there, is the goodest woman! She does   115
    so love 'em all over, in terms of Justice, and the style of
    authority, with her hood upright—that I beseech you
    come away, gentlemen, and see't.
Quar. 'Slight, I would not lose it for the Fair; what'll you do,
    Ned?   120
Winw. Why, stay here about for you; Mistress Wellborn
    must not be seen.
Quar. Do so, and find out a priest i' the meantime; I'll bring
    the licence. Lead, which way is't?
Edg. Here, sir, you are o' the backside o' the booth already,   125
    you may hear the noise.   [*Exeunt.*]

103. touch'd?] *F3;* touch'd. *F.*   104. sir;] *F3;* Sir, *F.*   107. vapours;]
F3; vapours, *F.*

   109–10. *wrestle . . . Mayor*] 'before the Lord Maior, Aldermen, and
Shiriffes of London placed in a large Tent neare vnto Clarkenwell . . .
wrestling is . . . practised on *Bartholomew* day in the after noone' (Stow, i.
104).
   111. *circling boy*] found only here, ? connected in some way with IV. iv.
125–7; perhaps, suggests Professor Leech, an attendant bully, one who
circles round his chief.

Act IV. Scene IV.

[*Enter*] KNOCKEM, NORDERN, PUPPY, CUTTING, WHIT, WASP,
　　　　　Mistress OVERDO.

[*Kno.*] Whit, bid Val Cutting continue the vapours for a lift,
　　Whit, for a lift.

Nor. I'll ne mare, I'll ne mare, the eale's too meeghty.

Kno. How now! my Galloway Nag, the staggers? Ha! Whit,
　　gi' him a slit i' the forehead. Cheer up, man; a needle and　　5
　　thread to stitch his ears. I'd cure him now an' I had it,
　　with a little butter, and garlic, long-pepper, and grains.
　　Where's my horn? I'll gi' him a mash, presently, shall
　　take away this dizziness.

Pup. Why, where are you, zurs? Do you vlinch, and leave us　10
　　i' the zuds, now?

Nor. I'll ne mare, I is e'en as vull as a paiper's bag, by my
　　troth, aye.

Pup. Do my northern cloth zhrink i' the wetting, ha?

Kno. Why, well said, old flea-bitten, thou'lt never tire, I see.　15
　　　　　　　　　　They fall to their vapours, again.

IV. iv. 0.1–2. KNOCKEM . . . OVERDO.] KNOCKHVM. NORDERN. PVPPY. CVTTING.
WHIT. EDGVVORTH. QVARLOVS. OVERDOO. WASPE. BRISTLE. *F.*　　15.1. *They*
. . . *again.*] F *margin, ll. 16–19.*

　　IV. iv. 1. *lift*] shift, trick.

　　4. *Galloway Nag*] a small tough breed, 'the best kind of Scotish nags'
(according to Drayton, *Polyolbion*, iii. 28, margin).

　　5–6. *slit . . . ears*] cf. Markham, p. 64: for the staggers ('a dizzy madnesse
of the braine . . .'), '. . . with a knife make a hole of an inch long, overthwart
his forehead. . . Others . . . take felladine . . . to stoppe . . . his eares and . . .
stitch the tippes of his eares together that he may not shake the medecine
out.'

　　7. *long-pepper*] the fruit spike of *piper longum*, sometimes called 'tailed
pepper' in the 17th century.

　　11. *i' the zuds*] in difficulty or disgrace.

　　14. *northern . . . wetting*] a frequent complaint; cf. Dekker and Webster,
Westward Hoe, II. i. 41–2: 'old things must shrinke as well as new Northern
cloth.'

　　15. *flea-bitten*] of a horse, with bay or sorrel spots; *O.E.D.* quotes Barnabe
Googe, *Foure Bookes of Husbandrie*, 1577 (1586, II, f.116v): 'The flea bitten
horse proueth alwaies good and notable in trauell.'

Cut. No, sir, but he may tire, if it please him.

Whit. Who told dee sho ? that he vuld never teer, man ?

Cut. No matter who told him so, so long as he knows.

Kno. Nay, I know nothing, sir, pardon me there.

[*Enter*] EDGWORTH, QUARLOUS.

Edg. They are at it still, sir, this they call vapours.   20

Whit. He shall not pardon dee, captain, dou shalt not be pardon'd. Pre'de shweetheart, do not pardon him.

Cut. 'Slight, I'll pardon him, an' I list, whosoever says nay
to't.

Quar. Where's Numps ? I miss him.   25

Wasp. Why, I say nay to't.

Quar. O there he is!

Kno. To what do you say nay, sir ?

*Here they continue their game of vapours, which is nonsense: every man
to oppose the last man that spoke, whether it concern'd him, or no.*

Wasp. To anything, whatsoever it is, so long as I do not like it.

Whit. Pardon me, little man, dou musht like it a little.   30

Cut. No, he must not like it at all, sir; there you are i' the
wrong.

Whit. I tink I be, he musht not like it, indeed.

Cut. Nay, then he both must, and will like it, sir, for all you.

Kno. If he have reason, he may like it, sir.   35

Whit. By no meansh, captain, upon reason, he may like nothing upon reason.

Wasp. I have no reason, nor I will hear of no reason, nor I will
look for no reason, and he is an ass that either knows any,
or looks for't from me.   40

Cut. Yes, in some sense you may have reason, sir.

Wasp. Aye, in some sense, I care not if I grant you.

Cut. Pardon me, thou ougsht to grant him nothing, in no
shensh, if dou do love dyshelf, angry man.

Wasp. Why then, I do grant him nothing; and I have no sense.   45

Cut. 'Tis true, thou hast no sense indeed.

28.1-2. *Here ... no.*] F margin, *ll. 25-36.*

Wasp. 'Slid, but I have sense, now I think on't better, and I
　　will grant him anything, do you see?

Kno. He is i' the right, and does utter a sufficient vapour.

Cut. Nay, it is no sufficient vapour, neither, I deny that.　　50

Kno. Then it is a sweet vapour.

Cut. It may be a sweet vapour.

Wasp. Nay, it is no sweet vapour, neither, sir; it stinks, and
　　I'll stand to't.

Whit. Yes, I tink it doesh shtink, Captain. All vapour doesh　　55
　　shtink.

Wasp. Nay, then it does not stink, sir, and it shall not stink.

Cut. By your leave, it may, sir.

Wasp. Aye, by my leave, it may stink; I know that.

Whit. Pardon me, thou knowesht nothing; it cannot by thy　　60
　　leave, angry man.

Wasp. How can it not?

Kno. Nay, never question him, for he is i' the right.

Whit. Yesh, I am i' de right, I confesh it; so ish de little man
　　too.　　65

Wasp. I'll have nothing confess'd that concerns me. I am not
　　i' the right, nor never was i' the right, nor never will be i'
　　the right, while I am in my right mind.

Cut. Mind? Why, here's no man minds you, sir, nor anything
　　else.　　70

　　　　　　　　　They drink again.

Pup. Vriend, will you mind this that we do?

Quar. Call you this vapours? This is such belching of quarrel,
　　as I never heard. Will you mind your business, sir?

Edg. You shall see, sir.

Nor. I'll ne mair, my waimb warks too mickle with this　　75
　　auready.

Edg. Will you take that, Master Wasp, that nobody should
　　mind you?

70.1. *They drink again.*] F *margin, ll. 69–70.*

---

73. *your business*] from III. v. 252.

Wasp. Why? What ha' you to do? Is't any matter to you?

Edg. No, but methinks you should not be unminded, though.   80

Wasp. Nor I wu' not be, now I think on't; do you hear, new
    acquaintance, does no man mind me, say you?

Cut. Yes, sir, every man here minds you, but how?

Wasp. Nay, I care as little how, as you do; that was not my
    question.   85

Whit. No, noting was ty question; tou art a learned man, and I
    am a valiant man, i' faith la, tou shalt speak for me, and I
    vill fight for tee.

Kno. Fight for him, Whit? A gross vapour; he can fight for
    himself.   90

Wasp. It may be I can, but it may be, I wu' not, how then?

Cut. Why, then you may choose.

Wasp. Why, and I'll choose whether I'll choose or no.

Kno. I think you may, and 'tis true; and I allow it for a reso-
    lute vapour.   95

Wasp. Nay, then, I do think you do not think, and it is no
    resolute vapour.

Cut. Yes, in some sort he may allow you.

Kno. In no sort, sir, pardon me, I can allow him nothing.
    You mistake the vapour.   100

Wasp. He mistakes nothing, sir, in no sort.

Whit. Yes, I pre dee now, let him mistake.

Wasp. A turd i' your teeth, never pre dee me, for I will have
    nothing mistaken.

Kno. Turd, ha, turd? A noisome vapour; strike, Whit.   105

They fall by the ears.

[EDGWORTH *steals the licence out of the box, and exit.*]

Mrs. Overdo. Why, gentlemen, why gentlemen, I charge you
    upon my authority, conserve the peace. In the king's
    name, and my husband's, put up your weapons; I shall
    be driven to commit you myself, else.

105. strike,] *1716;* strike *F.*   105.1. *They . . . ears.*] *F margin, ll. 105–6.*
105.2. EDGWORTH . . . *exit.*] *G.*

109. *commit*] send to prison.

Quar. Ha, ha, ha.   110
Wasp. Why do you laugh, sir?
Quar. Sir, you'll allow me my Christian liberty. I may laugh,
    I hope.
Cut. In some sort you may, and in some sort you may not, sir.
Kno. Nay, in some sort, sir, he may neither laugh nor hope,   115
    in this company.
Wasp. Yes, then he may both laugh and hope in any sort,
    an't please him.
Quar. Faith, and I will then, for it doth please me exceed-
    ingly.   120
Wasp. No exceeding neither, sir.
Kno. No, that vapour is too lofty.
Quar. Gentlemen, I do not play well at your game of vapours,
    I am not very good at it, but—
Cut. Do you hear, sir? I would speak with you in circle!   125

            He draws a circle on the ground.

Quar. In circle, sir? What would you with me in circle?
Cut. Can you lend me a piece, a jacobus, in circle?
Quar. 'Slid, your circle will prove more costly than your
    vapours, then. Sir, no, I lend you none.
Cut. Your beard's not well turn'd up, sir.   130
Quar. How, rascal? Are you playing with my beard? I'll
    break circle with you.

            They draw all, and fight.

Pup. Nor. Gentlemen, gentlemen!
Kno. Gather up, Whit, gather up, Whit, good vapours.   [*Exit.*]
Mrs. Over. What mean you? are you rebels? gentlemen!   135
    Shall I send out a sergeant-at-arms, or a writ o' rebellion,

---

125.1. *He . . . ground.*] F margin, ll. *124–6.*   132.1. *They . . . fight.*] F
margin, ll. *131–2.*

114, 115. *sort*] (*a*) kind, fashion (cf. ll. 98–101); (*b*) group, company.
121. *exceeding*] being 'superior'.
127. *jacobus*] the gold 'sovereign' of 1603, current then for 20s., but by
1612 valued at 24s.

against you? I'll commit you, upon my womanhood, for
a riot, upon my justice-hood, if you persist.

[*Exeunt* QUARLOUS, CUTTING.]

Wasp. Upon your justice-hood? Marry shit o' your hood;
you'll commit? Spoke like a true Justice of Peace's wife,   140
indeed, and a fine female lawyer! Turd i' your teeth for a
fee, now.

Mrs. Over. Why, Numps, in Master Overdo's name, I
charge you.

Wasp. Good Mistress Underdo, hold your tongue.   145

Mrs. Over. Alas! poor Numps.

Wasp. Alas! And why alas from you, I beseech you? Or why
poor Numps, Goody Rich? Am I come to be pitied by
your tuft taffeta now? Why mistress, I knew Adam, the
clerk, your husband, when he was Adam scrivener, and   150
writ for twopence a sheet, as high as he bears his head
now, or you your hood, dame. What are you, sir?

The watch comes in.

Bri. We be men, and no infidels; what is the matter, here, and
the noises? Can you tell?

Wasp. Heart, what ha' you to do? Cannot a man quarrel in   155
quietness, but he must be put out on't by you? What are
you?

Bri. Why, we be His Majesty's Watch, sir.

Wasp. Watch? 'Sblood, you are a sweet watch, indeed. A
body would think, an' you watch'd well o' nights, you   160
should be contented to sleep at this time o' day. Get you
to your fleas, and your flock-beds, you rogues, your
kennels, and lie down close.

152.1. *The . . . in.*] *F margin, ll. 152–3.*

---

140. *commit*] cf. l. 109; here with quibble on the sense 'fornicate'.
148. *Goody*] Goodwife.   *Rich*] see note to l. 179 below.
149. *tuft taffeta*] Taffeta was 'a thin, fine silk fabric of even texture. . .
But plain taffeta was not rich enough for Elizabethan taste. It must be
"tufted" i.e. woven with raised stripes or spots' (Linthicum, *Costume in the
Drama*, 1936, pp. 123–4).

Bri. Down ? Yes, we will down, I warrant you; down with
        him in His Majesty's name, down, down with him, and   165
        carry him away, to the pigeon-holes.
Mrs. Over. I thank you honest friends, in the behalf o' the
        Crown, and the peace, and in Master Overdo's name, for
        suppressing enormities.
Whit. Stay, Bristle, here ish a noder brash o' drunkards, but   170
        very quiet, special drunkards, will pay dee five shillings
        very well. Take 'em to dee, in de graish o' God: one of
        'em does change cloth for ale in the Fair here, te oder ish
        a strong man, a mighty man, my Lord Mayor's man, and
        a wreshler. He has wreshled so long with the bottle, here,   175
        that the man with the beard hash almosht streek up hish
        heelsh.
Bri. 'Slid, the Clerk o' the Market has been to cry him all the
        Fair over, here, for my Lord's service.
Whit. Tere he ish, pre de taik him hensh, and make ty best on   180
        him.   [*Exit watch with* WASP, NORDERN, PUPPY.]
        How now, woman o' shilk, vat ailsh ty shweet faish ? Art
        tou melancholy ?
Mrs. Over. A little distemper'd with these enormities; shall I
        entreat a courtesy of you, Captain ?   185
Whit. Entreat a hundred, velvet voman, I vill do it, shpeak
        out.
Mrs. Over. I cannot with modesty speak of it out, but—
Whit. I vill do it, and more, and more, for dee. What, Urs'la,
        an't be bitch, an't be bawd, an't be!   190

                    [*Enter*] URSULA.

---

166. *pigeon-holes*] stocks.
176. *man with the beard*] 'a Jug, Fac'd, with a beard' (*N.I.*, I. iv. 13–14).
178. *Clerk o' the Market*] an official appointed 'to take tolls and manage
for its proprietors the general business of the Fair' (Morley, pp. 151–2).
179. *my Lord*] the Rich family to whom had been assigned at the disso-
lution 'the site and capital messuage and mansion house of the late monas-
tery . . . of St. Bartholomew' and hence the rights and tolls of the part of the
Fair held within its precincts, in particular of the Cloth Fair (Morley,
pp. 117–18).

Urs. How now, rascal ? What roar you for ? Old pimp.

Whit. Here, put up de cloaks, Ursh; de purchase; pre dee
now, shweet Ursh, help dis good brave voman to a jordan, an't be.

Urs. 'Slid, call your Captain Jordan to her, can you not ?   195

Whit. Nay, pre dee leave dy consheits, and bring the velvet
woman to de—

Urs. I bring her! Hang her: heart, must I find a common pot
for every punk i' your purlieus ?

Whit. O good voordsh, Ursh, it ish a guest o' velvet, i' fait la.   200

Urs. Let her sell her hood, and buy a sponge, with a pox to
her, my vessel is employed, sir. I have but one, and 'tis
the bottom of an old bottle. An honest proctor and his
wife are at it, within; if she'll stay her time, so.

Whit. As soon ash tou cansht, shweet Ursh. Of a valiant man   205
I tink I am the patientsh man i' the world, or in all
Smithfield.

[*Re-enter* KNOCKEM.]

Kno. How now, Whit ? Close vapours, stealing your leaps ?
Covering in corners, ha ?

Whit. No, fait, captain, dough tou beesht a vishe man, dy vit   210
is a mile hence, now. I vas procuring a shmall courtesy,
for a woman of fashion here.

Mrs. Over. Yes, captain, though I am Justice of Peace's wife,
I do love men of war, and the sons of the sword, when
they come before my husband.   215

Kno. Say'st thou so, filly ? Thou shalt have a leap presently;
I'll horse thee myself, else.

Urs. Come, will you bring her in now ? And let her take her
turn ?

Whit. Gramercy, good Ursh, I tank dee.   220

Mrs. Over. Master Overdo shall thank her.   [*Exit.*]

---

192. purchase;] *1716;* purchase, *F.*   198. her!] *1716;* her, *F.*   202.
vessel is] *F3;* vessell, *F.*   218. take] *1716;* talke *F.*

---

209. *Covering*] copulating (of stallions).

Act IV. Scene V.

[Enter to them] LITTLEWIT, WIN.

[*Lit.*] Good Gammer Urs; Win and I are exceedingly beholden to you, and to Captain Jordan, and Captain Whit.
Win, I'll be bold to leave you i' this good company, Win:
for half an hour, or so, Win, while I go, and see how my
matter goes forward, and if the puppets be perfect: and   5
then I'll come and fetch you, Win.

Win. Will you leave me alone with two men, John?

Lit. Aye, they are honest gentlemen, Win, Captain Jordan,
and Captain Whit, they'll use you very civilly, Win; God
b' w' you, Win.   [*Exit.*]   10

Urs. What's her husband gone?

Kno. On his false gallop, Urs, away.

Urs. An' you be right Bartholomew-birds, now show yourselves so: we are undone for want of fowl i' the Fair, here.
Here will be 'Zekiel Edgworth, and three or four gallants   15
with him at night, and I ha' neither plover nor quail for
'em: persuade this between you two, to become a bird o'
the game, while I work the velvet woman within (as you
call her).   [*Exit.*]

Kno. I conceive thee, Urs! go thy ways. Dost thou hear, Whit?   20
is't not pity my delicate dark chestnut here—with the fine
lean head, large forehead, round eyes, even mouth, sharp
ears, long neck, thin crest, close withers, plain back, deep
sides, short fillets, and full flanks; with a round belly, a
plump buttock, large thighs, knit knees, straight legs,   25
short pasterns, smooth hoofs, and short heels—should

IV. V. O.I. LITTLEWIT, WIN.] IOHN. WIN. VRSLA. KNOCKHVM. WHIT. OVERDOO.
ALES. *F.*   12. false] *F3;* false, *F.*   20. ways.] *1716;* waies, *F.*

IV. v. 11. *What*] for what end or purpose.
16. *plover, quail*] loose women.
21 ff.] cf. *Venus and Adonis*, 295–300, for a similar catalogue, and con-
clusion: 'Look what a horse should have he did not lack, Save a proud rider
on so proud a back.'

lead a dull honest woman's life, that might live the life of a
lady ?

Whit. Yes, by my fait and trot it is, captain: de honesht woman's leef is a scurvy dull leef, indeed, la.   30

Win. How, sir ? Is an honest woman's life a scurvy life ?

Whit. Yes, fait, shweetheart, believe him, de leef of a bond-
woman! But if dou vilt harken to me, I vill make tee a
free-woman, and a lady: dou shalt live like a lady, as te
captain saish.   35

Kno. Aye, and be honest too, sometimes: have her wires, and
her tires, her green gowns, and velvet petticoats.

Whit. Aye, and ride to Ware and Rumford i' dy coash, shee de
players, be in love vit 'em; sup vit gallantsh, be drunk,
and cost dee noting.   40

Kno. Brave vapours!

Whit. And lie by twenty on 'em, if dou pleash, shweetheart.

Win. What, and be honest still ? That were fine sport.

Whit. Tish common, shweetheart, tou may'st do it, by my
hand; it shall be justified to ty husband's faish, now: tou   45
shalt be as honesht as the skin between his hornsh, la!

Kno. Yes, and wear a dressing, top, and top-gallant, to compare with e'er a husband on 'em all, for a fore-top: it is the

30. leef] *This ed.;* life *F.*   40. dee] *This ed.;* de *F.*   44. it,] *HS;* it *F.*

---

36. *wires*] 'to beare vp the whole frame & body of the ruffe from falling
or hanging down' (Stubbes, *Anatomie of Abuses*, 1583, ed. Furnivall,
i. 52).

37. *tires*] dresses.

green gowns] with quibble: stained from the wearer's having been thrown
on to the grass; cf. ll. 91–2, v. iii. 86, v. vi. 48; *O.E.D.* quotes Munday,
Palmerin of England, 1602: 'At length he was so bold as to give her a green
gowne when I fear me she lost the flower of her chastity.'

38. *Ware and Rumford*] places for assignations; cf. Mrs Otter in *S.W.*,
III. ii. 73, 'taking a coach to goe to *Ware* to meet a friend', and *N.I.*, IV. iii.
70 ff.: 'he runnes . . . to *Rumford* . . . the next bawdy road: And takes me
out, carries me vp, and throw's me Vpon a bed'.

47. *top, and top-gallant*] in full sail.

48. *fore-top*] (*a*) top of a foremast; (*b*) the fore part of the crown of the
head or a lock of hair there (or part of a wig) sometimes ornamentally
arranged on the forehead.

vapour of spirit in the wife, to cuckold, nowadays; as it is
the vapour of fashion, in the husband, not to suspect.   50
Your prying cat-eyed-citizen is an abominable vapour.

Win. Lord, what a fool have I been!

Whit. Mend then, and do everything like a lady, hereafter;
never know ty husband, from another man.

Kno. Nor any one man from another, but i' the dark.   55

Whit. Aye, and then it ish no dishgrash to know any man.

[*Re-enter* URSULA.]

Urs. Help, help here.

Kno. How now ? What vapour's there ?

Urs. O, you are a sweet ranger! and look well to your walks.
Yonder is your punk of Turnbull, Ramping Alice, has   60
fall'n upon the poor gentlewoman within, and pull'd her
hood over her ears, and her hair through it.

ALICE *enters, beating the Justice's wife.*

Mrs. Over. Help, help, i' the King's name.

Alice. A mischief on you, they are such as you are, that undo
us, and take our trade from us, with your tuft taffeta   65
haunches.

Kno. How now, Alice!

Alice. The poor common whores can ha' no traffic, for the
privy rich ones; your caps and hoods of velvet call away
our customers, and lick the fat from us.   70

Urs. Peace, you foul ramping jade, you—

Alice. Od's foot, you bawd in grease, are you talking ?

Kno. Why, Alice, I say.

Alice. Thou sow of Smithfield, thou.

Urs. Thou tripe of Turnbull.   75

Kno. Cat-a-mountain-vapours! ha!

62.1. ALICE . . . *wife.*] F *margin, ll. 62–4.*   69. velvet] *1716;* veluet, F.

---

72. *in grease*] fat, ready for killing.
76. *Cat-a-mountain*] leopard or panther; cf. *Merry Wives of Windsor*, II.
ii. 27–9: 'your cat-a-mountain looks . . . your bold-beating oaths'.

Urs. You know where you were taw'd lately, both lash'd and slash'd you were in Bridewell.

Alice. Aye, by the same token, you rid that week, and broke out the bottom o' the cart, night-tub. 80

Kno. Why, lion face! ha! do you know who I am? Shall I tear ruff, slit waistcoat, make rags of petticoat! Ha! go to, vanish, for fear of vapours. Whit, a kick, Whit, in the parting vapour. [*They kick out* ALICE.] Come, brave woman, take a good heart, thou shalt be a lady, too. 85

Whit. Yes, fait, dey shall all both be ladies, and write Madam. I vill do't myself for dem. Do, is the vord, and D is the middle letter of Madam, DD, put 'em together and make deeds, without which all words are alike, la.

Kno. 'Tis true, Urs'la, take 'em in, open thy wardrobe, and fit 90 'em to their calling. Green gowns, crimson petticoats, green women! my Lord Mayor's green women! guests o' the game, true bred. I'll provide you a coach, to take the air in.

Win. But do you think you can get one? 95

Kno. O, they are as common as wheelbarrows where there are great dunghills. Every pettifogger's wife has 'em, for first he buys a coach, that he may marry, and then he marries that he may be made cuckold in't: for if their wives ride not to their cuckolding, they do 'em no credit. Hide, and 100 be hidden; ride, and be ridden, says the vapour of experience. [*Exeunt* URSULA, WIN, Mistress OVERDO.]

84. *They* . . . ALICE.] *G.*

---

77. *taw'd*] softened by beating (of hides).

78. *Bridewell*] '. . . for the Bawd, the Rogue, and Whore' (Dekker, *Honest Whore*, pt 2, V. ii. 44).

79. *rid*] in the cart for whores.

80. *night-tub*] tub for filth or night-soil.

82. *tear ruff*] G. compares Pistol in *2 Henry IV*, II. iv. 154–5, '. . . tearing a poor whore's ruff in a bawdy-house'.

waistcoat] a short garment worn by women about the upper part of the body, usually beneath an outer gown, but so as to be seen; when worn without the latter, apparently the mark of prostitutes, sometimes called *waistcoateers* (*O.E.D.*).

Act IV. Scene VI.

[*Enter*] TROUBLE-ALL.

[*Tro.*] By what warrant does it say so?

Kno. Ha! mad child o' the Pie-powders, art thou there? Fill
us a fresh can, Urs, we may drink together.

Tro. I may not drink without a warrant, captain.

Kno. 'Slood, thou'll not stale without a warrant, shortly.   5
Whit, give me pen, ink and paper. I'll draw him a warrant
presently.

Tro. It must be Justice Overdo's!

Kno. I know, man. Fetch the drink, Whit.

Whit. I pre dee now, be very brief, captain; for de new ladies   10
stay for dee.

Kno. O, as brief as can be, here 'tis already. Adam Overdo.

Tro. Why, now, I'll pledge you, captain.

Kno. Drink it off. I'll come to thee, anon, again.   [*Exeunt.*]

[*Enter*] QUARLOUS, EDGWORTH.

Quar. Well, sir. You are now discharg'd: beware of being   15
spied, hereafter.   QUARLOUS *to the cutpurse.*

Edg. Sir, will it please you, enter in here, at Urs'la's; and take
part of a silken gown, a velvet petticoat, or a wrought
smock; I am promis'd such: and I can spare any gentleman a moiety.   20

Quar. Keep it for your companions in beastliness, I am none
of 'em, sir. If I had not already forgiven you a greater tres-
pass, or thought you yet worth my beating, I would in-
struct your manners, to whom you made your offers. But
go your ways, talk not to me, the hangman is only fit to   25

IV. vi. 0.1. TROUBLE-ALL.] TROBLE-ALL. KNOCKHVM. WHIT. QVARLOVS.
EDGVVORTH. BRISTLE. WASPE. HAGGISE. IVSTICE. BVSY. PVRE-CRAFT. *F.*
16. QUARLOUS *to the cutpurse.*] *F margin, ll. 15–17.*

IV. vi. 7. *presently*] at once.
17–18. *take part of*] partake of, have a share in.
20. *moiety*] a half, a share.

discourse with you; the hand of beadle is too merciful a
punishment for your trade of life. [*Exit* EDGWORTH.] I
am sorry I employ'd this fellow; for he thinks me such:
Facinus quos inquinat, æquat. But, it was for sport. And
would I make it serious, the getting of this licence is no-   30
thing to me, without other circumstances concur. I do
think how impertinently I labour, if the word be not mine
that the ragged fellow mark'd: and what advantage I have
given Ned Winwife in this time now, of working her,
though it be mine. He'll go near to form to her what a de-   35
bauch'd rascal I am, and fright her out of all good conceit
of me: I should do so by him, I am sure, if I had the
opportunity. But my hope is in her temper, yet; and it
must needs be next to despair, that is grounded on any
part of a woman's discretion. I would give, by my troth,   40
now, all I could spare (to my clothes, and my sword) to
meet my tatter'd soothsayer again, who was my judge i'
the question, to know certainly whose word he has damn'd
or sav'd. For, till then, I live but under a reprieve. I must
seek him. Who be these?   45

Enter WASP *with the officers.*

Wasp. Sir, you are a Welsh cuckold, and a prating runt, and
no constable.
Bri. You say very well. Come put in his leg in the middle
roundel, and let him hole there.
Wasp. You stink of leeks, metheglin, and cheese. You rogue.   50
Bri. Why, what is that to you, if you sit sweetly in the stocks in
the meantime? If you have a mind to stink too, your
breeches sit close enough to your bum. Sit you merry, sir.

45.1. *Enter . . . officers.*] F *margin, ll. 46–7.*

---

29. Facinus . . . æquat] Lucan, *Pharsalia*, v. 290: 'Crime levels those
whom it pollutes' (J. D. Duff).
32. *impertinently*] to no purpose.
35. *form*] formulate.
46. *runt*] an ignorant, uncouth person.
50. *metheglin*] Welsh mead.

Quar. How now, Numps ?

Wasp. It is no matter, how; pray you look off.   55

Quar. Nay, I'll not offend you, Numps. I thought you had sat there to be seen.

Wasp. And to be sold, did you not ? Pray you mind your business, an' you have any.

Quar. Cry you mercy, Numps. Does your leg lie high   60 enough ?

Bri. How now, neighbour Haggis, what says Justice Overdo's worship, to the other offenders ?

Hag. Why, he says just nothing, what should he say ? Or where should he say ? He is not to be found, man. He ha'   65 not been seen i' the Fair, here, all this live-long day, never since seven o'clock i' the morning. His clerks know not what to think on't. There is no court of Pie-powders yet. Here they be return'd.

[*Enter others of the watch with* JUSTICE *and* BUSY.]

Bri. What shall be done with 'em, then, in your discretion ?   70

Hag. I think we were best put 'em in the stocks, in discretion (there they will be safe in discretion) for the valour of an hour, or such a thing, till his worship come.

Bri. It is but a hole matter if we do, neighbour Haggis; come, sir, here is company for you; heave up the stocks.   75

Wasp. [*Aside*] I shall put a trick upon your Welsh diligence, perhaps.

As they open the stocks, WASP *puts his shoe on his hand,
and slips it in for his leg.*

Bri. Put in your leg, sir.

Quar. What, Rabbi Busy! Is he come ?

They bring BUSY, *and put him in.*

69.1. *Enter* . . . BUSY.] G.   77.1-2. *As* . . . *leg.*] F *margin, ll. 73–8.*
79.1. *They* . . . *in.*] F *margin, ll. 80–2.*

___

70, 71, 72. *discretion*] (*a*) judgement; (*b*) prudence; (*c*) separation, cf.
O.E.D. 1614: 'certaine discretion of true Prophets from false'.
72. *valour*] amount, quantity.

Busy. I do obey thee; the lion may roar, but he cannot bite. I   80
am glad to be thus separated from the heathen of the land,
and put apart in the stocks, for the holy cause.

Wasp. What are you, sir?

Busy. One that rejoiceth in his affliction, and sitteth here
to prophesy the destruction of Fairs and May-games,   85
Wakes, and Whitsun-ales, and doth sigh and groan for the
reformation of these abuses.

[*They put* JUSTICE *in the stocks.*]

Wasp. And do you sigh and groan too, or rejoice in your affliction?

Jus. I do not feel it, I do not think of it, it is a thing without me.   90
Adam, thou art above these batt'ries, these contumelies.
In te manca ruit fortuna, as thy friend Horace says; thou
art one, *Quem neque pauperies, neque mors, neque vincula
terrent.* And therefore, as another friend of thine says (I
think it be thy friend Persius), *Non te quæsiveris extra.*   95

Quar. What's here! A stoic i' the stocks? The fool is turn'd
philosopher.

Busy. Friend, I will leave to communicate my spirit with
you, if I hear any more of those superstitious relics, those
lists of Latin, the very rags of Rome, and patches of   100
Popery.

Wasp. Nay, an' you begin to quarrel, gentlemen, I'll leave
you. I ha' paid for quarrelling too lately: look you, a
device, but shifting in a hand for a foot. God b' w' you.

---

90. *a thing without me*] again 'the lofty language of Stoicism. He begins
with the distinctions of Epictetus—τὰ ἐφ' ἡμῖν and τὰ οὐκ ἐφ' ἡμῖν' (G.).
See *Encheiridion,* I. i.

92–4. In . . . terrent] adapting Horace, *Sat.,* II. vii. 83–8: 'Who then is
free? The wise man, who has dominion over himself; whom neither
poverty nor death nor chains affright'; 'in her assaults upon you Fortune
is powerless' or 'maims herself'.

95. Non . . . extra] Persius, *Sat.,* i. 7: 'Look to no one outside yourself'
(G. G. Ramsay).

100. *lists*] strips (of cloth).

Latin] H. & S. quote *The Returne from Pernassus,* pt. II, II. iv [ed. Leish-
man, 1949, ll. 676–7]: 'this popish tongue of Latine'.

He gets out.

Busy. Wilt thou then leave thy brethren in tribulation?　　　105
Wasp. For this once, sir.　　　　　　　　　　　　　[*Exit.*]
Busy. Thou art a halting neutral—stay him there, stop him
　　—that will not endure the heat of persecution.
Bri. How now, what's the matter?
Busy. He is fled, he is fled, and dares not sit it out.　　　110
Bri. What, has he made an escape? Which way? Follow,
　　neighbour Haggis.　　　　　　　　　　[*Exit* HAGGIS.]

[*Enter*] PURECRAFT.

Pure. O me! In the stocks! Have the wicked prevail'd?
Busy. Peace, religious sister, it is my calling, comfort your-
　　self, an extraordinary calling, and done for my better　115
　　standing, my surer standing, hereafter.

The madman enters.

Tro. By whose warrant, by whose warrant, this?
Quar. O, here's my man dropp'd in, I look'd for.
Jus. Ha!
Pure. O good sir, they have set the faithful, here, to be won-　120
　　der'd at; and provided holes, for the holy of the land.
Tro. Had they warrant for it? Show'd they Justice Overdo's
　　hand? If they had no warrant, they shall answer it.

[*Re-enter* HAGGIS.]

Bri. Sure you did not lock the stocks sufficiently, neighbour
　　Toby!　　　　　　　　　　　　　　　　　　　　125
Hag. No! See if you can lock 'em better.
Bri. They are very sufficiently lock'd, and truly, yet some-
　　thing is in the matter.
Tro. True, your warrant is the matter that is in question; by
　　what warrant?　　　　　　　　　　　　　　　　130
Bri. Madman, hold your peace; I will put you in his room
　　else, in the very same hole, do you see?

104.1. *He gets out.*] F *margin, l. 103.*　　116.1. *The madman enters.*] F *margin, ll. 117–18.*　　118. man] *1716;* man! F.

Quar. How! Is he a madman?

Tro. Show me Justice Overdo's warrant, I obey you.

Hag. You are a mad fool, hold your tongue.   135

                      [Exeunt HAGGIS, BRISTLE.]

Tro. In Justice Overdo's name, I drink to you, and here's my

    warrant.   *Shows his can.*

Jus. [Aside] Alas, poor wretch! How it yearns my heart for

    him!

Quar. [Aside] If he be mad, it is in vain to question him. I'll   140

    try, though. *[To him]* Friend, there was a gentlewoman

    show'd you two names, some hour since, Argalus and

    Palemon, to mark in a book; which of 'em was it you

    mark'd?

Tro. I mark no name, but Adam Overdo; that is the name of   145

    names; he only is the sufficient magistrate; and that

    name I reverence; show it me.

Quar. [Aside] This fellow's mad indeed: I am further off,

    now, than afore.

Jus. [Aside] I shall not breathe in peace, till I have made him   150

    some amends.

Quar. [Aside] Well, I will make another use of him, is come

    in my head: I have a nest of beards in my trunk, one

    something like his.

             The watchmen come back again.

Bri. This mad fool has made me that I know not whether I   155

    have lock'd the stocks or no; I think I lock'd 'em.

Tro. Take Adam Overdo in your mind, and fear nothing.

Bri. 'Slid, madness itself, hold thy peace, and take that.

Tro. Strikest thou without a warrant? Take thou that.

---

134. warrant,] *F3;* warrant. *F.*   137. *Shows his can.*] *F margin, ll. 136-7.*
141. though. Friend,] *F3;* though, friend: *F.*   154.1. *The ... again.*] *F*
margin, ll. 155-7.   155-6. I have] *F3;* I I haue *F.*

---

138. *yearns*] moves to compassion; cf. *Merry Wives of Windsor,* III. v.
44-5: 'She laments, sir, for it, that it would yearn your heart to see it.'
    153. *nest*] collection.
    trunk] trunk-hose, stuffed breeches reaching to the knees.

The madman fights with 'em, and they leave open the stocks.

Busy. We are delivered by miracle; fellow in fetters, let us not　160
　　refuse the means; this madness was of the spirit: the
　　malice of the enemy hath mock'd itself.

　　　　　　　　　　　　　　　　　[*Exeunt* BUSY *and* JUSTICE.]

Pure. Mad, do they call him! The world is mad in error, but
　　he is mad in truth: I love him o' the sudden (the cunning
　　man said all true) and shall love him more, and more.　165
　　How well it becomes a man to be mad in truth! O, that I
　　might be his yoke-fellow, and be mad with him, what a
　　many should we draw to madness in truth, with us.　　[*Exit.*]

　　　The watch, missing them, are affrighted.

Bri. How now! All 'scap'd? Where's the woman? It is witch-
　　craft! Her velvet hat is a witch, o' my conscience, or my　170
　　key, t' one! The madman was a devil, and I am an ass; so
　　bless me, my place, and mine office.　　　　　　　[*Exeunt.*]

159.1. *The . . . stocks.*] F *margin, ll. 158–62.*　　168.1. *The . . . affrighted.*]
F *margin, ll. 169–72.*

---

171. *t' one*] the one or the other.

Act V

Scene I

[*Enter*] LEATHERHEAD, FILCHER, SHARKWELL.

[*Lea.*] Well, Luck and Saint Bartholomew! Out with the sign
of our invention, in the name of Wit, and do you beat the
drum, the while; all the foul i' the Fair, I mean all the dirt
in Smithfield (that's one of Master Littlewit's carriwitchets now), will be thrown at our banner today, if the   5
matter does not please the people. O the motions, that I
Lantern Leatherhead have given light to, i' my time,
since my Master Pod died! *Jerusalem* was a stately thing;
and so was *Nineveh*, and *The City of Norwich*, and *Sodom
and Gomorrah*; with the rising o' the prentices, and pull-   10
ing down the bawdy houses there, upon Shrove Tuesday;
but *The Gunpowder Plot*, there was a get-penny! I have
presented that to an eighteen-, or twenty-pence audience,
nine times in an afternoon. Your home-born projects
prove ever the best, they are so easy, and familiar; they   15
put too much learning i' their things now o' days: and that
I fear will be the spoil o' this. Littlewit? I say, Mickle-
wit! if not too mickle! Look to your gathering there, good
man Filcher.

0.1. LEATHERHEAD,] LANTHORNE, *F.*   10. prentices,] *F3;* prentises; *F.*

---

1. *sign*] the 'banner' of l. 5.
2. *invention*] work of imagination, play.
4–5. *carriwitchets*] quibbles.
8. *Pod*] 'Pod *was a Master of Motions before him*', Jonson's marginal note;
see III. iv. 121 n.; he is 'Captain' Pod in *E.M.O.*, IV. v. 62 and *Ep.*, xcvii.
11. *Shrove Tuesday*] which the apprentices notoriously celebrated by riot
and wreckage of brothels and theatres.
14. *projects*] conceptions, designs; cf. v. ii. 10.
18. *mickle*] great.

Fil. I warrant you, sir. 20

Lea. An' there come any gentlefolks, take twopence a piece,
    Sharkwell.

Shar. I warrant you, Sir, threepence an' we can. [*Exeunt.*]

Act V. Scene II.

The JUSTICE *comes in like a porter.*

[*Jus.*] This later disguise, I have borrow'd of a porter, shall
    carry me out to all my great and good ends; which, how-
    ever interrupted, were never destroyed in me: neither is
    the hour of my severity yet come, to reveal myself, where-
    in, cloud-like, I will break out in rain and hail, lightning 5
    and thunder, upon the head of enormity. Two main works
    I have to prosecute: first, one is to invent some satisfac-
    tion for the poor, kind wretch, who is out of his wits for
    my sake; and yonder I see him coming; I will walk aside,
    and project for it. 10

[*Enter*] WINWIFE, GRACE.

Winw. I wonder where Tom Quarlous is, that he returns not;
    it may be he is struck in here to seek us.

Grace. See, here's our madman again.

[*Enter*] QUARLOUS, PURECRAFT. QUARLOUS *in the habit of the mad-
    man is mistaken by* Mistress PURECRAFT.

Quar. [*Aside*] I have made myself as like him, as his gown and
    cap will give me leave. 15

Pure. Sir, I love you, and would be glad to be mad with you
    in truth.

Winw. How! my widow in love with a madman?

Pure. Verily, I can be as mad in spirit, as you.

v. ii. o.i. *The . . . porter.] F margin, ll. 1–3;* IVSTICE. WIN-WIFE. GRACE.
QVARLOVS. PVRE-CRAFT. *F.* 13.1–2. QUARLOUS[2] *. . .* PURECRAFT.] *F margin,
ll. 14–19.*

Quar. By whose warrant ? Leave your canting. Gentlewoman,   20
    have I found you ? (Save ye, quit ye, and multiply ye.)
    Where's your book ? 'Twas a sufficient name I mark'd, let
    me see't, be not afraid to shew't me.

                He desires to see the book of Mistress GRACE.

Grace. What would you with it, sir ?

Quar. Mark it again, and again, at your service.   25

Grace. Here it is, sir, this was it you mark'd.

Quar. Palemon ? Fare you well, fare you well.

Winw. How, Palemon!

Grace. Yes, faith, he has discover'd it to you, now, and there-
    fore 'twere vain to disguise it longer; I am yours, sir, by   30
    the benefit of your fortune.

Winw. And you have him, Mistress, believe it, that shall
    never give you cause to repent her benefit, but make you
    rather to think that, in this choice, she had both her eyes.

Grace. I desire to put it to no danger of protestation.   35

                  [*Exeunt* GRACE *and* WINWIFE.]

Quar. Palemon, the word, and Winwife the man ?

Pure. Good sir, vouchsafe a yoke-fellow in your madness;
    shun not one of the sanctified sisters, that would draw
    with you, in truth.

Quar. Away, you are a herd of hypocritical proud ignorants,   40
    rather wild, than mad. Fitter for woods, and the society of
    beasts, than houses, and the congregation of men. You are
    the second part of the society of canters, outlaws to order
    and discipline, and the only privileg'd church-robbers of
    Christendom. Let me alone. Palemon, the word, and   45
    Winwife the man ?

Pure. [*Aside*] I must uncover myself unto him, or I shall never
    enjoy him, for all the cunning men's promises. [*To him*]
    Good sir, hear me, I am worth six thousand pound; my

23.1. *He . . .* GRACE.] F *margin, ll. 22–4.*

20. *canting*] (pious) jargon, cf. l. 43.
34. *had . . . eyes*] The goddess of Fortune is usually represented as blind-folded.

love to you is become my rack; I'll tell you all, and the　50
truth, since you hate the hypocrisy of the party-coloured
brotherhood. These seven years, I have been a wilful holy
widow only to draw feasts and gifts from my entangled
suitors: I am also by office, an assisting sister of the dea-
cons, and a devourer, instead of a distributor of the alms.　55
I am a special maker of marriages for our decayed brethren with our rich widows; for a third part of their wealth,
when they are married, for the relief of the poor elect: as
also our poor handsome young virgins with our wealthy
bachelors, or widowers; to make them steal from their　60
husbands, when I have confirmed them in the faith, and
got all put into their custodies. And if I ha' not my bargain, they may sooner turn a scolding drab into a silent
minister, than make me leave pronouncing reprobation,
and damnation unto them. Our elder, Zeal-of-the-land,　65
would have had me, but I know him to be the capital
knave of the land, making himself rich by being made
feoffee in trust to deceased brethren, and coz'ning their
heirs by swearing the absolute gift of their inheritance.
And thus, having eas'd my conscience, and utter'd my　70
heart, with the tongue of my love:—enjoy all my deceits
together. I beseech you. I should not have revealed this to
you, but that in time I think you are mad; and I hope
you'll think me so too, sir?

Quar.　Stand aside, I'll answer you, presently.　75

He considers with himself of it.

50. you¹] *F3;* you, *F.*　51. truth,] *F3;* truth: *F.*　75.1. *He . . . it.*] *F
margin, ll.* 75-7.

63-4. *silent minister*] one of 'the silenc'd saints' whom Tribulation
Wholesome wished to 'restore' (*A.,* III. i. 38), i.e. those excommunicated
for non-compliance with the canons approved by the Hampton Court con-
ference of 1604.

68. *feoffee in trust*] a trustee invested with a freehold estate in land.

73. *in time*] ? at a suitable time; cf. Stubbes: 'The word of God is to be
preached night and day, in time, and out of time, in season and out of
season' (*op. cit.,* ii. 78).

Why should not I marry this six thousand pound, now I
think on't? And a good trade too, that she has beside, ha?
The tother wench, Winwife is sure of; there's no expectation for me there! Here I may make myself some saver;
yet, if she continue mad, there's the question. It is money   80
that I want; why should I not marry the money, when 'tis
offer'd me? I have a licence and all, it is but razing out one
name, and putting in another. There's no playing with a
man's fortune. I am resolv'd! I were truly mad, an' I
would not! [*To her*] Well, come your ways, follow me, an'   85
you will be mad, I'll show you a warrant!

> *He takes her along with him.*

Pure. Most zealously, it is that I zealously desire.

> *The* JUSTICE *calls him.*

Jus. Sir, let me speak with you.

Quar. By whose warrant?

Jus. The warrant that you tender, and respect so; Justice   90
Overdo's! I am the man, friend Trouble-all, though thus
disguis'd (as the careful magistrate ought) for the good of
the republic, in the Fair, and the weeding out of enormity. Do you want a house or meat, or drink, or clothes?
Speak whatsoever it is, it shall be supplied you; what want   95
you?

Quar. Nothing but your warrant.

Jus. My warrant? For what?

Quar. To be gone, sir.

Jus. Nay, I pray thee stay, I am serious, and have not many   100
words, nor much time to exchange with thee; think what
may do thee good.

Quar. Your hand and seal, will do me a great deal of good;
nothing else in the whole Fair, that I know.

Jus. If it were to any end, thou should'st have it willingly.   105

78. Winwife] *F3;* Winwife, *F.*   86.1. *He . . . him.*] *F margin, ll. 85–7.*
87.1. *The* JUSTICE *. . . him.*] *F margin, l. 88.*

_____

79. *make . . . saver*] compensate for loss (a gaming term).

Quar. Why, it will satisfy me, that's end enough, to look on;
  an' you will not gi' it me, let me go.

Jus. Alas! thou shalt ha' it presently: I'll but step into the
  scrivener's, hereby, and bring it. Do not go away.

                                      The JUSTICE *goes out.*

Quar. [*Aside*] Why, this madman's shape will prove a very   110
  fortunate one, I think! Can a ragged robe produce these
  effects? If this be the wise Justice, and he bring me
  his hand, I shall go near to make some use on't.

              [JUSTICE] *returns.*

He is come already!

Jus. Look thee! here is my hand and seal, Adam Overdo; if   115
  there be anything to be written, above in the paper, that
  thou want'st now, or at any time hereafter, think on't; it
  is my deed, I deliver it so; can your friend write?

Quar. Her hand for a witness, and all is well.

Jus. With all my heart.   120

            He urgeth Mistress PURECRAFT.

Quar. [*Aside*] Why should not I ha' the conscience to make
  this a bond of a thousand pound, now? or what I would
  else?

Jus. Look you, there it is; and I deliver it as my deed again.

Quar. Let us now proceed in madness.   *He takes her in with him.*

Jus. Well, my conscience is much eas'd; I ha' done my part;   126
  though it doth him no good, yet Adam hath offer'd satisfaction! The sting is removed from hence: poor man, he
  is much alter'd with his affliction, it has brought him
  low! Now, for my other work, reducing the young man I   130

109.1. *The* JUSTICE . . . *out.*] *F margin, ll. 109–10.*   113.1. *returns.*] *and
returns. F margin, l. 114.*   120.1. *He* . . . PURECRAFT.] *F margin, ll. 119–21.*
122. *pound, now?*] *HS; pound? now, F.*   125. *He* . . . *him.*] *F margin,
ll. 125–7.*

---

121. *conscience*] good sense, sound judgement; cf. *Timon of Athens,* II. ii.
185–6: 'Canst thou the conscience lack, To think I shall lack friends?'
  130. *reducing*] bringing back, recalling.

have follow'd so long in love, from the brink of his bane
to the centre of safety. Here, or in some such like vain
place, I shall be sure to find him. I will wait the good
time.

Act V. Scene III.

[Enter] COKES, SHARKWELL, FILCHER.

[Cok.] How now? What's here to do? Friend, art thou the
master of the monuments?

Shar. 'Tis a motion, an't please your worship.

Jus. [Aside] My fantastical brother-in-law, Master Bartholomew Cokes!   5

Cok. A motion, what's that?

He reads the bill.

'The ancient modern history of *Hero and Leander*, otherwise called *The Touch-stone of true Love*, with as true a
trial of friendship, between Damon and Pythias, two
faithful friends o' the Bankside?' Pretty i' faith, what's the   10
meaning on't? Is't an interlude? or what is't?

Fil. Yes, sir; please you come near, we'll take your money
within.

Cok. Back with these children; they do so follow me up and
down.   *The boys o' the Fair follow him.* 15

[Enter] LITTLEWIT.

Lit. By your leave, friend.

Fil. You must pay, sir, an' you go in.

Lit. Who, I? I perceive thou know'st not me: call the master
o' the motion.

v. iii. o.i. COKES, . . . FILCHER.] COKES. SHAKRVVEL. IVSTICE. FILCHER. IOHN.
LANTERNE. *F.*   6.i. *He . . . bill.*] F margin, *ll. 6–8.*   15. *The . . . him.*]
F margin, *ll. 14–16.*

v. iii. 11. *interlude*] a comedy or farce.

Shar. What, do you not know the author, fellow Filcher? You　20
　　must take no money of him; he must come in *gratis*: Mas-
　　ter Littlewit is a voluntary; he is the author.

Lit. Peace, speak not too loud, I would not have any notice
　　taken, that I am the author, till we see how it passes.

Cok. Master Littlewit, how dost thou?　　25

Lit. Master Cokes! you are exceeding well met: what, in your
　　doublet and hose, without a cloak or a hat?

Cok. I would I might never stir, as I am an honest man, and by
　　that fire; I have lost all i' the Fair, and all my acquaintance
　　too; didst thou meet anybody that I know, Master Little-　30
　　wit? My man Numps, or my sister Overdo, or Mistress
　　Grace? Pray thee, Master Littlewit, lend me some money
　　to see the interlude, here. I'll pay thee again, as I am a
　　gentleman. If thou'lt but carry me home, I have money
　　enough there.　　35

Lit. O, sir, you shall command it; what, will a crown serve
　　you?

Cok. I think it will. What do we pay for coming in, fellows?

Fil. Twopence, sir.

Cok. Twopence? there's twelvepence, friend; nay, I am a gal-　40
　　lant, as simple as I look now, if you see me with my man
　　about me, and my artillery, again.

Lit. Your man was i' the stocks, e'en now, sir.

Cok. Who, Numps?

Lit. Yes, faith.　　45

Cok. For what, i' faith? I am glad o' that; remember to tell me
　　on't anon; I have enough, now! What manner of matter is
　　this, Master Littlewit? What kind of actors ha' you? Are
　　they good actors?

Lit. Pretty youths, sir, all children both old and young, here's　50
　　the master of 'em—

[*Enter*] LEATHERHEAD.

38. will] *F3;* well *F.*　　46. faith?] *1716;* faith, *F.*

---

22. *voluntary*] volunteer, who usually served without pay.

Why?

Lea. (Call me not Leatherhead, but Lantern.)

LEATHERHEAD *whispers to* LITTLEWIT.

Lit. Master Lantern, that gives light to the business.

Cok. In good time, sir, I would fain see 'em, I would be glad drink with the young company; which is the tiring-house? 55

Lea. Troth sir, our tiring-house is somewhat little; we are but beginners, yet, pray pardon us; you cannot go upright in't.

Cok. No? Not now my hat is off? What would you have done with me, if you had had me, feather and all, as I was once today? Ha' you none of your pretty impudent boys, now, 60 to bring stools, fill tobacco, fetch ale, and beg money, as they have at other houses? Let me see some o' your actors.

Lit. Show him 'em, show him 'em. Master Lantern, this is a gentleman, that is a favourer of the quality. 65

Jus. [*Aside*] Aye, the favouring of this licentious quality is the consumption of many a young gentleman; a pernicious enormity.

Cok. What, do they live in baskets?

Lea. They do lie in a basket, sir, they are o' the small players. 70

He brings them out in a basket.

Cok. These be players minors, indeed. Do you call these players?

Lea. They are actors, sir, and as good as any, none disprais'd, for dumb shows: indeed, I am the mouth of 'em all!

Cok. Thy mouth will hold 'em all. I think, one Taylor would 75

52.1. LEATHERHEAD . . . LITTLEWIT.] *F margin, ll. 52–4.* 70.1. *He . . . basket.*] *F margin, ll. 69–70.*

52. (*Call . . . Lantern.*)] to prevent recognition; cf. III. vi. 132–3.

65. *quality*] (acting) profession; cf. Hamlet to the actors: 'Come, give us a taste of your quality' (II. ii. 460–1).

74. *mouth*] interpreter; cf. *Hamlet,* III. ii. 260–1: 'I could interpret between you and your love, if I could see the puppets dallying.'

75. *Taylor*] a three-fold allusion (*a*) to the timidity of tailors; (*b*) to the then recent occasion, on 7 October 1614, when John Taylor the water poet 'did agree with William Fennor . . . to answer me at a triall of *Wit* . . . on the *Hope* stage on the *Bank-side*'. Fennor defaulted and Taylor entertained the audience till the regular players took over. 'For 'tis not possible for any

go near to beat all this company, with a hand bound behind him.

Lit. Aye, and eat 'em all, too, an' they were in cake-bread.

Cok. I thank you for that, Master Littlewit, a good jest! Which
is your Burbage now ?   80

Lea. What mean you by that, sir ?

Cok. Your best actor. Your Field ?

Lit. Good, i' faith! You are even with me, sir.

Lea. This is he that acts young Leander, sir. He is extremely
belov'd of the womenkind, they do so affect his action, the   85
green gamesters that come here; and this is lovely Hero;
this with the beard, Damon; and this, pretty Pythias : this
is the ghost of King Dionysius in the habit of a scrivener :
as you shall see anon, at large.

Cok. Well they are a civil company, I like 'em for that; they   90
offer not to fleer, nor jeer, nor break jests, as the great
players do : and then, there goes not so much charge to the
feasting of 'em, or making 'em drunk, as to the other, by
reason of their littleness. Do they use to play perfect ? Are
they never fluster'd ?   95

Lea. No, sir, I thank my industry and policy for it; they are
as well-govern'd a company, though I say it—and here

---

one To play against a company alone' (Taylor, *Works*, 1630, pp. 143, 145);
(c) to the actor Joseph Taylor who was among the Lady Elizabeth's men in
1614, and probably in the cast of this play.

78. *eat 'em*] Tailors were proverbially voracious; cf. Massinger and Field,
The Fatal Dowry, 1632, v. i (ed. Gifford, iii. 447): 'As you are merely A
tailor, . . . You are a companion at a ten-crown supper . . . and may with one
lark, Eat up three manchets [loaves]'.

80. *Burbage*] for other references to the high reputation of the great tragic
actor (1573–1619) see Chambers, ii. 308. He had acted in *E.M.I.* (1598),
E.M.O. (1599), *S.* (1603), *V.* (1605), *A.* (1610), *C.* (1611).

82. *Field*] Nathan Field (1587–?1620) had been Jonson's 'schollar &
he had read to him the Satyres of Horace & some Epigrammes of Mar-
tiall' (*Conversations with Drummond*, xi. H. & S., i. 137). He appears in
the actor lists of *C.R.* (1600), *Poet.* (1601), *S.W.* (1609), and *B.F.* See
Chambers, ii. 316–18, Bentley, *Jacobean and Caroline Stage*, ii, 1941,
pp. 434–6.

88. *habit of a scrivener*] cf. v. iv. 345.

is young Leander, is as proper an actor of his inches; and
shakes his head like an ostler.

Cok. But do you play it according to the printed book ? I have   100
read that.

Lea. By no means, sir.

Cok. No ? How then ?

Lea. A better way, sir; that is too learned and poetical for our
audience; what do they know what Hellespont is ?   105
'Guilty of true love's blood ?' Or what Abydos is ? Or 'the
other Sestos hight ?'

Cok. Th' art i' the right, I do not know myself.

Lea. No, I have entreated Master Littlewit, to take a little
pains to reduce it to a more familiar strain for our people.   110

Cok. How, I pray thee, good Master Littlewit ?

Lit. It pleases him to make a matter of it, sir. But there is no
such matter I assure you: I have only made it a little
easy, and modern for the times, sir, that's all; as, for the
Hellespont, I imagine our Thames here; and then   115
Leander I make a dyer's son, about Puddle-wharf; and
Hero a wench o' the Bank-side, who going over one
morning, to old Fish-street, Leander spies her land at
Trig-stairs, and falls in love with her: now do I introduce
Cupid, having metamorphos'd himself into a drawer,   120

104. sir;] *G;* Sir, *F.*   118. -street,] *F3;* -street; *F.*

---

99. *like an ostler*] perhaps alluding to William Ostler (d. 16 December
1614) who as one of the 'Children of Queene Elizabeths Chappell' had
taken a part in *Poet.* in 1601, and, after joining the King's men, in *A.* (1610)
and *C.* (1611).

100. *the printed book*] Marlowe's *Hero and Leander*, 1598, from the first
four lines of which Leatherhead quotes in his next speech but one.

114. *modern*] commonplace, everyday; new-fashioned.

116. *Puddle-wharf*] between Blackfriars and Paul's Stairs, 'a water gate
into the Thames, where horses vse to be watered, & therfore being filed with
their trampling, and made puddle . . .' (Stow, ii. 13).

118. *old Fish-street*] a continuation eastwards of the present Knightrider
Street, which is even in Stow an alternative title for this chief resort of 'wet
Fishmongers' (i. 81).

119. *Trig-stairs*] at the end of Trig Lane, a little downstream from Paul's
Stairs (Stow, ii. 11).

and he strikes Hero in love with a pint of sherry; and
other pretty passages there are, o' the friendship, that
will delight you, sir, and please you of judgement.

Cok. I'll be sworn they shall; I am in love with the actors
already, and I'll be allied to them presently. (They re-   125
spect gentlemen, these fellows.) Hero shall be my fairing: but, which of my fairings? Le' me see—i' faith, my
fiddle! and Leander my fiddle-stick: then Damon, my
drum; and Pythias, my pipe, and the ghost of Dionysius,
my hobby-horse. All fitted.   130

Act V. Scene IV.

[*Enter*] *to them* WINWIFE, GRACE.

[*Winw.*] Look, yonder's your Cokes gotten in among his play-
fellows; I thought we could not miss him, at such a spectacle.

Grace. Let him alone, he is so busy, he will never spy us.

Lea. Nay, good sir.   COKES *is handling the puppets.*   5

Cok. I warrant thee, I will not hurt her, fellow; what, dost
think me uncivil? I pray thee be not jealous: I am toward
a wife.

Lit. Well, good Master Lantern, make ready to begin, that I
may fetch my wife, and look you be perfect; you undo me   10
else, i' my reputation.

Lea. I warrant you, sir, do not you breed too great an expectation of it, among your friends: that's the only hurter of
these things.

Lit. No, no, no.   [*Exit.*]   15

---

129. pipe,] *F3; Pipe F.*

v. iv. 0.1. *to* . . . GRACE.] *To them* WIN-WIFE. GRACE. KNOCKHVM. WHITT.
EDGVVORTH. WIN. *Mistris* OVERDOO. *And to them* WASPE. F.   5. COKES . . .
puppets.] *F margin, ll. 5–8.*

---

v. iv. 7. *toward*] in prospect of or preparation for.

Cok. I'll stay here, and see; pray thee let me see.

Winw. How diligent and troublesome he is!

Gra. The place becomes him, methinks.

Jus. [*Aside*] My ward, Mistress Grace, in the company of a
    stranger? I doubt I shall be compell'd to discover myself,   20
    before my time!

    [*Enter*] KNOCKEM, EDGWORTH, WIN, WHIT, Mistress OVERDO.
            The door-keepers speak.

Fil. Twopence apiece, gentlemen, an excellent motion.

Kno. Shall we have fine fireworks, and good vapours?

Shar. Yes, captain, and waterworks, too.

Whit. I pree dee, take a care o' dy shmall lady, there, Edg-   25
    worth; I will look to dish tall lady myself.

Lea. Welcome, gentlemen, welcome, gentlemen.

Whit. Predee, mashter o' de monshtersh, help a very sick lady,
    here, to a chair, to shit in.

Lea. Presently, sir.   30

        They bring Mistress OVERDO *a chair.*

Whit. Good fait now, Urs'la's ale and *aqua vitae* ish to blame
    for't; shit down, shweetheart, shit down, and shleep a
    little.

Edg. Madam, you are very welcome hither.

Kno. Yes, and you shall see very good vapours.   35

Jus. [*Aside*] Here is my care come! I like to see him in so good
    company; and yet I wonder that persons of such fashion,
    should resort hither!   *By* EDGWORTH.

Edg. This is a very private house, madam.

21.2. *The door-keepers speak.*] F *margin, ll. 22–4.*   23. vapours?] *1716;*
vapours! F.   30.1. *They . . . chair.*] F *margin, ll. 31–4.*   38. *By* EDG-
WORTH.] F *margin, ll. 36–8.*

---

    17. *troublesome*] laborious.
    26. *tall*] fine, comely; cf. *Midsummer Night's Dream*, v. i. 146: 'Anon
comes Pyramus, sweet youth and tall'.
    31. aqua vitae] ardent spirits.
    38. By] with reference to.

Lea. Will it please your ladyship sit, madam?   40

    The cutpurse courts Mistress LITTLEWIT.

Win. Yes, good-man. They do so all-to-be-madam me, I
    think they think me a very lady!

Edg. What else, madam?

Win. Must I put off my mask to him?

Edg. O, by no means.   45

Win. How should my husband know me, then?

Kno. Husband? an idle vapour; he must not know you, nor
    you him; there's the true vapour.

Jus. [*Aside*] Yea, I will observe more of this. [*To Whit*] Is this a
    lady, friend?   50

Whit. Aye, and dat is anoder lady, shweetheart; if dou hasht a
    mind to 'em give me twelvepence from tee, and dou shalt
    have eider-oder on 'em!

Jus. [*Aside*] Aye? This will prove my chiefest enormity: I will
    follow this.   55

Edg. Is not this a finer life, lady, than to be clogg'd with a hus-
    band?

Win. Yes, a great deal. When will they begin, trow, in the
    name o' the motion?

Edg. By and by, madam; they stay but for company.   60

Kno. Do you hear, puppet-master, these are tedious vapours;
    when begin you?

Lea. We stay but for Master Littlewit, the author, who is gone
    for his wife; and we begin presently.

Win. That's I, that's I.   65

Edg. That was you, lady; but now you are no such poor thing.

Kno. Hang the author's wife, a running vapour! Here be
    ladies, will stay for ne'er a Delia of 'em all.

Whit. But hear me now, here ish one o' de ladish, ashleep;
    stay till she but vake, man.   70

40.1. *The* . . . LITTLEWIT.] *F margin, ll. 39–42.*   70. vake,] *F3;* vake *F.*

41. *all-to-be-madam*] persistently call me madam: properly, *all* is inten-
sive and *to* = asunder, as in *all to-broken, all to-torn*, etc.
    68. *Delia*] the lady of Daniel's *Sonnets,* 1592.

[Enter] to them WASP. *The door-keepers again.*

Wasp. How now, friends? What's here to do?

Fil. Twopence a piece, sir, the best motion, in the Fair.

Wasp. I believe you lie; if you do, I'll have my money again, and beat you.

Winw. Numps is come!   75

Wasp. Did you see a master of mine come in here, a tall young squire of Harrow o' the Hill, Master Bartholomew Cokes?

Fil. I think there be such a one, within.

Wasp. Look he be, you were best: but it is very likely: I won- der I found him not at all the rest. I ha' been at the Eagle,   80 and the Black Wolf, and the Bull with the Five Legs and Two Pizzles (he was a calf at Uxbridge Fair, two years agone), and at the Dogs that dance the Morrice, and the Hare o' the Tabor; and miss'd him at all these! Sure this must needs be some fine sight, that holds him so, if it have   85 him.

Cok. Come, come, are you ready now?

Lea. Presently, sir.

Wasp. Hoyday, he's at work in his doublet and hose; do you hear, sir? Are you employ'd, that you are bare-headed,   90 and so busy?

Cok. Hold your peace, Numps; you ha' been i' the stocks, I hear.

Wasp. Does he know that? Nay, then the date of my authority is out; I must think no longer to reign, my government is   95 at an end. He that will correct another, must want fault in himself.

Winw. Sententious Numps! I never heard so much from him, before.

Lea. Sure, Master Littlewit will not come; please you take   100 your place, sir, we'll begin.

Cok. I pray thee do, mine ears long to be at it; and my eyes

70.1. *The door-keepers again.*] F *margin, ll. 71–3.*   96–7. fault in himself] F; fault himselfe *reset* F.

too. O Numps, i' the stocks, Numps? Where's your
sword, Numps?

Wasp. I pray you intend your game, sir, let me alone.   105

Cok. Well then, we are quit for all. Come, sit down, Numps;
I'll interpret to thee: did you see Mistress Grace? It's no
matter, neither, now I think on't, tell me anon.

Winw. A great deal of love, and care, he expresses.

Grace. Alas! would you have him to express more than he   110
has? That were tyranny.

Cok. Peace, ho; now, now.

Lea. *Gentles, that no longer your expectations may wander,*
Behold our chief actor, amorous Leander,
With a great deal of cloth lapp'd about him like a scarf,   115
For he yet serves his father, a dyer at Puddle-wharf,
Which place we'll make bold with, to call it our Abydus,
As the Bankside is our Sestos, and let it not be denied us.
Now, as he is beating, to make the dye take the fuller,
Who chances to come by, but fair Hero, in a sculler;   120
And seeing Leander's naked leg, and goodly calf,
Cast at him, from the boat, a sheep's eye, and a half.
Now she is landed, and the sculler come back;
By and by, you shall see what Leander doth lack.

Pup. Lean. *Cole, Cole, old Cole.*   125

106. Well then,] *F;* Well, then *reset F.*   110. to express] *F;* expresse
reset F.   114. *Leander,*] *HS;* Leander. *F.*

---

114. amorous Leander] Marlowe, *op. cit.,* I. 51. The puppet-play which
follows echoes in rhythm the *Damon and Pithias* (1571) of Richard
Edwardes, but involves the famous friends in an altercation which recalls
the fighting of the lackeys Jack and Will in that play. The odd references in
Satiromastix (1601) where Horace-Jonson is called 'old Coale' (I. ii. 330)
and 'puppet-teacher' (IV. iii. 174) and Crispinus and Demetrius are said to
be his 'Damons and thou their Pithyasse' (I. ii. 332) perhaps indicate that
Jonson had earlier written some such play for puppets.

119. fuller] more thoroughly.

121. leg . . . calf] cf. Marlowe, *op. cit.,* I. 61–6.

122. sheep's eye] 'an amorous looke, affectionate winke, wanton aspect,
lustfull iest, or passionate cast of the eye' (Cotgrave, 1611, s.v. *œillade*).

125. old Cole] name for a pander (l. 157 below); H. & S. cf. Marston, *The*

Lea. *That is the sculler's name without control.*

Pup. Lean. *Cole, Cole, I say, Cole.*

Lea. *We do hear you.*

Pup. Lean. *Old Cole.*

Lea. *Old Cole? Is the dyer turn'd collier? How do you sell?*   130

Pup. Lean. *A pox o' your manners, kiss my hole here, and smell.*

Lea. *Kiss your hole, and smell? There's manners indeed.*

Pup. Lean. *Why, Cole, I say, Cole.*

Lea. *It's the sculler you need!*

Pup. Lean. *Aye, and be hang'd.*   135

Lea. *Be hang'd; look you yonder,*
Old Cole, you must go hang with Master Leander.

Pup. Cole. *Where is he?*

Pup. Lean. *Here, Cole, what fairest of fairs*
Was that fare, that thou landedst but now at Trig-stairs?   140

Cok. What was that, fellow? Pray thee tell me, I scarce
understand 'em.

Lea. *Leander does ask, sir, what fairest of fairs*
Was the fare that he landed, but now, at Trig-stairs?

Pup. Cole. *It is lovely Hero.*   145

Pup. Lean. *Nero?*

Pup. Cole. *No, Hero.*

Lea. *It is Hero*
Of the Bankside, he saith, to tell you truth without erring,
Is come over into Fish-street to eat some fresh herring,   150
Leander says no more, but as fast as he can,
Gets on all his best clothes; and will after to the Swan.

Cok. Most admirable good, is't not?

Lea. *Stay, sculler.*

Pup. Cole. *What say you?*   155

144. *that he*] *HS; thhe F; he F3.*   148. *Hero*] *1716; Hero. F.*

Malcontent, II. ii: 'an ould *Cole* that hath first bin fired, a pandresse, . . . who though thou canst not flame thyselfe, yet art able to get a thousand virgins tapers afire.'

130. collier] a term of abuse, from the blackness and reputation for cheating of charcoal-burners and -sellers; cf. *Twelfth Night*, III. iv. 132: '. . . Satan: hang him, foul collier!'

Lea. *You must stay for Leander, and carry him to the wench.*

Pup. Cole. *You rogue, I am no pander.*

Cok. He says he is no pander. 'Tis a fine language; I understand it, now.

Lea. *Are you no pander, Goodman Cole? Here's no man says*   160
    you are,
    You'll grow a hot Cole, it seems, pray you stay for your fare.

Pup. Cole. *Will he come away?*

Lea. *What do you say?*

Pup. Cole. *I'd ha' him come away.*   165

Lea. *Would you ha' Leander come away? Why 'pray, sir, stay.*
    You are angry, Goodman Cole; I believe the fair maid
    Came over wi' you o' trust: tell us, sculler, are you paid?

Pup. Cole. *Yes, Goodman Hogrubber o' Pickt-hatch.*

Lea. *How, Hogrubber, o' Pickt-hatch?*   170

Pup. Cole. *Aye, Hogrubber o' Pickt-hatch. Take you that.*

        The Puppet strikes him over the pate.

Lea. *O, my head!*

Pup. Cole. *Harm watch, harm catch.*

Cok. Harm watch, harm catch, he says: very good i' faith, the
    Sculler had like to ha' knock'd you, sirrah.   175

Lea. Yes, but that his fare call'd him away.

Pup. Lean. *Row apace, row apace, row, row, row, row, row.*

Lea. *You are knavishly loaden, sculler, take heed where you go.*

Pup. Cole. *Knave i' your face, Goodman rogue.*

Pup. Lean. *Row, row, row, row, row, row.*   180

Cok. He said knave i' your face, friend.

Lea. Aye, sir, I heard him. But there's no talking to these
    watermen, they will ha' the last word.

Cok. God's my life! I am not allied to the sculler, yet; he shall
    be Dauphin my boy. But my Fiddle-stick does fiddle in   185

---

166. *'pray,*] HS; *'pray' F.*   171.1. *The . . . pate.*] *F margin, ll. 171–4.*

169. Hogrubber] swineherd.

Pickt-hatch] noted for prostitutes; cf. *E.M.I.*, I. ii. 93: 'From the *Bur-
dello* it might come as well; The *Spittle:* or *Pict-hatch*'.

185. *Dauphin my boy*] alluding to the (lost) ballad which Edgar quotes in
Lear, III. iv. 100.   *my Fiddle-stick*] Leander; v. iii. 128.

and out too much; I pray thee speak to him on't; tell him,
I would have him tarry in my sight, more.

Lea. I pray you be content; you'll have enough on him, sir.

Now, gentles, I take it, here is none of you so stupid,
But that you have heard of a little god of love, call'd Cupid.
Who out of kindness to Leander, hearing he but saw her,   191
This present day and hour, doth turn himself to a drawer.
And because he would have their first meeting to be merry,
He strikes Hero in love to him, with a pint of sherry.
Which he tells her, from amorous Leander is sent her,   195
Who after him, into the room of Hero, doth venter.

Pup. Jo[nas]. *A pint of sack, score a pint of sack, i' the Coney.*

                 Puppet LEANDER *goes into* Mistress HERO'S *room.*

Cok. Sack? You said but e'en now it should be sherry.

Pup. Jo. Why so it is; sherry, sherry, sherry.

Cok. 'Sherry, sherry, sherry.' By my troth he makes me   200
merry. I must have a name for Cupid, too. Let me see,
thou mightst help me now, an' thou wouldest, Numps, at
a dead lift, but thou art dreaming o' the stocks, still! Do
not think on't, I have forgot it: 'tis but a nine days' wonder, man; let it not trouble thee.   205

Wasp. I would the stocks were about your neck, sir; condition I hung by the heels in them, till the wonder were off
from you, with all my heart.

Cok. Well said, resolute Numps: but hark you friend, where
is the friendship, all this while, between my drum,   210
Damon, and my pipe, Pythias?

Lea. You shall see by and by, sir!

197.1. Puppet . . . room.] *F margin, ll. 196–8.*   209. said,] *F3;* said *F.*

---

197. the Coney] name of a room in the tavern.
198. *Sack . . . sherry*] a ridiculous objection, as sack was the general
name for white wines imported from Spain, including sherry; cf. Markham, *The English Hus-wife,* 1623, p. 149: 'Your best Sacke are of *Seres* in
Spaine.'
203. *dead lift*] 'a hopeless exigence' (Johnson).
206–7. *condition*] on condition that.

Cok. You think my hobby-horse is forgotten, too; no, I'll see
'em all enact before you go; I shall not know which to
love best, else.   215

Kno. This gallant has interrupting vapours, troublesome
vapours, Whit, puff with him.

Whit. No, I pre dee, captain, let him alone. He is a child i'
faith, la.

Lea. *Now, gentles, to the friends, who in number are two,*   220
And lodg'd in that ale-house, in which fair Hero does do.
Damon (for some kindness done him the last week)
Is come fair Hero, in Fish-street, this morning to seek:
Pythias does smell the knavery of the meeting,
And now you shall see their true friendly greeting.   225

Pup. Pyth. *You whore-masterly slave, you.*

Cok. Whore-masterly slave you? Very friendly, and familiar,
that.

Pup. Dam. *Whore-master i' thy face,*
Thou hast lien with her thyself, I'll prove't i' this place.   230

Cok. Damon says Pythias has lien with her, himself, he'll
prove't in this place.

Lea. *They are whore-masters both, sir, that's a plain case.*

Pup. Pyth. *You lie, like a rogue.*

Lea. *Do I lie, like a rogue?*   235

Pup. Pyth. *A pimp, and a scab.*

Lea. *A pimp, and a scab?*
I say between you, you have both but one drab.

Pup. Dam. *You lie again.*

Lea. *Do I lie again?*   240

Pup. Dam. *Like a rogue again.*

Lea. *Like a rogue again?*

Pup. Pyth. *And you are a pimp, again.*

Cok. And you arc a pimp again, he says.

---

213. *hobby-horse . . . forgotten*] the frequently quoted (e.g. *Hamlet*, III. ii.
146) refrain of a lost popular song.
236. scab] scoundrel.

Pup. Dam. *And a scab, again.*   245
Cok. And a scab again, he says.
Lea. *And I say again, you are both whore-masters again,*
  And you have both but one drab again.

                    They fight.

Pup. Dam. Pyth. *Dost thou, dost thou, dost thou?*
Lea. *What, both at once?*   250
Pup. Pyth. *Down with him, Damon.*
Pup. Dam. *Pink his guts, Pythias.*
Lea. *What, so malicious?*
  Will ye murder me, masters both, i' mine own house?
Cok. Ho! well acted my drum, well acted my pipe, well acted   255
  still.
Wasp. Well acted, with all my heart.
Lea. *Hold, hold your hands.*
Cok. Aye, both your hands, for my sake! for you ha' both
  done well.   260
Pup. Dam. *Gramercy, pure Pythias.*
Pup. Pyth. *Gramercy, dear Damon.*
Cok. Gramercy to you both, my pipe, and my drum.
Pupp. Dam. Pyth. *Come now we'll together to breakfast to Hero.*
Lea. *'Tis well, you can now go to breakfast to Hero,*   265
  You have given me my breakfast, with ohone and 'honero.
Cok. How is't, friend, ha' they hurt thee?
Lea. O no!
  Between you and I, sir, we do but make show.
  Thus, gentles, you perceive, without any denial,   270
  'Twixt Damon and Pythias here, friendship's true trial.
  Though hourly they quarrel thus, and roar each with other,
  They fight you no more, than does brother with brother.
  But friendly together, at the next man they meet,

248.1. *They fight.*] F *margin, l.* 247.

---

  252. Pink] stab.
  261. pure] good, fine (in the general approbatory sense common later in
the century: *O.E.D.*, 1675).
  266. ohone and 'honero] alas! Scots (from Gaelic) *ochone, ochonarie.*

They let fly their anger, as here you might see't.　　　275

Cok. Well, we have seen't, and thou hast felt it, whatsoever
　　thou sayest. What's next? What's next?

Lea. This while young Leander, with fair Hero is drinking,
　　And Hero grown drunk, to any man's thinking!
　　Yet was it not three pints of sherry could flaw her,　　　280
　　Till Cupid, distinguish'd like Jonas the drawer,
　　From under his apron, where his lechery lurks,
　　Put love in her sack. Now mark how it works.

Pup. Hero. *O Leander, Leander, my dear, my dear Leander,*
　　I'll for ever be thy goose, so thou'lt be my gander.　　　285

Cok. Excellently well said, Fiddle, she'll ever be his goose, so
　　he'll be her gander: was't not so?

Lea. Yes, sir, but mark his answer, now.

Pup. Lean. *And sweetest of geese, before I go to bed,*
　　I'll swim o'er the Thames, my goose, thee to tread.　　　290

Cok. Brave! he will swim o'er the Thames, and tread his
　　goose, tonight, he says.

Lea. Aye, peace, sir, they'll be angry, if they hear you eaves-
　　dropping, now they are setting their match.

Pup. Lean. *But lest the Thames should be dark, my goose,*
　　　my dear friend,　　　295
　　Let thy window be provided of a candle's end.

Pup. Hero. *Fear not, my gander, I protest, I should handle*
　　My matters very ill, if I had not a whole candle.

Pup. Lean. *Well then, look to't, and kiss me to boot.*

Lea. Now, here come the friends again, Pythias and Damon,　　　300
　　And under their cloaks, they have of bacon, a gammon.

DAMON *and* PYTHIAS *enter.*

Pup. Pyth. *Drawer, fill some wine here.*

Lea. How, some wine there?
　　There's company already, sir, pray forbear!

277. sayest.] *F3;* sayest, *F.*　　280. *her.] F3;* her. *F.*　　297. *not,] F3;* not *F.*
301.1. DAMON . . . enter.] *F margin, ll. 300–2.*

290. tread] copulate with.

Pup. Dam. *'Tis Hero.*   305

Lea. *Yes, but she will not be taken,*
    After sack, and fresh herring, with your Dunmow-bacon.

Pup. Pyth. *You lie, it's Westfabian.*

Lea. *Westphalian you should say.*

Pup. Dam. *If you hold not your peace, you are a coxcomb, I*
    would say.   310

LEANDER and HERO are kissing.

Pup. Pyth. *What's here? What's here? Kiss, kiss, upon kiss.*

Lea. *Aye, wherefore should they not? What harm is in this?*
    'Tis Mistress Hero.

Pup. Dam. *Mistress Hero's a whore.*

Lea. *Is she a whore? Keep you quiet, or sir knave out of door.*   315

Pup. Dam. *Knave out of door?*

Pup. Hero. *Yes, knave, out of door.*

Pup. Dam. *Whore out of door.*

Here the Puppets quarrel and fall together by the ears.

Pup. Hero. *I say, knave, out of door.*

Pup. Dam. *I say, whore, out of door.*   320

Pup. Pyth. *Yea, so say I too.*

Pup. Hero. *Kiss the whore o' the arse.*

Lea. *Now you ha' something to do: you must kiss her o' the*
    arse she says.

Pupp. Dam. Pyth. *So we will, so we will.*   [*They kick her.*]   325

Pup. Hero. *O my haunches, O my haunches, hold, hold.*

Lea. *Stand'st thou still?*

    Leander, where art thou? Stand'st thou still like a sot,

310.1. LEANDER . . . *kissing.*] F margin, *ll. 310–12.*   311. Pup. Pyth.]
PVP.[P] *HS;* PVP. *F.*   318.1. Here . . . *ears.*] F margin, *ll. 318–22.*
325. *They kick her.*] G.

---

307. Dunmow-bacon] The famous flitch presented to any couple who
could satisfy a jury of six bachelors and six maidens of Little Dunmow in
Essex that they had spent the first year of married life without quarrelling
or wishing they had tarried.

309. Westphalian] large numbers of pigs are still reared on the plains of
this German province to produce the still famous hams.

And not offer'st to break both their heads with a pot?
See who's at thine elbow there! Puppet Jonas and Cupid.　330

Pup. Jo. *Upon 'em, Leander, be not so stupid.*

They fight.

Pup. Lean. *You goat-bearded slave!*

Pup. Dam. *You whore-master knave.*

Pup. Lean. *Thou art a whore-master.*

Pup. Jo. *Whore-masters all.*　335

Lea. *See, Cupid with a word has ta'en up the brawl.*

Kno. These be fine vapours!

Cok. By this good day they fight bravely! Do they not,
Numps?

Wasp. Yes, they lack'd but you to be their second, all this　340
while.

Lea. *This tragical encounter, falling out thus to busy us,*
It raises up the ghost of their friend Dionysius:
Not like a monarch, but the master of a school,
In a scrivener's furr'd gown, which shows he is no fool.　345
For therein he hath wit enough to keep himself warm.
'O Damon,' he cries, 'and Pythias; what harm
Hath poor Dionysius done you in his grave,
That after his death, you should fall out thus, and rave,
And call amorous Leander whore-master knave?'　350

Pup. Dam. *I cannot, I will not, I promise you, endure it.*

331.1. *They fight.*] *F margin, l. 331.*　347. *Damon,*] *1716;* Damon *F.*
351. *you,*] *1716; you* F.

343–4. Dionysius . . . school] The younger 'Dionysius quidem tyrannus
Syracusis expulsus Corinthi pueros docebat: usque eo imperio carere non
poterat' (Cicero, *Tusculan Disputations,* III. xii. 27).

Act V. Scene V.

[Enter] to them BUSY.

Busy. Down with Dagon, down with Dagon; 'tis I, will no
longer endure your profanations.

Lea. What mean you, sir?

Busy. I will remove Dagon there, I say, that idol, that
heathenish idol, that remains (as I may say) a beam, a   5
very beam, not a beam of the sun, nor a beam of the moon,
nor a beam of a balance, neither a house-beam, nor a
weaver's beam, but a beam in the eye, in the eye of the
brethren; a very great beam, an exceeding great beam;
such as are your stage-players, rhymers, and morrice-   10
dancers, who have walked hand in hand, in contempt of
the brethren and the cause, and been borne out by instruments, of no mean countenance.

Lea. Sir, I present nothing, but what is licens'd by authority.

Busy. Thou art all licence, even licentiousness itself, Shimei!   15

Lea. I have the Master of the Revels' hand for't, sir.

Busy. The Master of Rebels' hand, thou hast; Satan's! Hold
thy peace, thy scurrility, shut up thy mouth, thy profession is damnable, and in pleading for it, thou dost plead
for Baal. I have long opened my mouth wide, and gaped,   20
I have gaped as the oyster for the tide, after thy destruc-

v. v. 18. scurrility,] *F3;* scurrility *F.*

---

v. v. 1. *Dagon*] national god of the Philistines; in general sense, an idol.

12–13. *instruments*] agents (turning again to Leatherhead).

13. *countenance*] credit or repute in the world; cf. Lyly, *Euphues,* 1579
(Arber, p. 50): 'Philautus . . . both for his owne countenaunce, and the
great countenaunce which his father had while he liued, crept into credit
with Don Ferardo.'

15. *Shimei*] In his cursing and stone-throwing it is rather Busy himself
who resembles the son of Gera (2 Samuel xvi. 5–13).

16. *Master of the Revels*] at this time licenser of plays (see W. W. Greg,
Some Aspects and Problems of London Publishing, 1550–1650, Oxford, 1956,
pp. 103 ff.).

20. *for Baal*] i.e. for the licentious rites of idolatry.

21. *gaped . . . oyster*] cf. Eachard, *The Ground and Occasions of the Con-*

tion: but cannot compass it by suit, or dispute; so that I
look for a bickering, ere long, and then a battle.

Kno. Good Banbury-vapours.

Cok. Friend, you'd have an ill match on't, if you bicker with   25
him here; though he be no man o' the fist, he has friends
that will go to cuffs for him. Numps, will not you take our
side?

Edg. Sir, it shall not need; in my mind, he offers him a fairer
course, to end it by disputation! Hast thou nothing to say   30
for thyself, in defence of thy quality?

Lea. Faith, sir, I am not well studied in these controversies,
between the hypocrites and us. But here's one of my
motion, Puppet Dionysius, shall undertake him, and I'll
venture the cause on't.   35

Cok. Who? My hobby-horse? Will he dispute with him?

Lea. Yes, sir, and make a hobby-ass of him, I hope.

Cok. That's excellent! Indeed he looks like the best scholar of
'em all. Come, sir, you must be as good as your word, now.

Busy. I will not fear to make my spirit, and gifts known! Assist   40
me, zeal; fill me, fill me, that is, make me full.

Winw. What a desperate, profane wretch is this! Is there any
ignorance, or impudence like his? To call his zeal to fill
him against a puppet?

Quar. I know no fitter match, than a puppet to commit with   45
an hypocrite!

Busy. First, I say unto thee, idol, thou hast no calling.

Pup. Dion. You lie, I am call'd Dionysius.

Lea. The motion says you lie, he is call'd Dionysius i' the
matter, and to that calling he answers.   50

Busy. I mean no vocation, idol, no present lawful calling.

Pup. Dion. Is yours a lawful calling?

26. here;] *G;* here, *F.*   27. him.] *F3;* him, *F.*   29. need;] *G;* need, *F.*

---

tempt of the Clergy and Religion . . . , 1698, p. 62: 'Our Souls are constantly
Gaping after thee, O Lord, yea verily, our Souls do gape, even as an Oyster
gapeth' (G.).

45. *commit with*] join battle with (*committere pugnam*).

Lea. The motion asketh, if yours be a lawful calling?

Busy. Yes, mine is of the spirit.

Pup. Dion. Then idol is a lawful calling.   55

Lea. He says, then idol is a lawful calling! For you call'd him
    idol, and your calling is of the spirit.

Cok. Well disputed, hobby-horse!

Busy. Take not part with the wicked, young gallant. He
    neigheth and hinnyeth, all is but hinnying sophistry. I   60
    call him idol again. Yet, I say, his calling, his profession is
    profane, it is profane, idol.

Pup. Dion. It is not profane!

Lea. It is not profane, he says.

Busy. It is profane.   65

Pup. Dion. It is not profane.

Busy. It is profane.

Pup. Dion. It is not profane.

Lea. Well said, confute him with 'not', still. You cannot bear
    him down with your base noise, sir.   70

Busy. Nor he me, with his treble creaking, though he creak
    like the chariot wheels of Satan; I am zealous for the
    cause—

Lea. As a dog for a bone.

Busy. And I say, it is profane, as being the page of Pride, and   75
    the waiting-woman of Vanity.

Pup. Dion. Yea? What say you to your tire-women, then?

Lea. Good.

*Pup. Dion. Or feather-makers i' the Friars, that are o' your
    faction of faith? Are not they with their perukes, and their   80
    puffs, their fans, and their huffs, as much pages of Pride, and*

59. wicked,] *1716;* wicked *F.*

---

71. *creak*] (*a*) cry harshly (of e.g. geese); cf. *O.E.D.*, 1580: 'To Gagle, or
creake like a goose'; (*b*) to grate shrilly (of axles).

79. feather-makers . . . Friars] cf. Dekker and Webster, *Westward Hoe,*
v. i. 161–3: 'as fantasticke . . . to the eye, as fether-makers, but as pure about
the heart, as if we dwelt amongst em in Black Fryers'.

81. puffs] round bunches of ribbons or small feathers, or of hair (formed
by rolling in the ends).

*waiters upon Vanity ? What say you ? What say you ? What
say you ?*

Busy. I will not answer for them.

Pup. Dion. *Because you cannot, because you cannot. Is a bugle-*   85
*maker a lawful calling ? Or the confect-maker's (such you
have there) ? Or your French fashioner ? You'd have all the
sin within yourselves, would you not ? Would you not ?*

Busy. No, Dagon.

Pup. Dion. *What then, Dagonet ? Is a puppet worse than these ?*   90

Busy. Yes, and my main argument against you, is, that you are
an abomination : for the male, among you, putteth on the
apparel of the female, and the female of the male.

Pup. Dion. *You lie, you lie, you lie abominably.*

Cok. Good, by my troth, he has given him the lie thrice.   95

Pup. Dion. *It is your old stale argument against the players, but
it will not hold against the puppets; for we have neither male
nor female amongst us. And that thou may'st see, if thou
wilt, like a malicious purblind zeal as thou art !*

The Puppet takes up his garment.

Edg. By my faith, there he has answer'd you, friend; by plain   100
demonstration.

Pup. Dion. *Nay, I'll prove, against e'er a Rabbin of 'em all,
that my standing is as lawful as his; that I speak by inspiration, as well as he; that I have as little to do with learning as
he; and do scorn her helps as much as he.*   105

Busy. I am confuted, the cause hath failed me.

Pup. Dion. *Then be converted, be converted.*

Lea. Be converted, I pray you, and let the play go on!

Busy. Let it go on. For I am changed, and will become a beholder with you!   110

99.1. *The Puppet . . . garment.*] F margin, *ll. 98–100.*

85–6. bugle-maker] maker of black tube-shaped glass beads.
86. confect-maker's] that of a maker of sweetmeats.
87. fashioner] tailor.
90. Dagonet] 'kynge Arthurs foole' (Malory, ed. Vinaver, ii. 462).
92. *male*] cf. Deuteronomy xxii. 5.

N

Cok. That's brave i' faith; thou hast carried it away, hobby-
horse; on with the play!

The JUSTICE *discovers himself.*

Jus. Stay, now do I forbid, I Adam Overdo! Sit still, I charge
you.

Cok. What, my brother-i'-law!   115

Gra. My wise guardian!

Edg. Justice Overdo!

Jus. It is time, to take enormity by the forehead, and brand
it; for I have discover'd enough.

Act V. Scene VI.

[Enter] to them, QUARLOUS *(like the madman),*
PURECRAFT *(a while after).*

Quar. Nay, come, mistress bride. You must do as I do, now.
You must be mad with me, in truth. I have here Justice
Overdo for it.

Jus. Peace, good Trouble-all; come hither, and you shall
trouble none. I will take the charge of you and your   5
friend too; you also, young man, shall be my care, stand
there.   *To the cutpurse.*

Edg. Now, mercy upon me.   *The rest are stealing away.*

Kno. Would we were away, Whit; these are dangerous vapours; best fall off with our birds, for fear o' the cage.   10

Jus. Stay, is not my name your terror?

112.1. *The* JUSTICE . . . *himself.] F margin, ll. 113–15.*

v. vi. 0.1–2. *to . . . after).] To them,* QVARLOVS. *(like the Mad-man)* PVRECRAFT.
(a while after) IOHN. *to them* TROVBLE-ALL. VRSLA. NIGHTIGALE. *F.*   6.
too;] *F3;* too, *F.*   7. *To the cutpurse.] To the Cutpurse, and Mistresse* Lit-
wit. *F margin, ll. 5–7.*   8. *The rest . . . away.] F margin, ll. 9–11.*

---

111. *carried it away]* had the advantage, brought it off.

v. vi. 10. *cage]* prison.

Whit. Yesh, faith, man, and it ish for tat we would be gone, man.

[Enter] LITTLEWIT.

Lit. O gentlemen! did you not see a wife of mine? I ha' lost
my little wife, as I shall be trusted: my little pretty Win, I　15
left her at the great woman's house in trust yonder, the
pig-woman's, with Captain Jordan, and Captain Whit,
very good men, and I cannot hear of her. Poor fool, I fear
she's stepp'd aside. Mother, did you not see Win?

Jus. If this grave matron be your mother, sir, stand by her, *et*　20
digito compesce labellum, I may perhaps spring a wife for
you, anon. Brother Bartholomew, I am sadly sorry, to see
you so lightly given, and such a disciple of enormity; with
your grave governor Humphrey: but stand you both
there, in the middle place; I will reprehend you in your　25
course. Mistress Grace, let me rescue you out of the hands
of the stranger.

Winw. Pardon me, sir, I am a kinsman of hers.

Jus. Are you so? Of what name, sir?

Winw. Winwife, sir.　　　　　　　　　　　　　　　　　　30

Jus. Master Winwife? I hope you have won no wife of her, sir.
If you have, I will examine the possibility of it, at fit lei-
sure. Now, to my enormities: look upon me, O London!
and see me, O Smithfield! the example of justice, and
Mirror of Magistrates; the true top of formality, and　35
scourge of enormity. Hearken unto my labours, and but
observe my discoveries; and compare Hercules with me,
if thou dar'st, of old; or Columbus; Magellan; or our
country-man Drake of later times: stand forth you weeds
of enormity, and spread. (*To* BUSY). First, Rabbi Busy,　40

40. *To* BUSY.] F *margin, l. 40.*

---

19. *stepp'd aside*] gone astray (though the only *O.E.D.* quotation for this
sense is from Burns, s.v.19d; but cf. 2b).

20–1. et . . . labellum] Juvenal, *Sat.*, i. 160: 'restrain your lips wtih your
finger' (lest you be an informer).

21. *spring*] properly to cause (a partridge) to rise from cover.

N*

thou super-lunatical hypocrite. (*To* LANTERN.) Next,
thou other extremity, thou profane professor of puppetry,
little better than poetry. (*To the horse-courser, and cutpurse.*) Then thou strong debaucher, and seducer of
youth; witness this easy and honest young man. (*Then*   45
captain WHIT *and* Mistress LITTLEWIT.) Now thou
esquire of dames, madams, and twelvepenny ladies: now
my green madam herself, of the price. Let me unmask
your ladyship.

Lit. O my wife, my wife, my wife!   50
Jus. Is she your wife? *Redde te Harpocratem!*

Enter TROUBLE-ALL, URSULA, NIGHTINGALE.

Tro. By your leave, stand by, my masters, be uncover'd.
Urs. O stay him, stay him, help to cry, Nightingale; my pan,
my pan.
Jus. What's the matter?   55
Nigh. He has stol'n Gammer Urs'la's pan.
Tro. Yes, and I fear no man but Justice Overdo.
Jus. Urs'la? Where is she? O the sow of enormity, this! (*To*
URSULA *and* NIGHTINGALE.) Welcome, stand you there;
you, songster, there.   60
Urs. An' please your worship, I am in no fault: a gentleman
stripp'd him in my booth, and borrow'd his gown, and his
hat; and he ran away with my goods, here, for it.
Jus. (*To* QUARLOUS.) Then this is the true madman, and you
are the enormity!   65
Quar. You are i' the right, I am mad, but from the gown outward.

41. *To* LANTERN.] *F margin, ll. 41–2.*   43–4. *To . . . cutpurse.*] *F margin,
ll. 43–5.*   45–6. *Then . . .* LITTLEWIT.] *F margin, ll. 47–50.*   51.1. *Enter*
TROUBLE-ALL,] *F margin, ll. 52–3.*   52. by,] *G; by F.*   58–9. *To . . .*
NIGHTINGALE.] *F margin, ll. 58–61.*   59–60. there; you,] *F3; there, you F.*
64. *To* QUARLOUS.] *F margin, ll. 64–6.*

51. Redde te Harpocratem] 'make yourself like Harpocrates', god of
silence. H. & S. cf. Catullus, lxxiv. 4: 'patruum reddidit Harpocratem', 'he
laid his uncle under the seal of silence'.

Jus. Stand you there.

Quar. Where you please, sir.

　　Mistress OVERDO *is sick: and her husband is silenc'd.*

Mrs. Over. O lend me a basin, I am sick, I am sick; where's　70
　　Master Overdo ? Bridget, call hither my Adam.

Jus. How ?

Whit. Dy very own wife, i' fait, worshipful Adam.

Mrs. Over. Will not my Adam come at me ? Shall I see him no
　　more then ?　　　　　　　　　　　　　　　　　　　　75

Quar. Sir, why do you not go on with the enormity ? Are you
　　oppress'd with it ? I'll help you: hark you, sir, i' your ear
　　—your 'innocent young man', you have ta'en such care of,
　　all this day, is a cutpurse, that hath got all your brother
　　Cokes his things, and help'd you to your beating, and the　80
　　stocks; if you have a mind to hang him now, and show him
　　your magistrate's wit, you may: but I should think it
　　were better, recovering the goods, and to save your esti-
　　mation in him. I thank you sir for the gift of your ward,
　　Mistress Grace: look you, here is your hand and seal, by　85
　　the way. Master Winwife, give you joy, you are Palemon,
　　you are possess'd of the gentlewoman, but she must pay
　　me value, here's warrant for it. And honest madman,
　　there's thy gown, and cap again; I thank thee for my wife.
　　(*To the widow.*) Nay, I can be mad, sweetheart, when I　90
　　please, still; never fear me. And careful Numps, where's
　　he ? I thank him for my licence.

Wasp. How!　　　　　　　　　　　　　WASP *misseth the licence.*

Quar. 'Tis true, Numps.

Wasp. I'll be hang'd then.　　　　　　　　　　　　　95

Quar. Look i' your box, Numps. [*To* JUSTICE.] Nay, sir,
　　stand not you fix'd here, like a stake in Finsbury to be

69.1. Mistress . . . *silenc'd.*] F *margin, ll. 70–4.*　　86. Winwife,] *G;* Winwife *F.*　　90. *To the widow.*] F *margin, ll. 89–90.*　　93. WASP . . . *licence.*]
F *margin, ll. 93–5.*

83–4. *estimation*] repute.

97. *a stake in Finsbury*] cf. Stow, i. 104: 'before the Maior . . . in Fens-

shot at, or the whipping post i' the Fair, but get your wife
out o' the air, it will make her worse else; and remember
you are but Adam, flesh and blood! You have your   100
frailty, forget your other name of Overdo, and invite us
all to supper. There you and I will compare our discoveries; and drown the memory of all enormity in your
biggest bowl at home.

Cok. How now, Numps, ha' you lost it? I warrant, 'twas   105
when thou wert i' the stocks: why dost not speak?

Wasp. I will never speak while I live, again, for ought I know.

Jus. Nay, Humphrey, if I be patient, you must be so too; this
pleasant conceited gentleman hath wrought upon my
judgement, and prevail'd: I pray you take care of your   110
sick friend, Mistress Alice, and my good friends all—

Quar. And no enormities.

Jus. I invite you home with me to my house, to supper: I will
have none fear to go along, for my intents are *ad correc-*
tionem, non ad destructionem; ad ædificandum, non ad   115
diruendum: so lead on.

Cok. Yes, and bring the actors along, we'll ha' the rest o' the
play at home.   [*Exeunt.*]

The end.

---

burie field, to shoote the Standard, broad Arrow . . . some three or four
dayes after [Bartholomew day], in one afternoone and no more'.

114–16. ad . . . diruendum] 'for correction not destruction, building up
not tearing down'; cf. Horace, *Epist.*, I. i. 100: 'diruit, aedificat'; Sallust,
Catiline, xx. 12: 'nova diruunt, alia aedificant' expanded in *C.*, I. 392–5
(cf. H. & S., ii. 118).

The EPILOGUE.

Your Majesty hath seen the play, and you
    Can best allow it from your ear, and view.
You know the scope of writers, and what store
    Of leave is given them, if they take not more,
And turn it into licence: you can tell   5
    If we have us'd that leave you gave us, well:
Or whether we to rage, or licence break,
    Or be profane, or make profane men speak?
This is your power to judge, great sir, and not
    The envy of a few. Which if we have got,   10
We value less what their dislike can bring,
    If it so happy be, t' have pleas'd the King.

3–5. *what . . . licence*] Horace, *Ars Poetica*, 51: 'dabiturque licentia sumpta pudenter', which J. himself translates (H. & S. viii. 309): 'All men will . . . give, being taken modestly, this leave.'

BARTHOLOMEVV
FAIRE

OR

Variety of fancies vvhere you may find
a faire of vvares, and all to please your mind,

With

The severall enormityes and misdemea-/nours, which are there
seene and acted. . . . 1641.

BArtholomew Faire begins on the twenty fourth day of *August,* and is
then of so vast an extent that it is contained in no lesse then four
several parishes, namely, Christ Church, Great and Little Saint
Bartholomewes, and Saint Sepulchres. Hither resort people of all
sorts, High and Low, Rich and Poore, from cities, townes, and coun-
trys; of all sects, Papists, Atheists, Anabaptists, and Brownists: and
of all conditions, good and bad, vertuous and vitious, Knaves and
fooles, Cuckolds and Cuckoldmakers, Bauds, and Whores, Pimpes
and Panders, Rogues and Rascalls, the little Loud-one and the witty
wanton.

And now that wee may the better take an exact survay of the whole
Faire, First let us enter into Christ Church Cloysters, which are now
hung so full of pictures, that you would take that place or rather mistake it for Saint *Peters* in *Rome;* onely this is the difference, those
there are set up for worship, these here for sale. But by the way, I'le
tell / [p. 2] you a tale of a precise puritan, who came in all hast from
Lincolne to *London,* purposely to see the Faire, where he had never
bin before, and coming out of newgate marget, through Christ-
Church into the Cloysters, and elevating the snow bals of his eyes, he
presently espyes the picture of Christ and his twelve Apostles, with
the virgin Mary, and many other Saints departed; at which sight the
very thought and strong conceit of superstition set such a sharp edge
upon the pure mettle of his inflam'd zeale, that very manfully like a
man of valour, and son of mars, he steps to a stall wel stor'd with two-
peny halberts, and woodden backswords, where having arm'd him-

selfe *Cap a Pea*, (as he thought) he begins in a violent passion, to exclaime against the Idolatry of the times, that it was growne abominable; protesting that the whore of *Babilon* was crept into Christ Church, and that the good motions of the Spirit had brought him to towne, to make a sacrifice of those Idle *Idolls*, to his just anger and holy indignation, which begot no small laughter to the multitude, which throng'd about him, that put him into such a chafe, in so much that at the last, like *Rosicleare*, the Knight of the sunne, or *Don Quixot*, most furiously he makes an assault, and battery upon the poore innocent pictures, till the shopkeepers apprehending him had him before a Constable, who forthwith comitted my little hot furie to the stockes, where we will leave him to coole his heeles, whilst we take a further view of the Faire. And now being arriv'd through the long walke, to Saint Bartholomewes / [p. 3] hospitall; that place (me thinkes) appeares to me, a sucking Exchange, and may be so termed, not unfitl[y]; for there many a handsome wench exchanges her maidenhead for a small favour, as a moiety of bonelace, a slight silver bodkin, a hoopt-ring, or the like toye; for shee comes not thither with her sweet-heart, to serve her owne turne only, but also to satisfie his desire; according to the old saying, one good turne deserves another.

Let us now make a progresse into Smith-field, which is the heart of the Faire, where in my heart I thinke there are more motions in a day, to be seene, then are in a terme in Westminster Hall to be heard. But whilst you take notice of the severall motions there, take this caution along with you, let one eye watch narrowly that no ones hand make a motion into your pocket, which is the next way to moue you to impatience.

The Faire is full of gold and silver-drawers: Iust as Lent is to the Fishmonger, so is Bartholomew Faire to the Pickpocket; It is his high harvest, which is never bad, but when his cart goes up holborne.

The Citty-marshalls are as dreadfull to these yongsters, as the Plague is to our London Actors: That restraines them from playing, and they hinder these from working; you may quickly know these nimble youthes, and likely find them very busie-bodyes in quarrells, which nothing concerne them, and sometimes in discourse with their wenches, (the sisters of the scabard) for the most part to be found in a croud or throng of people. Their but-/[p. 4]tockes walke up and down the Faire very demurely; The end of their preambulation is to be taken up by some countrey-Gull, or city-cockscombe, and then your hand is no sooner in one of their plackets, but theirs is as nimble in one of your pockets; and if you take not heed of them, they will give you fairings with the poxe. Some of your cutpurses are in fee with cheating costermongers, who have a trick now and then to throw downe a basket of refuge peares, which prove choake-peares to those that shall loose their hats or cloaks in striving who shall gather fastest. They have many dainty baits to draw a bit, and (if you be not vigilant) you shall hardly escape their nets: fine fowlers they are, for every finger of theirs is a lime-twigge, with which they catch dotterels. They are excellently well read in Physiognomy; for they will know how strong you are in the purse by looking in your face; and for the more certainty thereof, they will follow you close, and never leave you till you draw your purse, or they for you, which they'l be sure to have, (if you looke not to it) though they kisse new-gate for it. It is remarkable, and worth your observation, to behold and heare the strange sights, and confus'd noise in the Faire. Here a Knave in a fooles coate, with a trumpet sounding, or on a drumme beating, invites you and would faine perswade you to see his puppets; There a Rogue like a wild woodman, or in an Antickship like an Incubus, desires your company, to view his motion; on the other side, Hocus Pocus with three yards of tape or ribbin in's hand, shewing his art of Legerdemaine, to the admiration and astonishment of a company of cockoloaches. /[p. 5] Amongst these you shall see a gray goose-cap (as wise as the rest,) with a what do ye lacke, in his mouth, stand in his boothe, shaking a rattle, or scraping on a fiddle, with which children are so taken that they presently cry out for these fopperies; And all these together make such a distracted noise, that you would thinck Babell were not comparable to it. Here there are also your gamesters in action; some turning of a whimsey, others throwing for Pewter, who can quickly dissolve a round shilling into a three halfepeny saucer. Long-lane at this time looks very faire, and puts out her best cloaths, with the wrong side outward, so turn'd for their better turning off; And cloth Faire, is now in great request: well fare the Alehouses therein; yet better may a man fare (but at a dearer rate) in the pig-market, alias Pasty-nooke, or Pye corner, where pigges are al houres of the day on the stalls piping hot, and would cry (if they could speak) come eate me, but they are so damnable deare, and the reckonings for them are so saucy, that a man had as good licke his fingers in a baudy house, as at this time come into one of those houses, where the fat greasy Hostesse instructs Nick Froth her tapster, to aske a shilling more for a pigs head of a woman big with child, in regard of her longing, then of another ordinary customer: these unconscionable exactions, & excessive inflammations of reckonings made that angle of the Faire too hot for my company; therefore I resolv'd with myself to steere my course another way, and having once got out, not to come again in hast.

Now farewell to the Faire; you who are wise, Preserve your Purses, whilst you please your eyes.

FINIS.

APPENDIX II (cf. I. iii. 88)

From *The Brownists Conventicle* 1641

The Grace before Dinner

Corroborate these thy good gifts unto our use, I beseech thee good Father, and make us thankful for all these thy bountiful blessings upon this boord, to nourish our corrupt bodies. These are boyl'd Chickens (I take it) let this dish of Chickens put us in mind of our Saviour, who would have gathered *Hierusalem* together as an Hen gathereth her chickens, but she would not: but let us praise God for these chickens, which are set before us, being six in number. Let this leg of Mutton call us to remembrance, that king *David* was once a Shepherd; and so was *Christ* the son of *David*, that good Shepherd, who having an hundred sheep, and losing one, to find that left ninetie and nine in the wildernesse. Here is an excellent Loyne of Veale, let that prompt[1] us to remember the Parable of the Prodigall child, whom to welcome home, the Father caused the fat calfe to be killed, which I thinke would not yeeld a better rump and kidney than is now visible before our eyes. And by this cramm'd and well fed capon, let us be mindfull of the cock, which crowed three times, when Peter had as often denyed his Master, for which he went out and wept bitterly. These Rabbets recollect us to think (having fur upon their backs) of the two wicked Elders, that lay in wait to entrap the chastity of *Susanna*: but I feare I have too much over-shot my selfe in alleaging any example out of the prophane Apocrypha . . . Gamond of . . . bacon . . . [Gadarene] swine . . . Sturgeon . . . that whale which swallowed Jonas. Pippins . . . put us in mind of . . . the forbidden Tree. Thus briefly, as I can, I have gone thorow every dish on the boord, for every sundry dish ought to have a severall blessing. And let us fall too, and feed exceedingly, that after our full repast, wee may the better prophesie.

[1] *1641*: prompts

Index to Annotations

'Pers.' refers to 'The Persons of the Play', 'Ind.' to 'The Induction on the Stage' and 'Epil.' to the Epilogue. References in brackets are to unannotated passages.

abeyance, I. v. 21
about, bring, Ind. 105
——, come, I. iii. 58
above board, III. iv. 83
Adams, Ind. 40
advance, II. ii. 95
advis'd, IV i. 66
affect, IV. iii. 3
after-game, II. iii. 40
again', I. i. 36 (cf. II. iv. 12, III. iv. 24, 30)
all-to-be-madam, V. iv. 41
anatomy, III. vi. 14
Andronicus, Ind. 107
angerly, I. v. 3
answer, *vb*, IV i. 63
antics, Ind. 130
apocryphal, III. vi. 52
apostle-spoons, I. iii. 100
apple-john, I. iii. 54
apprehend, I. ii. 4 (cf. I. ii. 36, I. iv. 65, 66)
apprehension, I. v. 133
aqua cœlestis, I. ii. 66
aqua vitae, V. iv. 31
Arches, Ind. 5
Argalus, IV. iii. 68
arras, Ind. 8
arsedine, II. ii. 19
Arthur of Bradley, II. ii. 127
asweare, IV. i. 63
aunt, II. ii. 132
a very less, I. i. 9–10
avoid, II. vi. 33
away with, I. vi. 98

Baal, V. v. 20
baby, Prol. 5 (cf. Ind. 165, II. ii. 30)
Banbury, Pers. 5 (cf. III. ii. 96)
banquet, III. iv. 141
Bartholomew, French, II. vi. 140
baste, II. v. 67
beak, II. iv. 44
beard, man with the, IV. iv. 176
bears within, Ind. 52–3
beauteous discipline, I. vi. 1
beaver, I. i. 22
Bedlam, I. ii. 51 (cf. III. vi. 129)
bees, I. iv. 78
bench, Ind. 106
Bermudas, II. vi. 72–3
black, II. vi. 42
blue, IV. i. 72
blue-starch-woman, I. iii. 132
bobchin, III. iv. 81
book-holder, Ind. 45.1
both-hands, I. iv. 38
bower, II. v. 39 (cf. III. ii. 55)
brabble, III. i. 5
break, II. v. 64
bridale, I. iii. 122
Bridewell, IV. v. 78
broker, II. v. 108
Brome, Ind. 8
Brutus, Lucius Junius, II. i. 48
Bucklersbury, I. iv. 113–14
Budge-row, I. i. 23
buff, I. iii. 67
bugle-maker, V. v. 85–6
Burbage, V. iii. 80
buy, III. v. 275

171

hobby-horse-man, Ind. 21
hogrubber, v. iv. 169
hood, *sb.*, I. iv. 81
——, French-, I. v. 15
——, *vb*, I. ii. 25
Horace, (*Ars Poetica* 51) Epil. 3–5,
　(*Epist.* I. i. 100) v. vi. 115, (*Sat.*
　I. iii. 26–7) II. i. 5, (*Sat.* II. vii.
　83–8) IV. vi. 92–4
horn-thumb, II. iii. 29
horse, II. ii. 30
—— -courser, Pers. 19
—— -leech, II. iii. 13
Hospital, the, Ind. 5–6
hum-ha-hum, I. iii. 97
humour, Ind. 12
hundred, III. ii. 137

idle, II. i. 37, IV. i. 52
ignorance, original, I. iii. 144
impertinently, IV. vi. 32
incubee, II. ii. 84
indenture, draught of, II. iv. 46
inginer, II. ii. 16
innocence, I. iii. 141
Inns o' Court, Ind. 34–5
inspiration, any other learning than,
　I. iii. 142–3
inspir'd, II. v. 74
instrument, v. v. 12–13
intelligence, II. i. 37
intend, III. iii. 44 (cf. v. iv. 105)
interlude, v. iii. 11
invention, v. i. 2
I wusse, I. iv. 52

jack, I. i. 17, III. i. 29, iv. 67
jacobus, IV. iv. 127
jaundice, I. iii. 80–1
Jeronimo, Ind. 107
Jew's trump, III. iv. 73
Jordan, II. iii. 32
jowl, II. v. 82
Judaism, I. vi. 94–5
juniper, III. ii. 68
Juvenal, (*Sat.* i. 40–1) I. iii. 76,
　(*Sat.* i. 160) v. vi. 20–1

keeps . . . a coil, I. iv. 33–4
kemb'd, I. ii. 75

Kindheart, Ind. 16
knot, *sb.*, II. ii. 52

lac'd, II. v. 81
lace, *sb.*, I. ii. 7
lading, II. ii. 40
lay aboard, III. ii. 131
leap-frog chance, I. i. 9
learning, any other . . . than inspira-
　tion, I. iii. 142–3
leer, *adj.*, Ind. 121
legend, III. vi. 70
less, a very, I. i. 10
lie, *vb*, IV. ii. 92
lift, *sb.*, IV. iv. 1
——, dead, v. iv. 203
lime-bush, III. v. 16
link, *sb.*, I. iii. 74
lion-chop, II. iii. 48
list, *sb.*, IV. vi. 100
——, *vb*, IV. i. 74
little-long-coats, I. iv. 111
long-pepper, IV. iv. 7
lottery, Ind. 95
Lubberland, III. ii. 75
Lucan, (*Pharsalia* v. 290) IV. vi. 29
lyam-hound, I. iii. 12
Lynceus, II. i. 4

Magistrates, Mirror of, Ind. 144
make . . . saver, v. ii. 79
—— . . . unready, I. v. 157
making, to, IV. iii. 40
male (putteth on apparel of the
　female), v. v. 92–3
mallanders, II. v. 167–8
malt-horse, II. vi. 103–4
man with the beard, IV. iv. 176
mark, *sb.*, I. iv. 22
Marlowe, (*Hero and Leander*) v. iii.
　100, iv. 114, 121
marry gip, I. v. 15
Martial, (*Ep.* I. xxvii. 5–7) I. iii. 25–
　6, (*Ep.* III. xciii) I. iii. 70–5, (*Ep.*
　XI. c) II. v. 98
masque, III. iv. 88
Master of the Revels, v. v. 16
maypole, I. iii. 122
meet, *adj.*, II. iii. 17
melicotton, I. ii. 15